PLANNING AND ENVIRONMENTAL IMPACT ASSESSMENT IN PRACTICE

Edited by
Joe Weston

Contributing Authors:
Peter Bulleid, Richard Frost, Michael Lee-Wright, Andrew McNab,
Richard Read, Elizabeth Street

LONGMAN

Addison Wesley Longman
Addison Wesley Longman Limited,
Edinburgh Gate, Harlow,
Essex CM20 2JE, England
and associated companies throughout the world

First published 1997

British Library Cataloguing in Publication Data
A catalogue entry for this title is available from the British Library

ISBN 0-582-27325-0

Typeset in 10/12pt New Baskerville by 32
Produced through Longman Malaysia, PA

CONTENTS

LIST OF FIGURES AND TABLES

ABOUT THE AUTHORS

Joe Weston is Senior Lecturer in environmental impact assessment at Oxford Brookes University and a member of the Royal Town Planning Institute. He has experience in both local government and private practice planning. Before taking up his post at Oxford Brookes he worked for six years in development control at the Vale of White Horse District Council. During the 1970s and 1980s Joe was an active campaigner with Friends of the Earth where he sat on the Board of Directors and for three years was chair of the organisation's campaign strategy committee. As well as his interest in EIA Joe teaches environmental law to planners and has published articles on risk assessment and aspects of land contamination.

After qualifying in environmental science and landscape architecture, **Peter Bulleid** worked for 15 years in planning, dealing with the design and management of the environment. He had a five year spell in consultancy advising on environmental impact assessment and environmental management before becoming the Environmental Systems Manager of Railtrack.

Michael Lee-Wright is a member of the Royal Town Planning Institute with over 20 years of experience in planning and development work. After 12 years of development control and local plan work in the private sector, he moved into consultancy, advising public and private sector clients on a variety of development projects. The 1990s have increased his involvement in EIA work and the co-ordination of multidisciplinary environmental and planning teams. Michael is a member of the Council of the Institution for Environmental Sciences, and has published a number of articles on planning and environmental issues. He currently heads the Environmental Management Division of G.L. Hearn and Partners and is based in London.

Andrew McNab is Director of Scott Wilson Resource Consultants, a major environmental consultancy which has widespread respect within the planning and EIA industry. Andrew has more than 20 years' experience in planning, both in the private and public sectors. His special expertise is in rural resource planning, tourism and EIA.

Richard Read graduated in geography from Leicester University in 1969. After three years working for the London Borough of Hammersmith as a planning assistant he studied full time for a postgraduate diploma in town planning at the then named Oxford Polytechnic. After a short interval with Derbyshire County Council he worked for Mid Glamorgan. The time in South Wales was originally spent working on strategic planning issues, then subsequently development control. Over the last ten years he has headed up the development control group for Hampshire County Council and has had to deal with a wide range of planning issues. These have included oil exploration, many gravel proposals, landfill and the Portsmouth 'Burner'. He has also planning policy responsibilities which include nursing a minerals and waste local plan for the County through the maze of statutory procedures.

Richard Frost is a qualified planner with a special interest in EIA. While a Research Associate in the Impact Assessment Unit of the School of Planning, Oxford Brookes University, he has been involved in research into the strategic environmental assessment of road schemes, reviewing the quality of ESs and maintaining a national database and collection of ESs. He is currently researching a PhD on EIA monitoring and audit.

Dr Elizabeth Street is Principal Planning Officer with Kent County Council where her work includes the appraisal of environmental statements, developing Kent's air quality management system and defining sustainable development in the Thames Gateway using GIS mapping techniques. She was trained in Canada in planning and environmental assessment and has over 25 years' experience, working in both Canada and the UK. Dr Street has worked in local government, private practice and as an academic. She has written extensively on environmental impact assessment and strategic environmental impact assessment.

ABBREVIATIONS

ADAS	Agricultural Development Advice Service
AONB	Area of Outstanding Natural Beauty
BATNEEC	best available technique not entailing excessive costs
BPEO	best practical environmental option
CCGT	combined cycle gas turbine
CPRE	Council for the Protection of Rural England
DoE	Department of the Environment
DTI	Department of Trade and Industry
EC	European Community
EEC	European Economic Community
EIA	environmental impact assessment
EIS	Environmental Impact Statement
EMS	environmental management systems
EPA	Environmental Protection Act
ES	Environmental Statement
ETB	English Tourist Board
EU	European Union
GIS	geographical information systems
HMIP	Her Majesty's Inspectorate of Pollution
HMSO	Her Majesty's Stationary Office
IEA	Institute of Environmental Assessment
IPC	Integrated Pollution Control
JEL	*Journal of Environmental Law*
JPL	*Journal of Planning and Environmental Law*
LPA	local planning authority
MAFF	Ministry of Agriculture Fisheries and Food
MoD	Ministry of Defence
NEPA	National Environmental Policy Act (USA)
NNR	National Nature Reserve
NRA	National Rivers Authority
PPG	Planning Policy Guidance note
PWR	pressurised water reactor
Regulations	Town and Country Planning (Assessment of Environmental Effects) Regulations 1988 (as amended)

RSPB	Royal Society for the Protection of Birds
RTPI	Royal Town Planning Institute
SEA	strategic environmental assessment
SNH	Scottish National Heritage
SPA	Special Protection Area
SSSI	Site of Special Scientific Interest
UK	United Kingdom

The NRA and HMIP, together with the Waste Regulation Authorities, have now become the Environment Agency. They appear here because the cases discussed in the book took place prior to the formation of the new agency.

ACKNOWLEDGEMENTS

The creation of a book is never the work of an individual. There are always many hands which help to mould, shape and produce the completed work. That is obviously the case in a book such as this and it is important that I thank my co-authors for their skill, efficiency and co-operation, without which, as they say, none of this would have been possible. I also need to thank my colleagues at Oxford Brookes University's School of Planning, in particular John Glasson, Riki Therivel and Elizabeth Wilson, all of whom helped and contributed in one form or another. Then there is the contribution made by my family: Anna, who never once complained, even when I spent most of Christmas sitting, tapping away, at a 'laptop'; Michael who accepted, with fairly good grace, the missed fishing trips; and Alice, who cheerfully ignored the tapping away at the 'flaptop' and insisted on explaining everything I didn't want to know about horses anyway!

This though is for Andrew Lees, whose environmental impact assessment was always spot on.

INTRODUCTION

EIA IN THE UK

Joe Weston

This book

Less than a year after the introduction of the Town and Country Planning (Assessment of Environmental Effects) Regulations 1988 Steven Mertz (1989) posed the not unreasonable question: 'The European Economic Community Directive on environmental assessments: how will it affect United Kingdom developers?'[1]. Eight years and over 2000 environmental assessments on, it seems appropriate to look again at that question and to ask now: what has been the effect of the environmental impact assessment regulations on the UK's land use planning system? The intention of this book is to provide a response to that question by focusing on the experience of practitioners in the implementation of the UK's Environmental Impact Assessment process.

Planning policy and even regulations and legislation seem to be constantly changing with continuous updating to accommodate new areas of concern and rulings by the courts. Any work which examines the planning system runs the risk of falling foul of such changes and of becoming dated very quickly. By focusing on the early implementation of and refinements to the environmental impact assessment system, and by claiming to be no more than an examination of those first years, we hope in this book to avoid such risks. By its very nature therefore the book is reflective. It examines the role and use of environmental impact assessment in the UK's planning system since its formal introduction in 1988 through to the beginning of 1996.

Perhaps the very first task is to define some of the terms to be used in the book. The terms used in the discussion of this topic vary considerably but essentially environmental impact assessment, usually abbreviated to EIA, is the most common, although as a term it does largely come from the US National Environmental Policy Act 1969 (NEPA). In the UK the government has always preferred the use of the less dramatic term 'environmental effects' rather than environmental impacts. This has generally led to the dropping of the middle word from the topic's title in the UK and hence the term 'environmental assessment' abbreviated to EA. However, since the introduction in 1990 of a system for the environmental assessment of development plans, the use of EA has become more closely associated with that process. Environmental assessment of development plans is a partial system of strategic environmental assessment (SEA) which is a process for examining the environmental consequences of adopting particular policies, programmes and plans. The EU has produced a draft directive on SEA and it is certain to grow in importance. It is not, however, the subject of this book and will only be discussed in passing. To avoid confusion, in this book the phrase 'environmental impact assessment' and 'EIA' will be used.

The other important abbreviation used here is ES which refers to the Environmental Statement, a document produced by a developer and submitted with a planning application to fulfil the requirements of the Regulations. Again, in a great deal of the literature the word 'impact' is retained and thus reference is sometimes made to an EIS. For the purposes of this study an ES and an EIS should be seen as meaning the same.

It is also essential to make clear that this is not a handbook explaining the process and methodology of EIA; there are already many, perhaps too many, such works. Those works have their utility but they are often less than effective in addressing the major issues created by the imposition of the EIA process on the UK's land use planning system. There is little or no 'science' here, for, as we shall see, the crucial issues facing EIA in the UK are related not to the scientific assessment of environmental impacts but to the political nature of UK planning. One major shortcoming of some works on EIA is that they tend to be written by people with limited practical experience of development control and development promotion. That is not the case here. The contributors to this work include people who are very much involved in the practice of development, from either a local authority or a consultancy perspective. The assembled authors represent some of the most experienced practitioners in the EIA business and bring a unique focus to the theoretical and conceptual debates surrounding EIA. In sharing their experiences they provide the insight necessary for a reflective work such as this – an opportunity to examine the way EIA has been introduced into an already complex development control system and the impact that this has had on that system.

The importance of definitions

Definitions are crucial to understanding both the nature and the development of EIA. The meaning of terms we use every day is often clouded by our own perspectives and understanding of the world. Take a simple term like 'the countryside' for example. In most western societies this is a term which has only positive connotations: it means a place of beauty, a place of relaxation, of leisure, a place to escape to from the often alienating routine of our urban way of life. Michael Redclift (1984)[2] contrasts this with the way the term is understood in many developing countries where it means a place of danger, of poverty, of disease, a place to escape from.

We take the baggage of our own understanding of a word or a phrase with us when we examine issues and debates. This can lead to misunderstandings and to difficulties of interpretation, particularly when the terms we are referring to are in such everyday use as 'the environment'. This is a term which seems to have been on everyone's lips for a generation now and yet it is rarely defined. Nowhere in the planning acts or the EEC Directive which brought in formalised EIA is 'the environment' defined and yet it is the whole focus of the policies and programmes of which EIA forms part.

In its widest sense 'the environment', as a term, becomes almost meaningless for it encompasses everything. Einstein is often quoted as saying 'The environment is everything that isn't me'. This is of course the common dictionary definition where environment is simply defined as 'surroundings'; and yet it is not the meaning ascribed to it in everyday use. Its more common use tends to narrow its meaning to include simply the biophysical world. This is the way the UK's Environmental Protection Act 1990 (EPA) limits and defines 'environment'. For the purposes of that Act:

> The 'environment' consists of all, or any, of the following media, namely, the air, water and land; and the medium of air includes the air within buildings and the air within other natural or man-made structures above or below ground'[3].

If Einstein's definition is too wide to be of use then the EPA's is far too narrow. Not only does it largely neglect the built environment it also ignores the people, animals and plants that inhabit the environment. Ball and Bell (1994) define 'environmental law' as being related to 'the physical surroundings that are common to all of us, including air, space, waters, land, plants and wildlife'[4]. That definition at least widens 'environment' to include the created physical world as well as the natural. Yet the use of the term 'common to us all' provides new difficulties for we do not experience 'the environment' in a common way. Just as the people of the developing world understand and experience 'the countryside' very differently from the people of the so-called developed world, so different groups within society experience 'the environment' differently. A piece of 'wasteland' to some is a 'wildlife site' to others, it may be a 'development site' to another group and a 'playground' to children and so on. Our understanding and experience of 'the environment' is shaped by our relationship to it and the way we use and interact with it. The environment is not therefore something which is objectively experienced but something which is full of different and often competing values and interests. In this way the physical world is socially, culturally, economically and politically constructed and reconstructed and the physical world cannot be set apart from the forces that shape it. Any meaningful definition of 'environment' must therefore be able to relate the physical world to those forces. In this Salter's (1992) definition would seem the most appropriate.

> It could be said to consist of the physical space on earth, and the inhabitants who live in that space and of all the processes in that space which interact with its inhabitants[5].

Those 'processes' would include the economic and social impacts upon the physical world as well as the physical world's impact upon economic and social factors. That interaction is what creates the environment and the way we see and experience our world. It is a dynamic process which ensures that the environment is changing all the time, both naturally and through human action. Because of that change it is pointless to discuss 'environmental protection' for 'the environment' cannot be protected in any meaningful way; all that can be achieved is the management of that change in the best interests of the planet and its inhabitants.

One tool for managing environmental change is land use planning which, in the UK at least, has always recognised the interrelationship and interaction between economic, social and political forces and the environment. Yet planning, as a means of managing the environment, is only as effective as the powers granted to it by government and the socio-legal system in which it operates. This can be a fundamentally important restriction on environmental management; especially when the law, as in the UK, traditionally only sees the environment in terms of property rights and where environmental decisions are made on the basis of a policy principle that sets a presumption in favour of development[6].

A further, and significant, feature of the UK's legal tradition is the way the courts take a very literal approach to the interpretation of legislation and regulations. The semantic meaning of individual words is central to the way courts make decisions and set precedents. As Alder (1993)[7] argues, this is a particularly important feature of the law when UK courts are interpreting EU legislation. The directives and regulations which come from Brussels are based upon a wholly different European tradition which relies more on the context and spirit of the law than on the meaning of individual words. This difference in approach is crucial to an understanding of the introduction and operation of formalised EIA in the UK.

The concept of EIA

EIA also needs to be defined and many people have attempted to do this in ways which express the full extent of its role and purpose in environmental management. Perhaps the most comprehensive definition of EIA is Walthern's (1992) adaptation of Munn's (1979):

> a process for identifying the likely consequences for the biogeophysical environment and for man's health and welfare of implementing particular activities and for conveying this information, at a stage when it can materially affect their decisions to those responsible for sanctioning proposals[8].

Walthern (1992), however, also puts it more succinctly:

> EIA is a process having the ultimate objective of providing decision makers with an indication of the likely consequences of their actions[9].

Here Walthern is acknowledging that decision makers are not simply those who provide the formal authorisation for the activity or development to take place. The decision maker in this sense can also mean the promoter of a project who, armed with the EIA, can decide whether to pursue the project or not, alter and amend the project and mitigate against impacts at an early stage so as to avoid failure at the authorisation stage.

The EIA process has been developing since the 1960s when it was first given formalised status through the USA's NEPA which required EIAs for federally funded or supported projects which were likely to have environmental effects. Yet, as Fortlage (1990) argues, environmental assessment has been with us for much longer[10]. Indeed in the UK a formalised system of EIA was resisted by successive governments because, they argued, the UK planning system had, since its creation, made an assessment of the environmental impact of development through the development control process. They believed EIA would only add unnecessary complications to a well tried and effective system[11]. Promoters of EIA have always argued that the difference between the assessment of environmental impacts carried out by traditional development control and EIA is the latter's more rational, systematic and holistic approach[12]. Yet the reasons for adopting a formalised EIA procedure go deeper than simply a perceived need for a more rational approach to project assessment. Indeed the introduction of EIA through the American NEPA was as much a response to political pressure from the growing environment lobby as it was an attempt to introduce a new planning technique[13]. The NEPA used EIA as a policy implementation measure rather than simply a planning technique and the introduction of EIA was part of a whole redirection of the planning process[14]. Indeed the NEPA established policy principles for the enhancement of the environment which EIA would implement. In this sense EIA is seen to have objectives of its own which are to minimise harm to the environment and those who inhabit and rely upon it[15]. Many early proponents of EIA saw it in this light and considered that its main value would be in the prevention and mitigation of the adverse environmental effects of development[16]. Grove-White (1984), for example, held the view that the 'underlying principle behind EIA, which I fully endorse, was in the NEPA's 1969 words "to create and maintain conditions under which man and nature can exist in productive harmony for present and future generations"'[17]. According to an OECD report published in 1979 the purpose of EIA is to 'safeguard the environment'[18]. EIA should therefore be seen in the context of this political aspiration and in the context of its introduction in the 1960s, a period of social, economic and political change when the environment was, perhaps for the first time, becoming an internationally popular political cause.

This view, that EIA is a process with its own inherent goals and objectives, runs through much of the literature on the subject, with much emphasis placed on the role of EIA in the prevention of environmental harm. Glasson *et al.* (1994) argue that EIA is a systematic process for the examination of environmental impacts of development and 'the emphasis, compared with many other mechanisms for environmental protection, is on prevention'[19]. Jorissen and Coenen (1992) describe EIA as an 'instrument of preventative environmental management'[20].

This underpinning purpose is important for our understanding of the whole process for it requires that EIA takes place at a much earlier stage of project development than traditional planning or development control assessments. Selman (1992) emphasises this by arguing:

> EIA should ideally ensure that thorough examination of a proposal takes place at the earliest possible opportunity, preferably to coincide with the earliest stages of project planning, so that design and performance standards can be influenced from the outset[21].

Walthern (1992) goes further:

> Indeed, the greatest contribution of EIA to environmental management may well be in reducing adverse impacts before proposals come through to the authorization phase[22].

The EIA process

As a systematic, rational, process EIA must logically take place within some kind of framework. Not only must that framework be able to provide the systematic appraisal of environmental effects, it must, according to Glasson *et al.* (1994), be cyclical and iterative to allow feedback and reassessment at every stage of the process[23]. The large collection of EIA handbooks that exist broadly agree on the content of that framework, with some emphasising the importance of one stage over another, and they tend to provide step by step advice on the procedures and content of each stage of the process. Most would agree that 'good' EIA would contain the following stages.

- Project/action identification: This will include an examination of alternatives such as processes and locations as well as the scale and dimensions of the project or action.
- Project screening: Determining whether the project requires an EIA and deciding whether the scale or other factors can be reduced to avoid formal EIA.
- Scoping: Narrows the scope of the EIA to the most likely significant impacts and defines the 'environment' to be assessed. This will include the geographical level of the study, i.e. local, regional, national, transnational.
- Project/action description: A detailed description of the project or activity is assembled to ensure that all facets, and therefore all potential impacts, are identified.

- Baseline environmental conditions description: This requires a thorough investigation or audit of the environment into which the project or activity is to be introduced.
- Identification of key or significant impacts: This is where the previous stages are brought together to ensure that all significant impacts are identified. It should be emphasised here that impacts can be both positive and negative.
- Impact prediction: Evaluation and assessment of the significance of impacts.
- Mitigation: The measures proposed to reduce the significance of impacts, including any redesign or reduction in scale of the project or activity.
- Public participation and consultation: This should not be seen as simply taking place at this point in the process but ideally should take place continuously from the first stage onwards. Public participation and consultation with public bodies can be particularly crucial to the success of the scoping stage.
- ES preparation and presentation: Under the NEPA system a draft ES is produced and is subject to scrutiny and public comment before the final version is produced. Under such a system many versions could be produced to reflect changes in the project or activity which have occurred during the EIA process.
- Review: This is the more formal ES appraisal stage where the authorisation body, together with the public and consultative bodies, consider the content, quality and the methodologies contained in the ES.
- Decision making: The formal authorisation stage will depend upon the decision-making system and may require separate appraisal of other factors outside the remit of EIA such as national security and economic policy.
- Monitoring: The monitoring of the impacts as they take place during construction/implementation and operation.
- Auditing: Assesses the quality of the EIA process by comparing predicted and actual impacts[24].

This dynamic, systematic and interactive approach was in many ways at the heart of the NEPA system which placed a great deal of emphasis on public participation, scoping, the publication of a draft ES for public comment and the redrafting of the ES following that comment and reassessment. The NEPA system also made provision for post decision and implementation monitoring to assess the accuracy of the impact predictions[25]. Jorissen and Coenen (1992) argue that in the US system an examination of alternatives is considered to be central to the whole EIA process[26]. As such, EIA is seen as a complete process that is much more than an aid to project authorisation. It is an aid to decision making but those decisions are made constantly throughout the process, from project inception to construction and beyond to operation and decommissioning.

For Haigh (1983) the main advantage of EIA is that it is a process which is 'self-contained and capable of being applied even without the infrastructure necessary of a fully fledged planning system. Hence its attractions to those countries who can see the inadequacy of their sectoral licensing procedures but whose planning system is still primitive'[27]. The interesting question for this book is what happens when EIA is introduced within an existing complex and legalistic planning system such as the UK's.

Introduction of EIA

As stated above successive UK governments had been opposed to the formalised introduction of EIA. There were a number of reasons for this. Firstly they took the view that the UK's development control system was already carrying out the function of environmental assessment; secondly they saw EIA as a further impediment to industrial development; and thirdly they disliked having new regulations imposed from outside[28]. As we shall see, this resistance to EIA was not completely dissolved when its introduction became mandatory following the introduction of an EEC Directive in 1985.

That Directive[29] was first suggested in the EEC's second action programme for the environment in 1977 and was published in draft form in 1980. However, progress from the action programme to the draft directive was not simple, with some commentators estimating that between 20 and 50 versions were produced before the final draft was published[30].

The cause for the delay in producing the draft directive was the resistance by member states, not only the UK, to some of the proposed requirements. Creating a system which would be acceptable to all members was not an easy process and even the published draft directive was subject to criticism and opposition. Haigh (1983) argues that even after the publication of the draft the UK's attitude towards the Directive appeared to be 'total opposition'[31]. Criticism of the draft was not limited to the Government; the Royal Town Planning Institute (RTPI) felt that the 'proposed Directive, by its very nature, is not best suited to the British planning system as it would excessively codify and formalise procedures of which, so far, there is limited experience and therefore their benefits are not yet proven'[32].

This is not to say that there was total opposition to EIA in the UK. Indeed the RTPI's submissions, although critical, did accept that the proposals were better than nothing. Moreover between 1970 and 1987 some 250 EIA type exercises were carried out in the UK on a non-statutory basis, including those for the Vale of Belvoir coalfield, the Lock Lomond pumped storage electricity scheme and a number of EIAs for motorways[33]. Indeed, for many large developments EIA had long been the norm in the UK since the early 1970s[34]. The problem for the UK Government was not the principle of EIA, for it had produced and published guidance on its preparation, it was having a formalised system forced on it by the EEC.

The Directive

Despite much rhetoric over loss of sovereignty during and following the Maastricht Treaty debate, the UK has been bound by EEC law since it joined the community in 1973[35]. The EEC has since become the European Union (EU) and it affects UK planning and environmental law through its policies and its regulations. In effect UK law *constitutes* the EU law in practice in that EU legislation, directives and regulations are implemented through UK law. The majority of EU environmental controls are in the form of Directives which are binding on member states and require changes to domestic law for their implementation[36].

The Directive on assessment of effects of certain public and private projects on the environment (85/337/EEC), finally adopted in 1985, was enacted under the terms of Article 100 of the Treaty of Rome which deals with the removal of unfavourable competitive conditions[37]. In fact most environmental Directives are produced under the terms of Article 100 which is basically intended to protect the free market operating within the community. By introducing EIA across the whole community the EEC hoped to ensure that the same development restraints and conditions operated equally throughout so that no single state would have more rigorous regulations than others. This is a very different rationale to the reasons behind the introduction of EIA in the USA. However, the Directive on EIA also fell within the terms of Article 235 which is for the implementation of other community objectives not specifically covered by other Articles. In this case the objective was 'the protection of the environment and quality of life'[38]. This 'objective' of the community was not part of the Treaty of Rome and was not in force at the time of the publication of the draft directive on EIA in 1980. Significantly protecting the environment only became a full objective as a result of a decision by the European Court of Justice in 1983, two years before the adoption of the Directive and three years after the publication of the draft[39].

The Directive required EIA to be carried out prior to the authorisation of development projects which were likely to have a significant effect on the environment. These projects were divided into two groups, Annex I projects for which EIA was mandatory and Annex II where EIA was largely discretionary but normally required when the project was likely to give rise to significant environmental effects. Annex I projects include crude oil refineries; thermal power stations; radioactive waste disposal installations; chemical installations; motorways and major roads; trading ports; certain waste incineration plant; and waste treatment plant or landfill. Annex II lists over 90 development projects which would be subject to EIA should they be likely to have significant environmental effects.

The Directive did not define 'significant effects' which inevitably causes ambiguity and inconsistency between member states. In the UK, as we shall see, there has been an attempt to define the term through threshold indicators which are wholly arbitrary and are not indications of significant effects in themselves. In December 1995 the EU's Environment Ministers agreed the terms of an amendment to the Directive which creates a new Annex IIa which will set out the criteria for selecting projects for assessment. Although lengthy the Annex basically relates impacts to a project's characteristics such as size, location, duration and complexity[40]. As we shall see below this is very similar to the UK's project screening criteria.

Other ambiguities within the Directive include the assessment of alternatives. The key requirement of the Directive is set out in Article 8 which requires that the information gathered through the EIA process must be taken into consideration in the authorisation procedure. That information is required under the terms of Article 5(1) and is set out in full in Annex III:

Information referred to in Article 5(1)

(1) Description of the project, including in particular:
   - a description of the physical characteristics of the whole project and the land-use requirements during the construction and operational phases;
   - a description of the main characteristics of the production processes, for instance, nature and quantity of the material used;
   - an estimate, by type and quantity, of expected residues and emissions (water, air and soil pollution, noise, vibration, light, heat, radiation, etc.) resulting from the operation of the proposed project.

(2) Where appropriate, an outline of the main alternatives studied by the developer and an indication of the main reasons for his choice, taking into account the environmental effects.

(3) A description of the aspects of the environment likely to be significantly affected by the proposed project, including in particular, population, fauna, flora, soil, water, air, climatic factors, material assets, including the architectural and archaeological heritage, landscape and the interrelationship between the above factors.

(4) A description of the likely significant effects of the proposed project on the environment resulting from:
   - the existence of the project,
   - the use of natural resources,
   - the emissions of pollutants, the creation of nuisances and the elimination of waste;
   and the description by the developer of the forecasting methods used to assess the effects on the environment.

(5) A description of the measures envisaged to prevent, reduce and where possible offset any significant adverse effects on the environment.

(6) A non-technical summary of the information provided under the above headings.

(7) An indication of any difficulties (technical deficiencies or lack of know-how) encountered by the developer in compiling the required information[41].

Here an examination of alternatives, considered by many to be essential to the EIA process, is only required 'where appropriate' with again no guidance given as to the circumstances where it would be appropriate to carry out that examination. Nor is there any indication of what would constitute the 'main' alternatives to any given project. Is the Directive referring to alternative locations or processes or both? The revised Directive agreed in 1995 will require developers to 'outline' the main alternatives 'studied' and to provide reasons for their choice[42]. Once again the scope for a minimalist approach is obvious.

This lack of definition within the Directive provides scope for differing interpretations between member states. Ultimately this must lead to variations between the systems used in different EU countries, thus negating one aim of the Directive which was to harmonise regulations across the community.

The emphasis placed by the Directive on the collection and presentation of information leads to the wrongful assumption that the document which contains that information, the ES, is the final result of the EIA. Ball and Bell (1994) describe the ES as the 'end product of the assessment ... and is submitted on behalf of the developer'[43]. Even Walthern (1992) refers to the ES as the 'outcome' of an EIA when in fact, as we have seen, it is simply a part or stage of the whole EIA process[44].

Significantly, and surprisingly given the degree of agreement over the process, the Directive does not establish any real framework for carrying out an EIA. There is no requirement for scoping or review or indeed the later stages of the process, monitoring and auditing. These are all stages which are considered by many in the field to be key features for the success of the whole process. The amended Directive will make it compulsory for competent authorities to provide the scope of the assessment but only where they are requested to do so by the developer. This change does not appear to recognise the importance of scoping to the EIA process and is far removed from the compulsory scoping demanded by many proponents of best practice.

Objectivity has long been considered a problematic area of EIA, particularly where the developer is carrying out the assessment. Over the first eight years of formal EIA in the EU the quality and objectivity of EIAs has been a major topic of debate and research. The Directive provides no requirement for any kind of independent review of an ES, which injects a potential for bias and the use of EIA to simply justify projects. In a paper to a conference at Aston University in 1994 Carys Jones[45] estimated that, on the basis of the Lee and Colley ES review criteria[46], of all ESs submitted between 1988 and 1992 only 30% were assessed as being of good quality with 40% considered to be unsatisfactory. A study by Oxford Brookes University in 1995 demonstrated that there had been a general improvement in the quality of ESs since the 1992 research. The Oxford Brookes research showed that the percentage of 'satisfactory' ESs from pre-1991 was 36% whereas the post-1991 percentage was 60%[47].

The central requirements of the Directive are the gathering of environmental information and its presentation and, without any formal framework for assessment, it has largely failed to create the cyclical and dynamic process necessary for full EIAs to take place. The Directive did not, therefore, introduce a full EIA *process*; it simply ensured that information about the impact of a project on the environment is taken into 'consideration' before that project is granted formal authorisation.

The detailed system for the implementation of EU Directives is left to the individual member states but must, in theory, be carried out within set time periods. In the case of the EIA Directive, Article 12 required that it be implemented within three years, i.e. before 3 July 1988. Article 5 of the Treaty of Rome requires the repeal of incompatible domestic laws and member states must send a letter of compliance to the Commission to explain the means used to implement the terms of a Directive. Article 2(2) of the Directive permitted member states to integrate EIA 'into the existing procedures for consent to projects'; which is exactly what happened in the UK.

The UK's EIA regulations

In the UK the Government's hostility to the new EIA system was not diminished by the adoption of the Directive and it too took its time in making the necessary changes to the planning system. Bently (1988) reported that the Government's officer responsible for supervising the implementation of the Directive publicly admitted that Europe's EIA requirements 'cut right across the Government's present policy of deregulation and simplification of the planning system'[48]. Forced to accept the inevitability of introducing a system which would fulfil the requirements of the Directive, the Government revised its initial opposition and argued that EIA would only apply to very few projects and that Annex II projects would not normally be subject to EIA at all[49].

Following the publication of the Directive a long process of producing draft regulations, consultation and debate took place during which the Government was consistently accused of attempting to adopt this minimalist approach[50]. Draft regulations and circulars were published which explained the Government's interpretation of the Directive and the system it would introduce for its implementation. Milne (1988b) argued that the Government's less than enthusiastic response to the Directive led to muddled and ill considered proposals for its implementation[51]. The consultation exercise produced many specific criticisms and the Council for the Protection of Rural England (CPRE) even complained to the EC Commission on what it saw as the Government's 'weak' proposals for projects such as forestry and agriculture which were outside the scope of UK development control and yet required EIA under the terms of the Directive. The draft proposals made the Forestry Commission and the Ministry of

Agriculture, Fisheries and Food (MAFF) the 'competent authorities' for deciding when an EIA was required, even for their own schemes[52]. It was not until 1995 that the Government finally amended the Regulations to cover those projects not normally requiring planning permission or other authorisations.

Other complaints related more to the failure of the Directive to require a defined procedure for carrying out EIAs and the lack of any requirement to consider cumulative impacts of projects which fall just below the thresholds for Annex II[53].

When the Directive was finally implemented it came in the form of 21 different sets of regulations. These regulations covered the planning system, projects authorised under other systems such as power stations, afforestation and harbour works. For the purposes of this study the important regulations, and the regulations under which most EIAs are carried out, are the *Town and Country Planning (Assessment of Environmental Effects) Regulations 1988* and their sister regulations for Scotland.

The integration of EIA into UK planning

The first issue of relevance is the way the term 'environmental assessment' is defined within the UK system. We saw above that in theory EIA is a systematic appraisal which has a number of stages running from project identification through construction monitoring to operational auditing and beyond. This system is cyclical and iterative, in that the identification of adverse impacts at one stage can be re-fed into a previous stage to alter the design of a project and that whole process is an aid to decision making in the broadest sense in that decisions are made at every stage of the process. The Department of the Environment (DoE) Circular 15/88: *Town and Country Planning (Assessment of Environmental Effects) Regulations 1988* defines environmental assessment thus:

> the whole process required to reach the decision, i.e. the collection of information on the environmental effects of a project, the consideration of that information which must be carried out by the local planning authority and the final judgement resulting in development consent or refusal[54].

This is a much narrower view of the process with only one decision seen as of relevance and with the process ending at that decision. In essence the EIA process has been adapted to fit within the existing UK planning system. It has not been imposed upon the system, therefore changing the nature of development control. It has simply been made to fit the existing system which has maintained its long established decision-making procedures. As we shall see from the following examination of the UK's EIA planning regulations, the principles of development control decision making have been largely untouched by the implementation of the Directive.

The 1988 Regulations carry through the requirements of the Directive by providing the legal mechanism under which certain development projects are assessed. Major development projects are divided into the two categories from the Directive; Schedule 1 projects where an environmental assessment is mandatory and Schedule 2 projects where developments only require an EIA when they are likely to give rise to 'significant environmental effects'. This phrase is the first difficult problem, for before a decision can be made as to whether a Schedule 2 project requires an EIA, and is therefore controlled by the terms of the Regulations, an assessment as to whether the development is likely to have 'significant environmental effect' must be carried out. DoE Circular 15/88, which was published to accompany the Regulations, provides some limited help and suggests a test of 'significance':

i) whether the project is of more than local importance, principally in terms of physical scale;

ii) whether the project is in a particularly sensitive location – e.g. National Park, SSSI, AONB and may have significant effects because of its location rather than its scale;

iii) whether the project is likely to give rise to complex or adverse effects – e.g. discharge of pollutants.

The Circular also suggests thresholds:

- pig rearing – 400 sows, 5,000 fattening pigs
- opencast mines – more than 50 ha
- manufacturing plants of 20–30 ha or above
- industrial estates of 20 ha+
- urban development – 10,000 square metres of shops, offices or other commercial uses
- local roads – within 100 m of SSSI, NNR or conservation area
- other infrastructure projects – 100+
- waste disposal – 75,000 tonnes p.a.+[55]

At the time of the publication of the Regulations there was concern that the planning profession, which would have the primary role of implementing the new system, was still largely ignorant of the implications of the new Regulations and that confusion over 'significant environmental effects' would remain long after the publication of Circular 15/88[56]. Indeed determining whether a Schedule 2 project will require an EIA remains a grey area even after eight years of experience. There have been two notable court cases, however, which provide guidance. Both cases *Reg. v Swale Borough Council and Medway Ports Authority, ex parte The Royal Society for the Protection of Birds* and *Reg. v Poole Borough Council ex parte Beebe and others*[57] were where local planning authorities had granted planning permission for development without an ES being submitted. In the Swale case it was held that the decision to require an ES for Schedule 2 projects was wholly discretionary and could not be challenged in law unless that decision was taken unreasonably. In the Poole Borough Council case a more substantive point was made. Here the court went to the central requirement of the Regulations. Regulation 4(2) establishes the core duty imposed by the Regulations and states:

> 4(2) The local planning authority or the Secretary of State or an inspector shall not grant planning permission pursuant to an application to which this regulation applies unless they have first taken the environmental information into consideration[58].

The court held that the only purpose of an environmental assessment was to produce the 'environmental information' that has to be considered by the decision maker. This requirement to 'take into consideration' the environmental information does not necessarily mean very much and in many respects provides the key to an understanding of the relationship between EIA and the UK development control system. Section 54a of the Town and Country Planning Act 1990 requires that planning applications and other planning decisions must be made in accordance with the development plan unless material considerations indicate otherwise. Section 70 of the Act requires that in the determination of planning applications regard should be had to all 'material considerations'. Clearly the 'environmental information' required by the EIA Regulations is a material consideration. This must be the case because the Regulations specifically require the information to be considered before an application to which they apply can be determined. Yet Carnwarth (1991) places the requirement of Regulation 4(2) into context:

> The Law is fond of imposing duties on authorities to 'have regard to' things or take them into account. They must have regard to the development plan and other material considerations; they must have regard to the 'desirability of conserving the natural beauty and amenity of the countryside'; and they must 'take into consideration the ES and EI'. Such requirements on their own have little practical effect. Legally an authority may conscientiously have 'regard to' something, and conscientiously put it into the waste paper bin[59].

In the Poole Borough Council case the court took the view that the council, the decision-making body, had all the necessary information available to it and therefore the production of an ES was unnecessary[60]. In a Scottish Office appeal case the Reporter took the view that an environmental assessment would not have raised issues that would not have become apparent 'through the process of planning application, consultations with relevant responsible bodies, district council decision appeal and public inquiry'[61]. The case was an appeal against a decision by the local planning authority to refuse planning permission for an opencast coal mine near Airdrie. The Reporter was even unmoved by a letter from a European Commissioner who supported the view of local people that the project might give rise to significant environmental effects.

These decisions are wholly compatible with the terms of the Regulations and advice of Circular 15/88. At paragraphs 43 and 44 the Circular makes clear that inadequacies of an ES or even the absence of an ES, is not grounds for invalidating a planning application. The duty on the developer is simply to provide the 'environmental information' required in Schedule 3 of the Regulations; there is no requirement to provide that information in a particular form. Schedule 3 defines the ES as 'comprising a document or series of documents providing … the information specified in paragraph 2' and paragraph 2 defines what is called the 'specified information'.

SCHEDULE 3

2 The specified information is –

(a) a description of the development proposed, comprising information about the site and design and size or scale of the development;

(b) the data necessary to identify and assess the main effects which that development is likely to have on the environment;

(c) a description of the likely significant effects, direct and indirect, on the environment of the development, explained by reference to its possible impact on –
human beings;
flora;
fauna;
soil;
water;
air;
climate;
the landscape;
the interaction between any of the foregoing;
material assets;
the cultural heritage;

(d) where significant adverse effects are identified with respect to any of the foregoing, a description of the measures envisaged in order to avoid, reduce or remedy those effects; and

(c) a summary in non-technical language of the information specified above[62].

Schedule 3 is sometimes referred to as the 'minimum regulatory requirements' of an ES[63]. However, the 'specified information' does not necessarily comprise all the 'environmental information' which Regulation 4(2) requires to be taken into consideration before a planning decision on a project can be made. The Regulations define the 'environmental information' thus:

'environmental information' means the environmental statement prepared by the applicant, any representations made by any body required by these Regulations to be invited to make representations or to be consulted and any representations duly made by any other person about the likely environmental effects of the proposed development[64].

At planning appeals DoE Inspectors have taken the view that this information includes representations made on the contents of the ES, information provided by third parties and information deduced through the cross-examination of expert witnesses during the public inquiry[65]. The ES is not, therefore, the end of the EIA process; it is simply a means of providing part, albeit a significant part, of the total environmental information required before a planning application can be determined.

This requirement to consider environmental information is not of course a new one for where environmental factors are material to a planning application they have always needed to be taken into consideration by the planning authority[66]. The real difference is that the Regulations require the developer to provide the bulk of this information with the planning application. Before formal EIA was introduced into the UK it was for the planning authority to amass the information necessary for it to make a decision. They had the right under the terms of the General Development Order to require the developer to supply such further information as they saw necessary to determine outline applications but that information would fall a very long way short of the requirements of the EIA Regulations. Prior to 1988 the level of information that has since been provided in an ES would only have been available once the application came before an Inspector or the Secretary of State at appeal. This is one of the greatest advantages of EIA, and perhaps the most significant change that has been made to the UK planning system. It provides the planning authority, together with consultees and the public, an opportunity to assess this information at a very much earlier stage in the development control process.

The Regulations do make provision for resolving disagreements between planning authorities and developers over the need for an EIA on Schedule 2 projects. Either before a planning application is made or after it is lodged the applicant can ask the 'competent authority', usually the local planning authority (LPA), if EIA is necessary (Regulation 5). The LPA has three weeks to respond and it must respond with full details of why it does or does not require an EIA (Regulation 9). If it fails to meet this deadline, or such other time limit as first agreed with the applicant, then the applicant can seek a direction from the Secretary of State for the Environment as to whether an EIA is necessary (Regulation 6). If the applicant disagrees with the LPA that an EIA is necessary then, after formal notification, there is again provision for a direction from the Secretary of State. The new Annex IIa of the amended Directive may require amendments to this part of the Regulations as competent authorities may be required to base their determination on the new thresholds rather than a case by case assessment.

Circular 15/88 makes clear that where an applicant volunteers an ES, even when the Regulations do not require such to be provided, and where the applicant has stated that the ES is submitted in accordance with the Regulations, then the LPA is entitled to deal with the proposed development in accordance with the Regulations.

If after three weeks from notification that the LPA requires an EIA the applicant has not responded or sought a direction from the Secretary of State, then the application is deemed to be refused and there is no right of appeal (Regulation 9).

The Secretary of State also has three weeks in which to make a decision on a direction but in effect he has as long as it takes as the Regulations make provision for him to come to a decision within three weeks or in such other time as the Secretary of State deems necessary (Regulation 6).

A planning application which is accompanied by an ES is subject to the publicity requirements of Article 8 of the General Development Procedures Order 1995. Regulation 13 requires that prior to the submission of the ES, if that takes place after the submission of the planning application, it is necessary for the developer to notify the public of the proposal through an advertisement in the local press and a site notice. The notice and advertisement must describe the proposal and give an address of where the ES may be viewed. The documents must be available for inspection for at least 20 days after the date of the notice and the LPA may not determine the application within 21 days of receipt of the application and the ES.

Unlike standard planning applications the Regulations make provision for prior consultation between the applicant and the statutory consultees, who are charged with a duty to provide such information as is available and necessary for the developer to carry out the EIA (Regulation 22). The developer may give notice of an intention to submit an application accompanied by an ES and the LPA must notify the statutory consultees (Regulation 8). These statutory consultees can include the Environment Agency, the Countryside Commission, English Nature and the equivalent bodies in Wales and Scotland.

Regulation 14 requires the LPA to ensure it has sufficient copies of the ES to carry out consultations in accordance with Article 10 of the General Development Procedures Order 1995. This will include consultation with bodies such as the Environment Agency, Utility Companies, Health and Safety Executive, Highway Authority etc.

An LPA has the power, under Regulation 21, to request further information if it believes that the information provided in the ES is inadequate in some way. However, this opportunity to review the ES and provide the cyclical interactive process of EIA is checked, to some extent, because the LPA cannot turn the application away if the requested additional information is not forthcoming. The only recourse in those circumstances is for the LPA to refuse planning permission, after which the developer enjoys the normal rights of appeal.

In assessing the ES local authorities need to be aware that they have this power to ask for further information for failure to exercise that power can be seen later, at an appeal for example, as tacit acceptance of the information provided. At an appeal for a quarry extension near Kilmarnock in Scotland the Reporter took the view that it was significant that the planning authority had not asked for further information when they were processing the application and had not raised any objections to the ES until the development came to appeal[67].

The LPA has 16 weeks, including the period of consultation with the statutory bodies and the public, in which to determine whether planning permission should be granted or not. A copy of their decision, together with conditions where approved, must be sent to the DoE (Regulation 23). If refused the applicant has the normal right of appeal.

The Regulations apply equally to local authorities even when making deemed consent applications. They do not apply in the same way to the Crown. Under the terms of Circular 18/84, where the Crown is to carry out development which would normally require planning permission it is only required to send details of proposals to the LPA and take account of its views[68]. Circular 15/88 states that where the Regulations would otherwise apply an ES will normally accompany the Circular 18/84 notification. Circular 15/88 also states that an ES will accompany DoE, Ministry of Defence and Department of Transport proposals provided national security is not threatened.

The role and potential of EIA is dependent upon the way it is operated and the overall context of its operation. In the UK it was introduced into an existing system of development control which had fixed decision-making procedures laid down by statute, court-made precedent and tradition. Because of this the introduction of EIA into Britain did not dramatically change the decision-making procedures. Environmental assessment was just slotted into an existing development control system to comply with the terms of European legislation while minimising the impact of that legislation on the existing system. Alder (1993) argues that EIA, in the UK:

> is not, as such, an environmental protection measure with positive goals. Environmental impact assessment is intended to enable decision-makers to make an informed choice between environmental and other objectives and for the public to be consulted. Nothing in the Directive requires any particular weight to be attributed to environmental factors or to public opinion[69].

This seems to be completely at odds with the theoretical understanding of EIA as an environmental management process with its own inherent aims and objectives. Salter (1992) goes further:

> So long as the procedures are in place and followed there is not any particular disadvantage to the United Kingdom in fully implementing the Directive in its present form because assessments in practice are not necessarily particularly influential[70].

Issues in EIA in the UK

The above discussion of the introduction of EIA into the UK and its role within the development control process has raised a number of key issues.

These issues include the roles and responsibilities of all the various participants in the process; the use and interpretation of the Regulations; the relationship between EIA and project decision making; and the ability of EIA to produce better, more environmentally sensitive, projects. Essentially these issues relate directly to some of the main stages of the EIA process that were discussed earlier such as project screening, scoping, public participation, review and decision making. The way those stages are carried out and managed is crucial to the success of the whole process and to an understanding of the role of EIAs within development control decision making.

At the heart of the issues addressed here is the question of how EIA, a rational, systematic environmental management process, is integrated into a sometimes irrational planning system which is in essence a political process: after all, planning determines who wins and loses in the constant and continuing battle over the crucial environmental resource of land. That struggle takes place because of the often adversarial nature of the UK planning system where developers must pit their power, influence, political and legal judgement, and sometimes cunning, against environmentalists, residents, interest groups and politicians. In such a system the 'science' of predicting individual impacts within EIA is largely secondary to the politics of the decision-making process, particularly when those predictions must first of all be believed by sceptical opponents and then attributed weight in the balancing act which is UK development control.

To assess these issues and EIA's position and role and its success in the UK we must examine how it is used in practice and how the participants in the whole process judge its utility and worth as a planning tool. Only then can we address the question raised by Mertz (1989) at the beginning of this Introduction.

EIA in practice

As was stressed earlier, this book makes only one real claim – that it is reflective. It examines EIA through the experience of practitioners and case studies, and through that examination draws some conclusions on the influence of formal EIA on the UK's land use planning system. The book has been structured around the important stages of the EIA process, discussed above, to highlight some fundamental issues in the introduction and development of EIA in the UK. Each chapter examines cases and issues from the individual perspective of the writer. There has been no editorial 'whip' to ensure all contributors 'toe the line', and yet there is very much common ground and agreement between the individual authors on the issues and problems facing EIA and its role within the planning process.

The first stage of EIA is project screening, determining which projects require full EIAs before a planning decision can be made. Given the vagueness of the Regulations and Circular 15/88 this is not a simple process. In Chapter 1 Peter Bullied looks at this initial stage and asks why so many formal environmental assessments have been carried out when the Government's original advice predicted that only a dozen or so each year would be required. As explained earlier, the Regulations only require EIA where there are 'significant environmental effects'. Peter Bullied discusses the definition of 'significance' and argues for early consultation with planning authorities to determine what those effects are and to establish whether an EIA is required or not or, indeed, whether something much smaller and simpler, like an issues report, would not be more appropriate in many cases.

After the decision is made to carry out an EIA the developer normally has to appoint consultants to carry out the work. It is far too simplistic to see EIA as something exclusively for 'scientists' to carry out. EIA is a planning tool within a land use decision-making process and system and in Chapter 2 Michael Lee-Wright discusses the crucial role of the planner in EIA and the need for a co-ordinated and multidisciplinary approach to the assessment process. Planners by training and by instinct should know what will be the material planning considerations in a given case and therefore have a central role in the scoping exercise.

There is a great deal of debate among both practitioners and theorists on the importance and relevance of the scoping exercise and what it entails. Some argue that scoping – the determination of what an EIA is to examine – is the most crucial of all the stages of EIA and should include early public participation to allow local people to become involved in identifying the issues they feel need to be resolved before a project can be permitted to go ahead. However, that approach has advantages and disadvantages for both the public and the promoters of schemes. In Chapter 3 Andrew McNab debates these fundamentally important issues within the context of case studies and arrives at some significant conclusions about the role of different groups within scoping and the EIA process as a whole.

The next important stage of EIA examined here takes place after the submission of the planning application and its accompanying ES. The review stage has been the subject of great debate ever since the introduction of EIA in 1988 and there are a number of different ES review systems in existence to help LPAs and consultees assess the adequacy of the information presented. Most recently and significantly perhaps is the simple checklist quality criteria provided in the DoE's *Evaluation of Environmental Information for Planning Projects: A Good Practice Guide* (1994)[71]. However, in Chapter 4 Richard Read reminds us that it is the whole of the environmental information which needs to be reviewed by planning authorities and not just the ES submitted with the planning application. He describes the review process that has been adopted by Hampshire

County Council and how that rational approach does not always result in a rational decision.

Consultation and public participation is both at the heart of and central to the success of good practice EIA and much of the focus of the book is on these aspects of the process. Despite the demands of advocates of best practice that the public should be involved throughout the EIA process, in most cases consultation on EIA takes place after the ES and planning application have been lodged with the LPA. In Chapter 5 we look at the consultation process through two case studies. These studies make the point that consultation is not simply a public participation exercise for it takes place between and within local authorities, an often hidden and neglected yet vital part of the process. Through the case studies presented in the chapter we are provided with a unique insight into the workings of the system and the complexity and controversial nature of the issues EIA explores.

Consultation with the public is, of course, a central feature of UK development control and is perhaps especially important where the local authority is both the developer and the planning authority. In this respect local authorities should aspire to best practice in order both to promote it in others and to ensure that they are serving the public interest in the best possible way. The second case study presented in Chapter 5 makes the case for this approach by providing a model for LPAs of how not to carry out EIA.

If nothing more, EIA should be an aid to the decision-making process and, arguably, if carried out objectively with full participation and consultation should help produce decisions which all parties will accept. However, once the EIA has been completed and the ES submitted and all the other material planning considerations have been taken into account by the planning authority, the resulting decision often leads to a planning public inquiry. Chapter 6 is based upon original research and examines the use of ES at public inquiries and discusses the weight given to the findings of an EIA by planning Inspectors and the Secretaries of State. The examples examined cover the full range of developments requiring EIA and include cases from Scotland, Wales and England. Public inquiries are at the head of the decision-making hierarchy in the UK planning system and set precedents for other cases as well as establishing procedural rules of thumb. In examining EIA inquiry decision letters we are looking at the role of EIA at the highest level of decision making and thus its significance to development control as a whole.

Once planning consent is granted and the project goes ahead the next stage in the EIA process is monitoring. This is not a requirement of the UK Regulations and yet it is often seen as a vital part of a full EIA system. In Chapter 7 Richard Frost discusses the extent to which the monitoring of major projects takes place and how the information produced by that monitoring is used. Drawing on experience from a wide range of projects and cases he makes the case for monitoring being as much in the interests of the developer as the environment.

Elizabeth Street has more experience of EIA than virtually any other local authority planner and no book on the subject would be complete without her contribution. Here in Chapter 8 Dr Street discusses ways in which the EIA process can be harnessed to achieve wider environmental benefits. From the information provided in individual ESs a cumulative picture of the local environment can be produced from which a database of information can be constructed to help identify problems and target solutions. In this chapter, perhaps more than elsewhere, we see the full potential of EIA and one of its most long term impacts on planning and environmental management.

Finally in Chapter 9 the lessons to be learned from the cases examined in this book are discussed to draw some final conclusions about the impact of EIA on the UK land use planning system. The UK's system is assessed against both concepts of best practice and the systems of other countries and while shortcomings and problems are identified the chapter concludes that EIA has brought some notable benefits to the development control process.

Here then before you is the practical experience and implications for the UK planning system of the introduction of EIA. It is, as was said at the outset, a look back at what has happened thus far and as such is reflective. This is not a 'best practice' guide, nor is it a 'tricks of the trade' handbook; it is more than that, for presented here we have the strengths and weaknesses of EIA in UK planning practice.

Notes and references

1 Mertz, S (1989) The European Economic Community Directive on environmental assessments: how will it affect United Kingdom developers?, *JPL*, pp 483–498.

2 Redclift, M (1984) *Development and the Environmental Crisis: Red or Green Alternatives?* London: Methuen, pp 45–48.

3 Environmental Protection Act 1990. London: HMSO.

4 Ball, S and S Bell (1994) *Environmental Law.* London: Blackstone Press, p 4.

5 Salter, J R (1992) Environmental assessment – the question of implementation, *JPL*, pp 313–318.

6 Alder, J (1993) Environmental impact assessment – the inadequacies of English law, *JEL*, Vol. 5, No. 2, 203–220.

7 *Ibid.*

8 Walthern, P (1992) An introductory guide to EIA, in Walthern, P (ed) *Environmental Impact Assessment: Theory and Practice.* London: Routledge, p 6. From Munn, R E (1979) *Environmental Impact Assessment: Principles and Procedures.* New York: Wiley.

9 Walthern, P (ed), *op. cit.* p 6.

10 Fortlage, C A (1990) *Environmental Assessment: A Practical Guide.* London: Gower Technical, p 1.

11 Haigh, N (1983) The EEC Directive on environmental assessment of development projects, *JPL*, p 585.

12 Glasson, J, R Therivel and A Chadwick (1994) *Introduction to Environmental Impact Assessment.* London: UCL Press, p 3.

13 Mertz, S, *op. cit.*

14 Roberts, R D and T M Roberts (1984) Planning procedures for environmental impact assessment, in Roberts, R D and T M Roberts (eds) *Planning and Ecology.* London: Chapman and Hall, p 100.

15 *Environmental Impact Assessment Review,* No. 1, Boston, MA: MIT Press, 1980. Quoted in Garner, J F (1983) Environmental impact statements in the United States and in Britain, in O'Riordan, T and R Kerry-Turner (eds) *An Annotated Reader in Environmental Planning and Management.* Oxford: Pergamon.

16 Jarman, D (1988) Conference makes assessment of impact on system, *Planning* 768.

17 Grove-White, R (1984) The role of environmental impact assessment in development control and policy decision making, in Roberts, R D and T M Roberts (eds), *op. cit.* p 131.

18 OECD (1979) *Environmental Impact Assessment,* Report.

19 Glasson, J *et al., op. cit.* p 3.

20 Jorissen, J and R Coenen (1992) The EEC Directive on EIA and its implementation in the EC member states, in Colombo, A G (ed) *Environmental Impact Assessment.* Dordrecht: Kluwer Academic, p 1.

21 Selman, P (1992) *Environmental Planning.* London: Paul Chapman.

22 Walthern, P (ed), *op. cit.* p 6.

23 Glasson, J *et al., op. cit.* p 3.

24 Adapted from Glasson, J *et al., op. cit.* p 4.

25 Roberts, R and T M Roberts, *op. cit.*

26 Jorissen, J and R Coenen, *op. cit.* p 6.

27 Haigh, N, *op. cit.*

28 Alder, J, *op. cit.*

29 Directive on assessment of the effects of certain public and private projects on the environment (85/337/EEC). Brussels: Commission for the European Communities, 1985.

30 Walthern, P (1992) The EIA directive of the European Community, in Walthern, P (ed), *op. cit.* p 192.

31 Haigh, N, *op. cit.*

32 Memorandum of Observations to Sub-committee G (Environment) of the European Communities Committee of the House of Lords on Draft EEC Directive COM(80) 313. London: RTPI, 1980, p 1.

33 Clarke, B D and R G Turnball (1984) Proposals for environmental impact assessment procedures in the UK, in Roberts, R D and T M Roberts, *op. cit.* p 125; Assessing the impact of new legislation, *Planning* 736.

34 Jarman, D, *op. cit.*

35 Chown, W (1993) The undeniable supremacy of EC law, in *New Law Journal,* 12 March.

36 Ball, S and S Bell, *op. cit.* p 49.

37 Alder, J, *op. cit.*

38 *Ibid.*

39 Redman, M (1993) European Community planning law, *JPL,* p 999.

40 Environmental assessment rules leave much to member states, *ENDS Report 252,* January 1996.

41 Directive 85/337/EEC, *op. cit.* Annex III.

42 *ENDS Report 252, op. cit.*

43 Ball, S and S Bell, *op. cit.*

44 Walthern, P, *op. cit.* p 6.

45 Jones, C (1994) ESs – numbers, quality and the EIA process. Paper presented to Conference on Assessing Environmental Statements, Aston University, 18 October.

46 Lee, N and R Colley (1990) Reviewing the quality of environmental statements. *Occasional Paper 24* (1st edition). Manchester: Department of Planning and Landscape, University of Manchester.

47 DoE (1996) *Changes in the Quality of Environmental Statements for Planning Projects.* London: HMSO.

48 Bently, J (1988) Three months to go, *Planning* 763; Wood, C (1988) EIA and BPEO: acronyms for good environmental planning, *JPL*, pp 310–321.

49 Wood, C, *op. cit.*

50 Milne, R (1988a) Explosion on impact, *Planning* 765.

51 Milne, R (1988b) Private doubts on assessment, *Planning* 754.

52 Bently, J, *op. cit.*

53 Groups unimpressed with impact Circular, *Planning* 756 (1988).

54 DoE (1988) Circular 15/88: *Town and Country Planning (Assessment of Environmental Effects) Regulations 1988.* London: HMSO.

55 *Ibid.* These thresholds are likely to change in light of the amendments to the Directive agreed in 1995. For example, intensive livestock rearing projects, where there are to be in excess of 85,000 broilers, 60,000 hens, 3,000 production pigs or 900 sows, will become Schedule 1 projects, i.e. EIA will be mandatory in all cases.

56 Profession told to wake up on impact, *Planning* 779 (1988).

57 *Reg. v Swale Borough Council and Medway Ports Authority, ex parte The Royal Society for the Protection of Birds*, 1991 JPL 39; *Reg. v Poole Borough Council ex parte Beebe and others*, 1991 JPL 643.

58 Regulation 4(2) Town and Country Planning (Assessment of Environmental Effects) Regulations 1988.

59 Carnwarth, R (1991) The planning lawyer and the environment, *JEL*, Vol. 3, No. 1, 57–67.

60 Ball, S and S Bell, *op. cit.* p 240.

61 Weston, J (1994) Assessments at the appeal cutting edge, *Planning* 1075.

62 Town and Country Planning (Assessment of Environmental Effects) Regulations 1988.

63 Glasson, J *et al., op. cit.* p 153.

64 Regulation 4(2) Town and Country Planning (Assessment of Environmental Effects) Regulations 1988.

65 Weston, J, *op. cit.*

66 Carnwarth, R, *op. cit.*

67 Weston, J, *op. cit.*

68 DoE (1984) Circular 18/84: *Crown Land and Crown Development.* London: HMSO.

70 Salter, J R (1992) Environmental assessment: the challenge from Brussels, *JPL*, pp 14–20.

71 DoE (1994) *Evaluation of Environmental Information for Planning Projects: A Good Practice Guide.* London: HMSO.

CHAPTER 1

ASSESSING THE NEED FOR EIA

Peter Bulleid

Introduction

Throughout this book, the message that EIA is both necessary and beneficial is put with force. Without wishing to detract from this I would like to take the opportunity of an early chapter to step back and look at a few of the underlying assumptions about how EIA can be used and where it fits into the planning system. I also want to examine some of the motives of the various players in this particular game and see to what extent EIA can and does fulfil their hopes. All these matters are relevant for they affect both how and why such studies are done.

It is not my intention to question the potential of EIA but to question whether a technique imported into this country and grafted onto an existing planning system fulfils that potential given the wide range of players in the environmental field. I therefore intend to examine the issues from the point of view of each of the key players in turn. If this process does not answer the questions it will at least highlight them and the reader, in considering his or her answers, may gain further insights into the value of EIA. Perversely I will then look at some cases where an EIA was not undertaken and why this came about.

Background

Joe Weston has covered, in some detail, the background history of the process but there are some points that I think are worth restating. Britain is a relatively small but intensively developed country and it is perhaps not surprising that environmental awareness arose early, as exemplified by the works of many of the pioneers of town planning. However, the physical constraints of land directed early efforts along the lines of zoning and the control of land use as a means of environmental protection. Thus a planning system was developed at an early stage which, from the 1947 Town and Country Planning Act, has evolved into a very sophisticated means of directing and controlling development. The system was also flexible enough to respond to changes in public concern and emphasis and by the mid-1980s planning statements accompanying applications would regularly embrace environmental issues.

Elsewhere, notably in America, concern over development and the effects of industry centred not so much on land but on the wider environmental effects, particularly pollution, arising as a result of those activities. By 1969 this concern became crystallised in the National Environmental Policy Act (NEPA) and ecological impact assessment became firmly established. This rapidly came also to embrace socio-economic effects, so evolving into environmental impact assessment, and by the late 1970s the technique was also being applied to policies and plans.

Europe, or at least the EEC, also began to be concerned with the environment in the 1970s. In general, and at the risk of a sweeping generalisation, its approach to planning and the environment mirrored that of America more closely than that of Britain. Finally, Directive 85/337/EEC on EIA was issued, and Britain was required to legislate within three years to implement the Directive's requirements.

With only days to spare, in July 1988, Britain found itself grafting a 'foreign' procedure onto an already highly developed planning system. If the worst fears of the Europhobes were confirmed, then the Europhiles saw a chance to combine the best of both systems in a typical British compromise. However, it was a compromise and therefore perhaps not the same system that would have been developed if we had had the luxury of a clean slate. After seven years of operating this enforced marriage, have the hopes and fears been realised?

The view from Whitehall

As Joe Weston argued in the Introduction, to suggest that Government welcomed EIA with open arms would be untrue. The EC Directive came well before Mrs Thatcher's green conversion and the length of time it took to pass the necessary legislation speaks volumes for the environmental commitment at that time. Nevertheless, bowing to the inevitable it passed the legislation and issued its guidance in 1989[1].

The HMSO publication *Environmental Assessment: A Guide to the Procedures* (1989), or the 'Blue Book', defined the Schedule 1 and Schedule 2 projects and, helpfully, provided in Appendix 2 guidance on what might be significant for projects falling within Schedule 2. Clearly, as Schedule 1 projects are few and far between and, if the significant thresholds for Schedule two projects are set fairly high, there are going to be relatively few EIAs required each year. At the time it was stated that the number would be a few dozen. In practice 467 were produced between July 1988 and December 1989 with a further 321 in 1991 so that the total is now in excess of 2000. So what went wrong?

Well it could simply have been a mistake. However, the Government has never been slow in estimating the likely cost to the nation when debating proposed European legislation and has tended to look on the black side. It is doubtful that it would have knowingly or mistakenly underestimated the numbers, and hence the burden, when arguing the case.

It would seem more likely that it was expressing a wish, as part of its guidance to developers and local authorities, over the interpretation of the legislation. It did not think many EIAs would be necessary. This view is perhaps confirmed by its attitude to appeals to the Secretary of State by applicants who consider that an EIA is unnecessary. The trend of these decisions has been to minimise the number undertaken.

This view is perhaps strengthened when one looks at its attitude to extensions to the list of projects covered by Schedule 2. While it has recently added windfarms, motorway service areas, coastal protection work and private toll roads to the list it has omitted other contentious proposals such as fish farms and golf courses[2]. The list may be growing but it is doing so at a slower rate than some would wish. Or, conversely, there are fewer EIAs being undertaken than would be the case without the Government's restraining hand.

However, amongst those pressing for change, and by implication additions, is the EU itself. Conscious of failings in the 1985 Directive and of changes since then, an amendment to the Directive has now been circulated for comment. It is understood that, amongst other things, this will considerably extend the range of infrastructure projects falling in Schedule 2 and at the same time produce fresh guidance on interpretation of 'significant impacts'. The thresholds are likely to be lowered so that substantially more proposals would in future require EIAs. While the final form of the amendment remains open to speculation, it appears certain not to minimise the burden on developer and planning system. If this was the Government's original hope then we are moving in the 'wrong' direction.

But does the Government have a point when it talks about burdens and the need to reduce them? The Department of the Environment estimates that its own modest additions of project categories to Schedule 2, outlined above, will potentially add a further 20 EIAs a year. Furthermore it estimates that these cost an average £25,000 each but, as we shall see later, this figure is open to question. Nevertheless it is clear that the Government does consider there is a direct financial cost and few would dispute this. Whether the above figures amount to a burden nationally is open to debate.

This direct cost on projects goes of course to the heart of the Government's concerns over Europe, or rather emerging European legislation. While not antipathetic to the environment, the present Government sees it as only one of a number of factors to be taken into account in planning. Decisions made *in vacuo* in Brussels will not necessarily lead to the best use of resources. Such decisions would more appropriately be made at a local level on a proposal by proposal basis, or so the argument runs. This is the very essence of subsidiarity. If an EIA is necessary, its scope and format are something to be decided at local level, and over-prescriptive regulation from Europe is likely to stifle necessary investment. Given this attitude it is surprising that the concept of scoping has taken so long to be accepted. The original proposed revised Directive would have made this mandatory and it would seem to be a handy mechanism by which the potential discouragement that over-enthusiastic EIA requirements might have on investment and development could be curbed.

In fact the Government has always managed both to have its cake and to eat it, at least with respect to its own proposals, such as the road buildings programme and other strategic proposals in the national interest. While a private developer may be subject to close scrutiny through his ES or a subsequent public inquiry of the alternatives he has considered, the Government is happy to rule this out of court in respect of its own proposals. Such an attitude – 'we are going to build a road and the ES is only there to formally record the likely environmental effects' – is not likely to engender confidence in the belief that EIAs are always the best mechanism for objective decision making.

The local authority perspective

To local authorities falls the main responsibility of administering the regulations concerning EIAs. These require a substantial amount of additional work and resources and, given the downward pressure on staff and costs, one might expect that EIAs would not be welcomed. Curiously the opposite is the case. Why should this be?

There are several reasons. The first is that most professional planners find the requirement for an ES to accompany a major application is genuinely helpful for coming to a balanced decision on the proposed development. A number of local authorities such as Kent County Council have issued helpful guidance on EIAs. Even though the final decision may be taken out of the local authority's hands and given to an Inspector or the Secretary of State, officers cannot advise their members on what position to take on the proposal without an EIA.

This is reasonable. It is the whole purpose of environmental assessment and on the whole it works. Unfortunately there are other reasons for EIAs being welcomed, which may only come to light in private conversations. The second is that an EIA both generates additional work and can be seen to an extent as enhancing the status of those charged with processing it. Moreover, for a manager under pressure to reduce costs and measure up to some performance indicator, the arrival of an ES in his group can be viewed as a manifestation of value. Then again it may be elected members who, faced with a controversial or sensitive proposal, see the need for an EIA as a means of gaining both time to judge a political climate and a possible reason upon which the ultimate decision may be hung. Many unpopular proposals are subject to objections on environmental grounds. An ES that shows no adverse environmental effect can be a very helpful tool in justifying an approval. Conversely if reasons are sought for refusal then most ESs will identify at least one adverse effect and so provide ammunition to use against the unwelcome proposal. This is what Alder (1993) alludes to in his statement quoted by Joe Weston[3].

Whatever the reasons for a local authority seeking an ES, very real doubts exist about the ability of many smaller authorities to interpret adequately the information provided. The range of professional skills in an authority is necessarily restricted and most unlikely to encompass all the issues arising from a major development.

Furthermore, even when it has the skill in house, the staff may not be practised in interpreting an ES or have adequate time to devote to it. One way of addressing this is the use of external consultants to review ESs, if the budget is available. I recall being briefed at short notice to oppose a major development in the Thames Valley and being handed an accompanying ES with the comment that it was very comprehensive. However, a quick review together with a site visit showed that there were significant errors, some 50 potential impacts not identified in the scoping and that the site was materially different from that described.

One of the intentions of the regulations is that an EIA should explore alternatives to the proposal. To a local authority, in considering land use in an area, a detailed consideration of alternatives would be most helpful, but unfortunately this is one area where most ESs are lacking. The original intention was, no doubt, that alternative technologies as well as sites were considered. However, in reality few applicants are realistically able to offer an alternative site, let alone a different technical solution, at least on smaller and medium sized projects. On the largest projects, e.g. the parts of the road programme or the nuclear industry, the Government takes the attitude that alternatives are national issues, outside local decision making. In that the alternative sites may be beyond the local authority boundary, this may not be unreasonable.

However, a number of local authorities, welcoming the requirement for EIAs but dissatisfied with the results, have taken the initiative. Kent, for example, recognising the value of the procedure has sought to ensure that there is some standardisation of contents and treatment of the individual issues in ESs. Regardless of whether the applicant welcomes such guidance and the obligations it places on them, the logic of improving the product for the user, the local authority, is indisputable. After six years the Government followed suit with its own document on the preparation of ESs, which was first published as a consultation draft[4]. It will almost certainly become the benchmark for future ESs, with the danger that it will be assumed that all ESs must treat all the issues to the suggested depth.

The developer

If there is any party that could be expected to have an ambivalent attitude to EIA it is the developer. The immediate reaction is understandably to look askance at a requirement to make public the aspects of their proposal, warts and all, so providing ready ammunition for objectors and regulators. Furthermore the requirement inevitably adds 'up front' costs, at a stage before funding is generally agreed, so increasing the financial risks. Add to this the potential delays the work will entail or, looked at another way, the need to start planning and programming earlier, and there seems to be little in it for the developer.

Of course the argument goes that the discipline that an EIA imposes on the project design and development leads to a reduction in risk and an optimisation in design that provide consequential savings. Thus the EIA can more than pay for itself. I am not sure that an applicant who has been through a long and hotly contested public inquiry where the ES has been debated in detail, for example, would rush to agree. Indeed the whole argument of consequential savings is questionable if the project is properly managed. You do not need to publish an ES to go through the discipline of considering alternatives and refining designs. What, for example, are hazard and operability studies (HAZOPS) and value management supposed to achieve?

Is it all stacked against the developer then? Perhaps not. Few potential developers can be so naive as to think that they do not nowadays require a basket of permissions and consents nor that all the regulatory bodies and statutory consultees will not want to know about various aspects of the proposal and its environmental effects. One single exercise that wraps up all the issues in a seamless manner makes sense. Furthermore, the funding agencies, particularly the banks, are increasingly sensitive to the environmental liabilities of lenders. They look to the ES for reassurance that their commitment is limited and under control. The bank's scrutiny of the ES may be more rigorous than that of the local authority. The long term effects of a bad investment can be more painful than those of a bad planning decision. It is this commercial discipline that concentrates the developer's mind wonderfully.

The consultants

Environmental consultancy work has mushroomed in the last decade and has been less affected by the recession than some other sections of the development industry. Some of this growth has undoubtedly been fuelled by Directive 85/337/EEC. Do consultants therefore see EIA as a breadwinner?

Well to some it may be a meal ticket but not necessarily an easy one. Most clients will be looking to award contracts on a competitive tender basis and will be keeping a close eye on costs. Nevertheless a major EIA is a substantial and no doubt very welcome piece of work for any consultancy. By the same token both the need for an EIA and its scope are issues that it is in the commercial interest of the consultant to bolster.

This raises the question of whom the consultant is serving. Hopefully in the long run it is 'the environment' or the public interest in the environment. To that extent any tendency to an over-comprehensive study can be said to be in the public interest. However, it may not necessarily be in the interest of the client who is paying the bill. The client does not want to take on the job of environmental protection, only to show that the proposal is acceptable. Is the consultant the last party one should look to to argue for or against the need for an EIA and the scoping of that EIA?

Indeed the reports on the quality of EIAs that have been carried out to date must have been a cause for thought amongst clients[5]. Some no doubt felt that they showed that the Regulations are not worth the paper they are written on. Others, though, must have wondered if all this money paid out to consultants was money well spent in terms of the quality of the product. Whatever the quality of ESs has been the fact remains that few consultants have built up a track record of actually negotiating away the need for an EIA.

The industry, conscious of the need and quality issues, has realised the benefits of self-regulation and has itself addressed the matter of quality. The Institute of Environmental Assessment now exists to register consultants, monitor performance and set guidelines and standards. Many individuals and practices have contributed time and resources to assisting with the generation of specialist guidelines on individual topics. As more EIAs are undertaken each year a number of firms are building a track record of achievement.

The public

If the developer can be expected to take a jaundiced view of the process then the public might be expected to take quite the opposite view. The requirement for EIA offers an unprecedented opportunity for access to information through the ES and a chance to influence decisions. However, these benefits have not always been realised in practice.

To start with, the scoping of the study will be carried out by the planners, who may have different objectives from the public, particularly a potential objector. Secondly the study, while being both factual and balanced, may still fail to address some of the issues that an objector feels important, while presenting other issues in a rather favourable light. Finally the very complexity of the issues, the impacts and the environment itself can be such that they are difficult to grasp for the layman, non-technical summary not withstanding.

An added difficulty is that the ultimate test of an ES comes with a public inquiry. Inquiries are notoriously difficult for the lay person and many objectors feel that they are poorly served by the system, often openly expressing frustration with the timetabling and procedures. Certainly if they expect to see value for money, then, considering the direct costs of the EIA, the time spent by planning officers and statutory consultees and the expenses of the public inquiry, the whole process may appear to be less than satisfactory. Perhaps it is these 'hidden' costs that the Government is concerned about as a 'burden'.

One final point is the dilemma that the public and potential objectors face if asked to contribute to the EIA and to the scheme development. Public participation is officially encouraged in the process but is not often practised. Will participation compromise any eventual objections? Could participation improve a scheme that was otherwise unacceptable to the extent that it received approval against objectors' wishes? Nevertheless, in spite of these potential flies in the ointment, the requirement for EIAs is universally welcomed by the public. The objections are almost solely confined to failings in the application of the requirements.

We can draw certain conclusions from this review of the different players on the environmental field. Firstly the very diversity of aspirations and objectives is obvious, and this review is not complete. To the list one should perhaps add regulatory bodies, statutory consultees to the planning process and voluntary bodies or interest groups for example. Secondly it is most unlikely that all will have the same opinion on what is, or is not, significant. Finally, it is very likely that there will be disagreement over whether an EIA will be required at all. It is these last two points, namely significance and whether an EIA is necessary, that I now want to explore.

Significant environmental effects

So what are these requirements and, given the differing objectives and concerns that all the parties bring to the table, how can they be resolved? Well, they are set out in EEC Directive 85/336 and more helpfully for us in the UK the 'Blue Book', which states in Schedules 1 and 2 the type of projects requiring EIAs and in Appendix 3 the contents of an ES. What could be simpler?

To start with this presents us with a very real philosophical problem or, if you prefer, a Catch 22. The purpose of the exercise is to study 'significant effects'. However, we can only determine what effects are significant once the study has been completed, so what are we to study? Come, come, I hear you say. This is a very academic objection. It is obvious for most developments that they are likely to have, say, visual, ecological and socio-economic effects; so study those. Quite right, but those are not necessarily the most significant. Experience tells us these things: first, the most significant effects are often secondary, on processes remote from the site and not manifest except in the longer term; second, that for potential objectors, concerns are likely to be very immediate, specific and personal in nature. Both of these are the least easy types of effects to predict with confidence even with a formal and structured scoping exercise.

Furthermore it is as well to remember that a development proposal does not materialise out of thin air. It is born from the interaction of forces arising from plans, policies, programmes and socio-economic factors, and the current proposal is only the manifestation of the resolution of this equation of forces. A good example of this is out of town shopping. Can Planning Policy Guidance notes 6 and 13 (PPGs 6 and 13) on planning for town centres and land use and transport[6] respectively hope to succeed by simply resisting existing pressure, if nothing is done to change the underlying demand and slow the economic vitality of such developments? So should the ES address such matters as underlying policies, particularly as part of its consideration of alternative processes, or should it be considered in isolation?

Lest we are tempted to recoil from this potentially vast and far reaching consideration of fundamental forces affecting both society and the environment by adopting the policy of considering the proposal in isolation, we must beware. No development can exist in total isolation. Significant effects may arise, indeed will arise, from the cumulative effects that it has with other developments, either existing or proposed. How should these cumulative effects be considered? Is it best for some authority to set local, regional or national limits, such as WHO air quality parameters, and each development show that it does not cause these to be exceeded? Should some arbitrary environmental bubble be defined, such as a local authority area, and all the processes and interactions within that be considered for their cumulative effect?

Just what is significant was an issue that was faced in America in the 1970s. National guidance noted that significance will vary depending upon the viewpoint adopted, i.e. local or global. For this reason a range of contexts for the development should be considered. Andrews et al. (1977) suggested that significance is related to the degree of deviation from some baseline condition, whether in magnitude or time[7]. Thus it is dependent upon the sensitivity of the environment rather than the context. This is the approach taken in much legislation where significance is defined by reference to some specified limit. For example cooling water discharges to rivers must not cause the overall water temperature to rise above a specified level appropriate to the nature of the fish community found in that river.

However, to illustrate the difficulties of judging what is significant Beanlands and Duinker (1982) suggested that the determination should be based on the perception of the decision-making authority, the public and those undertaking the assessment[8]. While this is an admirable recipe for ensuring the widest acceptability of the study it is not very helpful. To define 'significant' as anything that someone considers 'significant' is tautological to say the least.

Many though feel that significance can be defined in measurable terms in some cases or, failing that, at least in terms of past experience. Westman (1985) proposes a five-point checklist:

1. case studies – experience drawn from similar circumstances in the past;
2. modelling – both qualitative and quantitative to give guidance;
3. testing or laboratory studies – small scale practical simulations;
4. field experiments – again practical testing of ecosystem response to likely effects;
5. theoretical extrapolations – expert prediction based on theoretical knowledge[9].

To this is also added a consideration of likelihood in terms of both frequency and magnitude to ensure that the determination of significance is put on as objective a footing as possible. While this checklist, if applied completely, might be helpful and appropriate in connection with very substantial proposals, it would be somewhat onerous for smaller projects and unfortunately it is these smaller projects which are most contentious in terms of significance of effects.

Significance is still something with which we are grappling in this country. Some examples of current advice illustrate the point. The DoE Draft Guidance 1994 did not mention the word but suggested that a scoping report be produced which 'will describe the key environmental issues to be addressed' and so neatly avoids the issue[10]. Croner (1995) sees the need for 'impact screening', noting that interactions between effects such as mixing effluents need to be considered and that 'checklists and matrices have been developed as techniques for use in particular stages of the assessment process'[11]. DoE Circular 1/92 suggests that any Schedule 2 project affecting a designated site such as an SSSI or SPA should be considered significant but that if a local planning authority is in doubt about significant effects it should consult with the relevant statutory body[12]. These three approaches are all different in detail and unlikely to lead to the same conclusions.

The use of checklists to assist with impact identification is common. Indeed the 1989 DoE guidance is an example. Such lists certainly assist in systematising and summarising potential impacts. However, they are simplistic and cannot identify interaction or secondary effects and so are of limited assistance in determining significance. Matrices, such as that attributed to Leopold et al. (1971), are a development that can identify impacts with more precision and certainty[13]. They can, however, become extremely complex and, while still failing to identify significance, can overwhelm with detail.

Developments of the basic matrix can be used to trace secondary or higher order interactions or, by means of a scoring system, begin to identify significant effects. This unfortunately is not without its problems or, in advance of detailed study, will be subjective and the values ascribed including the type of scale used – nominal, ordinal or integral – open to dispute. There is also a tendency to become fascinated by the figures and be tempted to seek some grand index to summarise the likely overall impact of the proposal. Indices can be helpful but whether they offer significant benefits to, and are more cost effective than, informed opinion is open to question.

The ultimate refinement of this approach is the network, first advocated by Sorensen (1971), which traces secondary or higher order effects and allows an estimation of impact magnitude, importance and probability to be made[14]. Furthermore it lends itself to more sophisticated scaling methods and to identifying particular sections of the community that may be affected, but at a cost that is only likely to be justifiable for the largest and most controversial projects.

Indeed these increasingly complex and academic techniques are not met with wide acceptance. Fuller *et al.* (1994) warn:

> Finally, it was felt that normal methods of scoping should be used with caution. To use a check list or a matrix to determine the initial scope of an ES may result in a reluctance to eliminate issues from the EA. An appropriate use of such methods may be to use them literally as 'check list', i.e. the EA is scoped using professional expertise and consultation and then the formal methods are used to ensure that no important issues have been overlooked[15].

The danger that the process will identify insignificant or even non-existent effects for assessment is a very real one. The resulting reduction in the cost effectiveness of the process, demotivation of potential investors and loss of public confidence are exactly the sort of outcomes that the Government seeks to avoid.

Given these difficulties, and combining them with the different objectives of the various parties, which we have already discussed, what is surprising is that in less than ten years we have achieved anything at all. The quality of some published ESs may have left a lot to be desired and the practice of EIA may have been very variable, but in spite of this, we have forged a genuinely helpful tool to aid the decision-making process. The job now must be to improve the breed and to do this it is necessary to focus our efforts in future on what is genuinely significant.

The way ahead

It would be tempting to say that all that is needed is better guidance from the legislation and there is no doubt that this is true to an extent but it is not the whole story. It is clear that the original EEC Directive and the 1988 Regulations have needed review and amplification for some time.

The proposed alterations to the EEC Directive will extend the types of development that will require an EIA, a process that has in fact been ongoing in most countries already. It will also redefine the nature of developments that are likely to warrant an EIA, particularly in the difficult area of infrastructure. Thus rail development, for example, will be identified as requiring assessment if it is electrification or doubling. But necessary and helpful as these changes will be, they illustrate the difficulty of relying on statutory definition alone. For example, rail development that consists of new operating patterns or de-electrification or resignalling, which can double service frequency on a given route, are not included. Are they therefore definitively excluded or do we still have to rely on some interpretation of the catch-all clause about significance to define these types of development?

Perhaps most helpfully the draft directive proposed to make 'scoping' mandatory. This procedure, common, if not already mandatory, in many other countries, has not so far found favour with the Government here. Quite why this should be is unclear because it would appear to be helpful in achieving the balance and objectivity that the Government seeks. Indeed it is one of those rare procedures that appears to hold benefits for all the parties concerned.

The 'Blue Book' has always advised the desirability of early consultations between the developer and the local authority on the form and content of the study. Scoping formalises this process by making it mandatory and requiring both parties to agree on the general content of the final ES – in other words, what issues require to be addressed because of their significance. It is not the purpose of this chapter to deal with the mechanisms of scoping; however, it is worth noting here that it is intended to ensure that effort is not wasted. By implication this means expense and delay is not incurred on unnecessary work, unnecessary in terms of the significance either of the proposal's individual effects or of the total environmental impact.

Consultation, though, can serve a more fundamental purpose. It can materially assist all parties in understanding the proposal, in appreciating the responsibilities and concerns of others and in coming to a decision on the attitude that will be adopted to any planning application. There is often a tendency for developers to adopt a bullish approach or to assume that there will automatically be opposition to their proposals, neither of which are necessarily appropriate. Both lead to an attitude of secrecy to avoid giving information to potential opponents. In reality most statutory consultees and some community or interested groups are likely to take a precautionary approach and adopt a defensive stance to something presented to them for the first time. However, familiarity with the proposal or, better still, involvement in its evolution will usually result in, if not acceptance, then at least a constructive attitude.

Thus there is usually little to be lost and much to be gained by the developer, for a well managed programme of consultations. This can start at the feasibility stage, with the local authority and statutory consultees being informed that a study is being undertaken and being requested for relevant information. The circle can be widened at the design development stage and opportunities sought to offer the chance to influence the design. This helps to avoid features that might unnecessarily be unacceptable and also to encourage a sense of shared ownership. The development of the EIA can take place in parallel with this programme and, as a result, will be better focused and more relevant than one developed in isolation. A complimentary copy of all relevant documentation to the other interested parties at the application stage will at least demonstrate goodwill and facilitate the consultation process if not minimise the objections. Many experienced consultants will advise clients to follow such a programme as a matter of course, and in such cases scoping is almost a natural consequence.

Nevertheless it may be that the parties to any scoping process have such different objectives that there can be no meeting of minds. It is perfectly possible that in some cases no agreement can be reached on the most fundamental question of whether an EIA is required at all, the local authority insisting that one is required to make a decision on an application and the developer, or their professional adviser, arguing that the proposal is neither caught by the regulations nor significant. In fact, even before the scoping exercise, this issue can be explored as the 1988 Regulations made allowance for the developer to request the planning authority to express an opinion on the need for an EIA. There was also provision for a developer to appeal to the Secretary of State if dissatisfied with the local authority's requirement.

Potentially this is a very significant provision, one that could allow many proposals to escape the requirements for an EIA and a means by which the Government could keep a check on the number of EIAs undertaken. In practice it appears to have been little used. The DoE dealt with less than ten applications in 1993 which can be contrasted with several hundred ESs produced in the same period. This is curious as it would appear to be in the developer's interest to appeal and, if successful, avoid unnecessary work.

The inescapable logic of considering the environmental consequences of one's actions has become almost irresistible in the last ten years. Whatever the attitude to mandatory EIAs when first introduced in this country, the demand for them has diffused outward from the 1988 Regulations. Parliamentary committees now require an ES when considering private bills. The Transport and Works Act 1992, which sets a new procedure for obtaining consents for rail and some water transport and harbour works, specifically requires all applications for orders to be accompanied by an ES. The 1988 Regulations are reproduced in part in the guidance to the Act to show what is required in an EIA. Increasingly European legislation is likely to require EIA as a prerequisite of any planned changes, thus bypassing its own regulations and national legislation.

However, the Transport and Works Act again has the safeguard of applying to the Secretary of State for a waiver of the requirement for an EIA. This is very necessary if it is not to become an unwarranted burden, as many applications for orders will be for work which have negligible, if any, environmental effect at all. But again after two years of being in force, no waivers have been issued. The first is only now being made. There seems to be an acceptance within certain sectors of the development industry that an EIA will be required no matter how small the proposal.

Leaving aside the Government's original attitude, is this extension of EIA to all projects necessary and is it in the public's interest in terms of making the best use of resources? Why have the ability to appeal against the need for an EIA if it cannot or will not be exercised? To answer these questions I want to look at some examples of where appeals have been or are being made and examine their consequences.

Examples of EIA waivers

In 1993, Barton Willmore, acting for a client on land at Cheltenham, made a planning application for a retail store, petrol filling station and parking. The documentation did not include an ES but did cover the environment in some detail. The local planning authority determined that an EIA was required largely on account of it being a Schedule 2 project which would have a 'significant' impact on a sensitive site.

The company appealed to the Secretary of State for determination of the need for an EIA, arguing that the only category of development that applied was 'urban development' and that it failed to meet any of the thresholds for significance.

Furthermore, the site was not sensitive in terms of the criteria listed in Circular 15/88 nor, if it was to be treated as out-of-town shopping, did it meet the size criterion. The site's sensitivity rested largely on the interpretation of whether it was on land designated as Green Belt. The 1986 Local Plan did show it to be in the Green Belt, but the deposit Borough plan drew the boundary back from the site indicating an intention to release it from constraint.

The Secretary of State ruled that the proposal did not fall into either Schedule 1 or Schedule 2 and he did not even consider it necessary to respond on the issue of the Green Belt and site sensitivity. He directed that the application be determined on the submitted documentation.

The same firm also dealt with proposals to expand an existing new settlement on the outskirts of Aberdeen. Again the proposal was not in conflict with the Local Plan which showed the area as white land and the City Planning Department was not minded to require an ES. However, Scottish Natural Heritage (SNH) insisted that an EIA was undertaken. Detailed negotiations showed that the main concerns were visual intrusion to the existing residents, recreational use of adjacent land and land management of a small gorge. These could be adequately addressed by a well targeted study and good design but were not of sufficient importance to warrant an EIA. The suggestion to put the matter to the Secretary of State for determination was made but SNH moderated its requirements before this was done and agreement was reached on the work that would be undertaken.

Finally, a Railtrack proposal to replace two manned level-crossings on the East Coast Main Line with an overbridge carrying a minor road required an Order under the Transport and Works Act for the necessary powers. The initial reaction within the company was that an EIA was mandatory as the Regulations required all applications to be accompanied by an ES. However, informal discussions with the Department of Transport showed that this was, prima facie, a case for applying for a waiver to the EIA requirement, the reasons being that the proposal was welcomed by the local authority and that the few residents directly affected did not object. The main issues appeared to be the visual effect of the bridge and whether it affected an area of local nature conservation significance. In any event the whole scale of the development, a minor overbridge in an area not identified of any special value, was clearly substantially less than the developments in Schedule 2 of the EIA Regulations. Determination on this first application for a waiver is still awaited.

The above examples, while only three in number, still represent a significant proportion of those that, either formally or informally, have avoided an unnecessary EIA. They also illustrate some interesting points. First, relatively few firms are able to build up experience in this matter and so are able to advise clients with confidence. Second, each of the examples shows that pressure for an EIA can come from different parties, in these cases the local authority, a statutory consultee and, surprisingly, the developer itself. Third, in none of these cases could the environmental effects be regarded objectively as necessitating an EIA and the safeguard, built into the legislation, against generating unnecessary work is justifiably used to avoid unnecessary expense and delay.

Notes and references

1 DoE (1989) *Environmental Assessment: A Guide to the Procedures.* London: HMSO.
2 Town and Country Planning (Assessment of Environmental Effects) (Amendment) Regulations 1994 (Statutory Instrument 1994 No 677).
3 See the Introduction to this book, page 19.
4 DoE (1994a) *Evaluation of Environmental Information for Planning Projects: A Good Practice Guide.* London: HMSO; DoE (1994b) *Guide on Preparing Environmental Statements for Planning Projects (Consultation Draft).* London: HMSO.
5 Institute of Environmental Assessment (1993) *Practical Experience of Environmental Assessment in the UK.* East Kirkby, Lincolnshire: IEA.

6 DoE (1992) PPG6: *Town Centres and Retail Developments*. London: HMSO; DoE (1994) PPG13: *Transport*. London: HMSO.

7 Andrews, R N L, P Cromwell, C A Enk, E G Farnworth, J Hibbs and V L Sharp (1977) *Substantive Guidance for Environmental Impact Assessment*. Washington, DC: Institute of Ecology.

8 Beanlands, G E and P N Duinker (1982) *EIA in Canada – an ecological contribution*. Halifax: Institute for Resource and Environmental Studies, Dalhousie University.

9 Westman, W E (1985) *Ecology, Impact Assessment and Environmental Planning*. London: Wiley.

10 DoE (1994b) *op. cit.*

11 Croner Publications (continuously updated) *Croner's Environmental Management*. Kingston upon Thames: Croner Publications.

12 DoE (1992) Circular 1/92: *Planning Controls over Sites of Special Scientific Interest*. London: HMSO.

13 Leopold, L B, F E Clark, B B Hanshaw and J R Balsley (1971) A procedure for evaluating environmental impact, *Geological Survey Circular 645*. Washington, DC: US Department of the Interior.

14 Sorensen, J C (1971), A framework for identification and control of resource degradation and conflict in the multiple use of the coastal zone, Master's Thesis. Berkeley, CA: Department of Landscape Architecture, University of California.

15 Fuller, K, A Nixon, F Walsh and F Brook (1994) An eye to the future, *Environmental Assessment*, Vol. 2, No. 3.

CHAPTER 2

TAKING CHARGE OF THE ENVIRONMENTAL TEAM

Michael Lee-Wright

Introduction

Joe Weston's Introduction and Peter Bulleid's opening chapter have demonstrated that the need for a number of individual specialists to take part in EIA is apparent from the beginning of a project. In some cases, there will only be one or two topics requiring analysis as part of the EIA; more often in my experience, there will be at least four. Usually, there is a need for one or more of the many engineering disciplines such as transport planning or geotechnics. Any scheme involving unbuilt land (whether in town or not) will usually require an ecological assessment, and almost all will require an archaeological investigation. These are perhaps the most typical requirements of an EIA for new developments, but many also involve much more specialist analysis, especially where complex or interrelated effects need to be addressed.

Once the need for a variety of inputs to the project is established in this way, it is a short step to appreciate the need for effective team co-ordination. Landscape architects do not always fully appreciate the position of landscape in the wider scale of things; an ornithologist may focus excessively on the impacts on bird habitats; a highway engineer may be reluctant to compromise on accepted highway design criteria. The relative importance of these competing interests can only be established through the application of value judgements which, by common consent, are mainly reserved to democratically elected decision makers. However, before the community and its representatives can reach a view on the acceptability of a scheme in environmental terms, it is essential that all the available information is presented in a clear and impartial way. For different reasons, the client funding the EIA will expect the environmental work to be closely interrelated with their planning submissions, design philosophy, inquiry evidence and so on. This reflects the fact that EIAs are primarily carried out to satisfy planning requirements in connection with new development.

Leadership of the environmental team therefore requires a mixture of skills. The necessary qualities of a team leader include an understanding of diverse technical issues, expertise in evaluation (particularly of alternatives), familiarity with the planning and development process, management and communication skills. This is essentially the role of the 'planner': i.e. a member of the Royal Town Planning Institute (RTPI) with a particular interest or track record in environmental work. The criteria may, coincidentally, also fit outstanding professionals from other disciplines, but the RTPI planner ought to be the natural environmental team leader, owing to his or her unique training, role and perspective on the wider decision-making process. It is perhaps surprising that, at a time of recession in mainstream planning work since the statutory requirement for EIA first arose in 1988, planners have not always taken the lead in this field.

In this chapter we explore the relationship between the planning system and EIA, and look briefly at planning training in this context. In the second part, we look at how the planner might manage the environmental team in practice. Examples are given, based on hypothetical cases, in order to demonstrate the principles involved. The chapter concludes with comments about the interrelationship of EIA and the planning system in future years.

Understanding the planning context

The UK planning system has been around in various forms since at least the early days of this century. The phrase 'town planning' first appeared in an Act of 1909 which provided for planning 'schemes' to allow local authorities to control housing development areas. The Act was described by John Burns, President of the Local Government Board at the time, as hoping to secure 'the home healthy, the house beautiful, the town pleasant, the city dignified and the suburb salubrious'[1]. The 1909 Act built on public health legislation, providing an interesting link with today's concerns about health and the environment.

As the legislative basis for planning control was developed, notably through the effective nationalisation of the value of new development under the 1947 Town and Country Planning Act and the general increase in quasi-legal inquiry proceedings, so the scope of issues to be taken into account as material considerations in planning terms widened. The pace of legislation, policy statements and technical research also grew steadily throughout the post-war period, so that an interpretation of the effects on the environment was required of planning authorities and other decision makers long before the Regulations of 1988 introduced statutory EIAs to the planning system. It has been estimated that about 200–250 environmental assessments were carried out in the UK between 1972 and 1987, mostly in respect of major infrastructure projects[2]. In the USA, where planning control was held back by constitutional rights to property, legislation providing for EIA as part of the development process dates back as far as 1969. Even in the UK, government research led to a 'manual for practice' published in 1981, giving guidance on the assessment of major schemes[3]. The Department of Transport also developed its manual of environmental appraisal to provide guidance for highway planners[4].

Since the planning process is concerned with balancing competing interests and priorities, it is inevitably influenced by changing attitudes in society as a whole. Thus the history of post-war planning can be divided into various eras where it is possible to distinguish changes in emphasis. Since the consolidating 1971 Planning Act, for example, priorities have included housing improvement, transport capacity, urban renewal and townscape. To this list can now be added the environmental era, but already there are signs of a further shift towards rediscovering urban planning. The point is not that these are merely passing fashions. Each new priority tends instead to add to the list of planning issues, rather than substituting one for another. In much the same way, the 1988 Regulations now represent one of the layers of analysis required in order to evaluate new schemes from the planning point of view.

Central government guidance on the relationship of EIA to the planning process is actually quite thin. The main source of central government guidance is still the 'Blue Book', which reproduces the EEC Directive as an appendix, and gives guidance on the application of the 1988 UK Regulations for the planning system[5]. This makes it clear that

> Authorities already obtain from developers such information as they consider necessary to determine a planning application, including information about environmental effects.... What is new about EIA is the emphasis on systematic analysis ... the presentation of information ... and the scope for modifying or mitigating [environmental effects][6].

However, while some of the techniques for representation of environmental information are indeed new, the process of evaluating complex interactions arising from future development projects has long been a key activity for planners. A principal text on this subject is *Evaluation in the Planning Process*, which dates from 1975 and contains a selection of different means by which projects can be compared and assessed against policy objectives[7]. Similarly, Margaret Roberts's *Town Planning Techniques* (1974) illustrates the breadth of issues already being dealt with by planners long before the 1985 EEC Directive[8]. The matrix format now used to represent environmental effects was also in use by planners long before its application to environmental assessment.

Planners, training and EIA

The education of planners has also reflected the growing trend towards the wider and more complex understanding of project implications. Originally set up as the Town Planning Institute in 1914, the planners' professional body received its Royal Charter in 1971 as it began to move on from its public health origins with increasing speed. It is no coincidence that the emphasis of the planning education curriculum has been increasingly controversial in recent years, as the scope of the profession's concerns has steadily widened. The last policy statement, *The Education of Planners*, makes a distinction between the need for planners to possess 'knowledge about' certain matters and 'competence in other matters'. Including 'the environment and development' in the former category, it observes that 'the key attribute of a knowledgeable planner is the ability to make relationships across these areas of knowledge'[9].

Planning is concerned with the future, and notions of equity and the common good are fundamental to it. The European Council of Town Planners' Charter (1988) states that:

> Town planning ... operates in all social strata and on several interrelated spatial levels. It contributes to the creation of the present and future character of social, physical, economic, organisation and environmental quality.

The breadth of this canvas is only matched by the size and complexity of the environmental agenda which led to the adoption of a statutory system of EIA throughout Europe in 1985.

The qualities required to be developed through planning education are suitably diverse. The RTPI's guidance to planning schools lists the 'skills components' as including 'problem definition, the synthesis and application of knowledge to practice' and 'collaborative problem solving', as well as 'the ability to work effectively as members and leaders of planning teams'. These tasks are fundamental to an effective, project-oriented environmental assessment and equate to the essential co-ordinating role between those professions with more technical training and capabilities.

Quite apart from their background of vocational training, practising planners also learn quickly the importance of obtaining inputs from a wide variety of sources. Development controllers at the sharp end of the planning system have for a long time used a system of consultation procedures to ensure technical evaluation of schemes prior to a decision being made. Research recently carried out for the DoE showed that the consultation process is the principal means by which planning authorities assess the technical aspects of ESs submitted to them[10]. Long before the 1988 EIA Regulations, consultees were already well established as a means of vetting development proposals. Landscaping proposals were often referred to the district's own landscape staff for comment, while highway or drainage applications were usually assessed by the authority's own engineers. With the growth in private sector planning work since the 1970s, planners have developed this team response, to the extent that planners often now advise on the timing and context of specialist team appointments from the earliest stages of a project. Perhaps the ultimate confirmation of the central role of planners on the team is the growth of their appointments to large corporate landowners and developers during the 1980s and early 1990s.

The ES and the planning submission

Despite the interrelationship between planning applications and ESs there still exists a surprising degree of disharmony between the two. Research into the quality of ESs in the UK has found significant shortcomings, particularly during the first years of the system[11]. Notable criticisms were lack of objectivity, failure to deal with short term and residual impacts and superficial analysis. To this could be added the sheer inaccessibility of many ESs, due to poor presentation or lack of editing. Some of the earlier ESs amounted to little more than a collection of specialist reports about the likely effects of a development: far short of the new treatment of issues envisaged in the DoE 'Blue Book'.

The uncomfortable relationship between the ES and the planning submission reflects basic differences in their terms of reference. In the context of development proposals, the planning authority is required to determine planning submissions in accordance with the development plan, unless material considerations indicate otherwise[12]. Central government requires the policies of the development plan to concentrate on matters relevant to the 'use and development of land' but 'material considerations' can be much wider[13]. Therefore a planning submission must address both development plan policies and any other matters which might be 'material', if it is to be cast in the best light. The matters to be considered for inclusion in the EIA (where the likely effects are 'significant') are also quite extensive, but they are confined to a specific list taken from the EEC Directive and this list appears in full in Joe Weston's Introduction[14].

In practice, the natural science aspects have tended to dominate ESs and most non-specialists probably associate the ES more with ecology than any other single discipline.

That the early years of statutory EIA in the UK have not seen a very close correlation between the planning agenda and the EIA process is therefore perhaps not surprising since planners have failed to fulfil their potential as environmental team leaders.

Yet I estimate that consultancies engaged mainly in planning figure prominently in less than a quarter of even the mainstream development projects[15]. The figure is probably lower on more technical or specialist forms of development such as waste disposal or mineral extraction. Environmental or engineering consultants quite often appear as lead authors, and these may include planning staff within the team, but the planning perspective is likely to be less dominant in a non-planning practice. In my experience, the planner's share of ES co-ordination work broadly reflects these conclusions.

The preliminary project assessment

In the great majority of commercial development projects, the planner is on the scene first of all the consultants. This is because both speculative development projects and landowners' schemes are dependent above all on the prospect of securing planning permission. Thus the planning consultant is usually asked at the outset to take a view on all the considerations likely to affect the planning decision, including the need for EIA, its likely cost, scope, timing and conclusions. Alternatively, a planner in the client organisation, or someone occupying a similar role, takes a commercial view on the basis of his or her own experience of the planning system and EIA. It is at this early stage that many of the key decisions are taken about alternative schemes, quantity and location of development, etc.

Major infrastructure projects tend to require more work on technical and financial feasibility but planning advice will still usually be sought at an early stage. Even local authorities discharging their statutory functions have to pay some regard to planning policies! Similarly, projects which fall under other legislation, such as the Highways Acts, the Water Resources Act or the Transport and Works Act, will also be tested at some stage against national and local planning policies dealing with the environment.

During the early stages of a project, any areas of particular sensitivity will need to be the subject of a preliminary assessment by an appropriate specialist. This is usually the product of desk-based data research and on-site reconnaissance. The planner will generally agree the scope and terms with his or her client, and often acts as a central co-ordinator of the preliminary reports, drawing initial conclusions and shaping a wider view of project feasibility. All this may take place before the land is acquired, and the decision on whether to purchase property may turn on its outcome.

Example 1:

An area of farmland adjoining a market town in Hereford and Worcester is offered to house builders as a contribution to their long term landbank. Prior to entering into an option agreement to purchase, they carry out a planning and environmental feasibility study to identify the prospect of planning permission being granted for housing development in the foreseeable future. Inquiries reveal suspected archaeological remains in one field, and the land is found to be of better than average quality in agricultural terms. After considering these factors in relation to competing sites, the house builders reduce their offer and negotiations to purchase break down. The land is sold to an adjoining farmer who wants to expand his operations.

The approach which is taken to preliminary environmental work is of critical importance from the earliest stages of the project. Only after project feasibility has been established and the client is committed to proceeding can the real EIA process begin. Andrew McNab discusses scoping in Chapter 3; suffice it to say here that the later scoping of issues on the basis of the perceived significance of likely impacts will usually owe much to the earlier feasibility study. Hence the planner's approach in the early stages of the project can be fundamental to an efficient EIA later.

The need for specialists to be appointed early on in the project will nearly always be a matter of concern to a commercial developer or private client. As more of the public sector spending departments go over to a more strictly commercial basis, the same now applies to public sector schemes. From the client's point of view EIA has tended to suffer a bad press since its introduction, because of the perceived cost and delay. The increasing commercial need for enlightened corporate attitudes to environmental issues does not appear to have significantly reduced this caution. This is perhaps understandable when one considers that a typical EIA might take six months and cost in the region of £50,000.

As a direct consequence of the need to keep costs under control, the preliminary overview of environmental issues has become increasingly important. Investigations of, for example, published agricultural land quality information or land contamination records can be carried out as part of the earliest feasibility studies by the project planner.

Preliminary environmental information used to be confined to a paragraph or two on the impact on chalk downland, or the effects of tree loss. Today, however, even projects falling short of the threshold triggering the 1988 EIA Regulations might require work on each of these issues. Where once a summary of the rarity and loss of affected environmental interests was sufficient to judge most schemes, today there will probably be a need for a comparison of alternative solutions, an evaluation of the quality of the interests concerned, and an assessment of the likely impacts in relation to development plan and other policies. The conclusions from these studies may influence the outcome of a planning application and so it is vitally important to adopt a realistic approach at the outset. This demands a level of management and co-ordination not hitherto required.

As already noted, changes in planning priorities tend to add to the list of matters likely to affect project feasibility, rather than substituting one for another. Consequently, the issues to be addressed in the early stages of a project include all the potential environmental effects, as well as the implications for transport planning, commercial viability, the community, crime prevention, urban design, settlement planning and so on. The environmental team leader cannot be detached from these other priorities if the project is to fulfil its potential.

Identifying key issues

Planning techniques offer a variety of methods which help to identify the key issues in an EIA. In the case of complex or large scale projects, such as a new airport or a coastal superquarry, it will be necessary to conduct a vigorous analysis of likely impacts at the earliest possible stage of the project, and that process will need to be systematic and transparent for future reference. In the majority of cases, however, the key environmental issues are likely to be more straightforward, and can be presented in a relatively simple matrix. The central government publication *Policy Appraisal and the Environment* introduces a simple impact matrix which can be used or adapted to aid the early stages of an environmental project[16].

The formal scoping process involves data research and consultation with various environmental representative bodies and comes later. In the meantime, a preliminary assessment of environmental issues needs to be carried out in order to help estimate the feasibility of the project and the need for specialist team resources, and to give some idea of the time and cost implications of carrying out the work.

During the early stages of the project, the available detailed information will probably be very limited. The preparation of an impact matrix must therefore be carried out at a senior level by someone who has sufficient project experience to make reliable assumptions. Not all of these assumptions will be correct, but the main objective at this stage is to minimise unnecessary work later, rather than to achieve scientific accuracy.

Depending on the time available, it may be possible to carry out some sample data search work at this stage too. Any factual information on which the early stages of the project can be planned will increase its reliability. Planning authorities include a number of environmental designations in Local Plan proposals maps, and almost nationwide coverage will be achieved in some form within the next few years. Designated sites of nature conservation interest can be identified through English Nature or the County Ecologist, and archaeological sites through the National Monuments Records (NMR) or the County Sites and Monuments Records (SMR), although both may require specialist interpretation. Other records which can be consulted include Ancient Woodlands, Environmentally Sensitive Areas (for Agriculture), Source Protection Zones and Nitrate Sensitive Areas (for water quality), the Transport Policies and Programmes document (for transport schemes) and historic maps (showing past development which may have led to land contamination).

Example 2:

A consortium of haulage firms and development interests is considering the construction of a new road/rail freight transfer facility in the West Midlands, involving a section of new railway and the reopening of a disused railway. The project will be subject to the procedures in the Transport and Works Act 1980, requiring an ES to be prepared. A key part of the preliminary work is to identify which effects will require the most work and take the longest in programming terms. The matrix shows that noise effects, loss of trackside ecological habitats and the visual effects and spoil disposal associated with the new sections of track are of most potential concern. No fundamental conflicts arise with environmental interests, however, and the matrix is used to guide and programme the next stages of the work.

The environmental team leader will need to use all the available information on the project and the receiving environment to make a preliminary assessment of the key issues on which further work is required. The client will generally be impatient to obtain this early view so that his or her commercial judgement can be confirmed and so it is important to get it right even before the team is appointed.

Selecting the team

Once past the preliminary stage, EIA is a team activity. It is almost impossible to envisage circumstances where the range of issues could be adequately addressed by a single individual.

In order to build the team effectively, specialists with the right sort of experience must be selected from what is now an enormous range. The team members should not only be competent and suitably experienced, but also preferably based reasonably near to the site of the scheme to maximise cost-effectiveness.

There are also organisational and business considerations to take into account. Does the project require a relatively costly Public Limited Company with its corporate overhead costs, or will a small partnership serve equally well? Does the consultant firm have a reputation for allowing excessively junior staff to carry out complex tasks in order to boost profit margins? Are the technical capabilities of the practice matched by an understanding of commercial imperatives? Is the consultant able to take on the work without overstretching their resources?

In the cut-and-thrust of everyday business, many of these aspects of team creation are often dealt with superficially or not at all. Inevitably, the growing importance of the EIA to the client, time pressures and the sheer difficulty of assimilating all these aspects of the project tend to result in team selection being neglected. As is often the case in the wider business world, familiarity with methods of working often counts for more than precise suitability for the job. It is the role of the environmental team leader to fill this gap in expertise, and to offer a level of understanding of the environmental consultancy world which should greatly improve the match between requirements and resources.

The 1994 *Environment Business Directory* contains over 600 separate entries under the 'consultants' section. Consultancies active in the environmental field range in size from sole proprietor businesses to multinational companies[17]. There are also at least 40 environmental associations or representative organisations with differing degrees of independence and authority, although few have industry-wide acceptance or recognition. In this extensive field, the main environmental science qualification continues to be the university degree, not requiring on-the-job training and not designed as a specific vocational qualification. Yet in this comparatively unregulated field capabilities differ dramatically and few industry standards exist. Project team creation can consequently be a hazardous activity in the wrong hands.

The environmental team leader must achieve an understanding of both the likely issues to be addressed and the availability of resources in the wider market place if they are to select the best team for the job. This will involve not just finding a specialist to deal with a topic generally, but identifying the type of interests likely to be affected first, and then seeking a suitable consultant with skills in the relevant specialist fields. The degree of sophistication which can be applied to this process will be dependent on such matters as the scale of the project, the relative importance of environmental issues to its success, the available budget, the range of key issues and the expectations of the client. In every case, the team leader should be able to respond effectively to these demands.

Example 3:

An engineering firm based in the northwest of England has occupied an extensive site since the early nineteenth century, when its predecessors built a range of factory buildings. The company is anxious to invest in modern production floorspace, and wants to dispose of about half of its site to finance the scheme. Because of its location near to the city centre, the company is advised of its potential for a major mixed-use development which is likely to require an EIA. The local planning authority is known to have concerns about demolition of the old buildings, and other likely issues include visual impact, transport implications and socio-economic effects. The need for demolition consent is fundamental to the scheme, and researches as to capabilities identify an industrial archaeologist of repute who has experience of development issues, as well as prior knowledge of the site. Specialists in the other key fields are also matched carefully to the requirements of the project, and as a result of this the building was demolished with consent and planning permission finally granted after lengthy negotiations.

In view of the number and diversity of environmental consultancies now operating in the UK, a resource database of some sort is a prerequisite for team selection. Various published directories are available, of which the *Environment Business Directory* and the ENDS Directory[18] are perhaps the best known. However, the main problem in selecting a consultant for a particular project is that many consultants are multidisciplinary, and it is often difficult to establish their core expertise. Almost all practices will admit to strengths and weaknesses when pressed, but in an increasingly competitive market place a narrow specialist background is not something to broadcast. *Caveat emptor* applies here as elsewhere, and there is as yet no substitute for research, other than the appointment of a team leader with experience and knowledge of the resources available.

It is possible to distinguish two alternative approaches to team selection which may be chosen between at the outset, or mixed according to the demands of the project. At one extreme is what we might call the dispersal approach, where a deliberate choice is made to appoint specialists from different practices to work together as a team. This is often adopted where strict cost controls apply, and smaller practices are chosen, with lower overheads and fewer specialisms. Potential cost implications arising from the fragmentation of resources are usually more than compensated for by lower hourly fee rates, although flexibility and speed may be a problem. This approach is also more difficult where the client has a strict policy of Quality Assurance, since such procedures are rarely followed by small practices. Professional indemnity insurance cover for these practices may also be limited in value.

The opposite extreme to the dispersal approach involves the centralisation of resource requirements, generally within one or two multidisciplinary organisations. Such organisations are likely to be larger, with more than one geographical base and the potential for cross-fertilisation of ideas and solutions between otherwise unrelated disciplines. They are usually appointed where the credibility of the EIA may need the support of a well-known name, and in particular where the client itself is a large corporate entity. On the other hand, clients sometimes feel too reliant on a single consultant in this approach. The cost of commissioning these larger consultancy companies is also generally greater, and the original principals on whose reputation they are usually based may not be much involved in the day-to-day work.

Example 4:

An aggregates supplier working nationwide requires a steady supply of mineral-bearing land, preferably with planning permission for infilling with wastes after sand and gravel extraction. However, proximity to construction sites is desirable, because of the high cost of transporting bulky materials. The company therefore operates a land buying policy which includes both smaller sites to supply local markets and major extraction and landfill sites able to serve the largest centres of population. The difficulty of obtaining planning permissions in the face of frequent local opposition has led them to take a central role in the acquisition and promotion of new sites, using smaller and cheaper local consultants where necessary. However, their few strategic sites require a considerable investment to have a chance of receiving planning permission, often through a major planning inquiry. In those sites they consequently employ larger, well-known consultancy firms with extensive resources and a wider reputation.

The environmental team leader who advises on team creation must therefore be aware of the full extent of choices available if the right resources are to be selected at the start of the project. An understanding of the development context, the likely planning and environmental issues arising, the availability of different skills in the consultancy market place, and above all the client and project requirements, are fundamental to an effective environmental team.

Co-ordinating the team

Whether a single multidisciplinary team or a multi-sourced team is chosen, there will be a need for its management and co-ordination. True, experienced professionals will all be familiar with the data search–survey–analysis–reporting process, but each project differs in terms of client objectives, available budget, timescale and so on. This is in addition to the differing internal characteristics of each scheme.

If specialists are sought in relatively unusual fields, and particularly if a multi-sourced team is required, the environmental team leader may arrange and advise on some form of tendering process for the client. This can be quite time consuming if a clear brief is to be provided (although all too frequently it is not!). The appointment of a single-practice, multidisciplinary team may also require some form of competitive tendering, but the environmental team leader is then more likely to be appointed from within the successful consultants, and so is not usually on the scene as early in the project.

In advising on team selection, the environmental team leader will take into account the factors which contribute to efficiency and effectiveness already mentioned. Particularly important will be his or her preliminary assessment of the issues likely to be critical in the planning decision, whatever the legislative framework concerned. Nevertheless, the final choices as to resources and personnel will be made by the client.

Once appointments have been made, the environmental team will begin project familiarisation, before going on to carry out data searches, site reconnaissance and baseline surveys. Since there are often several specialisms represented, each of which may be provided by individuals at different levels of experience, there is considerable scope for communications to be delayed. The greatest problems at this stage are generally the need for rapid progress and the ever-present budgetary constraints which circumscribe all commercially led EIAs.

By the time an EIA gets under way, the client organisation will probably have been working on the project for at least a year – sometimes considerably longer. There is a need for effective team management at this stage, so that the latest drawings are circulated, individuals are kept informed of changes relevant to them, realistic deadlines are set for all team members and key information is fed back to the client regularly. If frequent meetings involving the whole team are arranged, communication may of course be enhanced. But the real trick is to ensure close and effective co-ordination on a tight budget timescale. This is difficult to achieve, unless the team leader has a strategic overview of both the development and the environmental issues surrounding the project.

The co-ordination of the environmental team follows the same principles throughout the scoping and consultation process: during survey work, through project design development and of course during the planning submission. It may extend to a planning inquiry, with the attendant need for detailed evidence from a variety of sources. The co-ordination role may also continue during the design stages, when detailed architectural or engineering work will often produce different implications for different interests. There may be a need for a 'watching brief' during construction, in case archaeological remains are discovered during excavation, to oversee the protection of trees or the translocation of protected species.

The management demands of an environmental team leader's work are in proportion to the diversity of resources required.

Clearly, larger scale projects with complex applications will usually demand more of the environmental team leader, but certain types of project which are not of themselves large in scale may also involve complex environmental issues. Engineering plant and infrastructure projects often fall into this category, where the size of the building footprint may be quite small compared with its implications for the receiving environment. Thus the importance of effective team leadership is not confined to larger projects.

Conducting planning negotiations

The overwhelming majority of EIAs are prepared at the expense of a client who is seeking some form of planning permission. Schemes which fall under other legislation, such as the Highways Acts, the Water Resources Act or the Transport and Works Act, may involve different procedures, but their essential purpose is the same. They allow for a degree of public participation or scrutiny so that the scheme's various implications can be considered before it goes ahead.

Once the planning submission has been made, accompanied by the ES, there is likely to be a more detailed response from the planning authority and others than has occurred at the earlier scoping stage. This is because more extensive consultation takes place at this stage, possibly with members of the public becoming aware of the scheme for the first time. It may also result from this first opportunity for trade-offs to be made by the planning authority between competing environmental or other interests. The whole process will certainly be sharpened by the knowledge of all concerned that, once permission has been granted, the fundamentals of the scheme will become established. In this context, the planning negotiations after submission of the ES are usually critical to the success of the project.

The post-submission planning negotiations can also add significantly to the project timescale, threatening the programming of the scheme and, in some cases, its viability. Essentially, the local authority planning officer occupies an environmental team manager's role for the decision maker, relying on the technical advice of specialists from within consultative organisations like English Nature, English Heritage and the Countryside Commission. In the same way, the need for effective communications within the project team requires a planner to occupy a co-ordinating role during negotiations. The 1988 Regulations allow for double the usual period for the consideration of a planning application in EIA cases (16 weeks), recognising the greater complexity of negotiations in such cases. In practice, this phase often takes much longer.

Example 5:

Private landowners are seeking planning permission for the extraction of a substantial quantity of limestone from farmland on the edge of the Mendip Hills. The project planner carries out a preliminary assessment which identifies the key issues as impacts on landscape, ecology and archaeology (there is a Roman Road nearby). Additional work is also required on highway access and agricultural land quality, as well as on developing the proposals for low-level restoration. Noise from blasting might be an issue, but development plan considerations demand an early submission, and potential policy objections make the landowners reluctant to commit more resources on baseline surveys in the early stages of the project. The application is submitted with an ES which offers commitments to noise surveys, ecological investigations and habitat creation. Once the application has been submitted, the planning requirements gradually become clearer and an ambient noise levels survey is commissioned. The commitments on archaeological investigations and habitat creation are finally accepted, and planning permission is granted subject to various matters laid down by conditions.

Negotiations after submission usually take the form of a series of meetings at which aspects of the project, environmental survey information and analysis are tested, challenged or reconsidered. Not knowing which issues are going to arise later in the negotiations, the project team will usually have to adopt a reactive approach at this stage. This may result in aspects of the scheme or its effects being reworked more than once, or it may require aspects of the ES itself to be readdressed. At all times there is a need for continuity. If work on all the different aspects of the project can be combined, then costs will be more effectively contained. Above all, it is essential to maintain an overview of priorities so that the fundamental objectives of the project are not compromised. Sometimes this will involve a decision not to accede to requested amendments to the scheme.

The need for ESs to give an impartial account of potential effects on the environment may be perceived to be in conflict with the client's development objectives. This perception can result in difficulties both at the ES preparation stage and with the planning submission. Clients may be uncomfortable with the idea of identifying harmful effects associated with their proposals, and may seek a dilution of the conclusions in the ES. One way to deal with this is by the preparation of a separate scheme brochure in addition to the ES. A scheme brochure is not bound by the need for impartiality, and can therefore adopt an advocacy role, explaining why the scheme is justified even in the context of the impacts that arise.

The main area where the planning system may be supportive of a scheme which carries significant environmental impacts is in relation to economic considerations. In terms of relative values, the global debate about growth versus environmental protection is just as relevant at the local level as it is internationally. Planning negotiations must therefore be conducted with an understanding of the social and political decision-making climate, as well as an awareness of the environmental implications of alternative courses of action.

Example 6:

An area of structural unemployment in Wales offers potential for a major new distribution facility because of its accessibility by rail and motorway. Commercial developers approach the local planning authority with proposals for a major scheme which could bring both a significant number of short-term construction jobs and a longer term economic benefit to the local economy. However, the only suitable site is within an extensive lowland area, valued for its archaeological potential. There is also a network of drainage ditches, some of which provide habitats for a wide range of plants, birds and invertebrates. The whole area has been designated a Site of Special Scientific Interest, but after extensive consultations a scheme is devised which retains the pattern of ditches and allows for prior archaeological surveys. Supplementary planting of hedgerows and the careful choice of cladding materials will mitigate impacts on longer-distance landscape views. After weighing carefully the residual environmental impacts against the potential economic benefits of the scheme, planning permission is granted subject to conditions.

The terms of both the 1985 EEC Directive on EIA and the 1988 UK Regulations include 'the effects on human beings' amongst the matters to be included in EIAs. A liberal interpretation of this would include such matters as community severance and economic benefits. However, these traditional preoccupations of planning control have rarely been fully integrated into ESs in the UK, possibly because of the way in which planning and environmental assessment have developed separately. Planning negotiations over the EIA must nevertheless be conducted with an awareness of these contradictions, not least because if the scheme has to be examined at inquiry any inconsistencies of approach or detail are likely to be painfully obvious.

The process of co-ordinating the environmental team during planning negotiations therefore requires a wide understanding of the context and parameters. Decisions will have to be made on how to respond to criticism, comments or requests for information from different parties to the process. Good judgement is required in order to decide between competing policy objectives, accepting one criticism in order to achieve another expression of support. An element of advocacy will be helpful in persuading others that the environmental effects of the project have been accurately represented and mitigated whenever possible. Above all, there must always be an understanding of the decision-making climate within which the scheme will be tested.

The role of the client

It is notable that a significant proportion of the authorship of ESs is attributed to the client organisation, rather than their consultants. In other words, the client occupies or claims the role of environmental team leader.

There are reasons why it is desirable to maintain a degree of separation between the two functions – principally because of the potential conflicts between the need to produce an impartial ES and the client's natural commitment to achieving the project. However, apart from these fundamental conflicts (which can arise to some extent for consultants too), there is no reason why the co-ordination and leadership of the environmental team cannot be carried out by an individual employed within the commissioning organisation. Indeed, most of the utility companies include within their staff individuals who can occupy an environmental team management role – either planners or professionals from a related discipline, but with a wider-than-usual perspective on the process. This is because the type of development with which they are widely concerned usually requires an ES before it can proceed, and so there is more justification for the appointment of permanent staff in this role. Nevertheless, recent cost-cutting exercises within some of these organisations suggest no enlargement of this role in the near future.

Example 7:

A waste disposal company wholly owned by a subsidiary of one of the privatised water companies seeks planning permission and, subsequently, HMIP consent for a combined heat and power plant burning household waste. For economic reasons, the plant needs to be sited close to the source of arisings, i.e. within an urban area. There is extensive opposition to the scheme once local people are aware of the proposals, mainly on the grounds of air pollution risks. At the inevitable public inquiry, a great deal of the evidence and press attention is expected to be focused on the technical and engineering aspects of the scheme: temperature of burn, consistency of feedstock, flue gas scrubbing system and safety procedures. The environmental effects resulting from the 'natural operation' state may therefore be less decisive in planning terms than the credibility of the plant's engineering design. In the circumstances, the decision is taken to nominate a senior environmental engineer from within the waste disposal company to lead the environmental team through EIA, planning submissions and inquiry. With the help of the project planner, he is able to bridge the gap between 'hard' engineering and 'soft' environmental considerations.

Apart from the difficulties of conflicting objectives for environmental team leaders working within the commissioning organisation, there may also be conflicting priorities. Often the planning negotiation stage will be a particularly busy time for the client in other respects, as the proposals achieve wide publicity, possibly for the first time. Members of the public, neighbouring landowners, joint venture partners and competitors may be seeking a dialogue over the scheme. Engineering design will be undergoing refinement, as will costings and programming. Legal advice may be needed as to liabilities, contracts and funding. It may be necessary to think about future tendering processes for design and construction. At this time, a team leader whose duties extend much beyond the planning and environmental aspects of the scheme is likely to have to prioritise heavily, and the environmental duties may suffer unduly.

As with all matters relating to planning, the right approach to team leadership will be a matter of judgement, according to the circumstances of each case. Clearly, a separation between the client's project management function and the environmental team leader's role is usually desirable. But in cases where the design of the scheme itself is fundamental to its perceived impact there may be advantage in managing the environmental team directly from within the client organisation. Whichever course is adopted, the appointed person will need to have an unusually wide perspective and must not become too involved in detail lest they lose sight of the overall objectives.

The future

As indicated at the beginning of this chapter and described by Joe Weston in his Introduction, formal EIA is still a relative newcomer to the UK planning system. It has been grafted onto a planning tradition which has always involved assessing and weighing the public benefits and disadvantages of a scheme before allowing it to proceed. The leadership of environmental teams therefore falls naturally under the general umbrella of the planning profession. Yet despite the logic of this, planners have so far not made much of a mark in EIA.

In my view, EIA and the techniques of analysis and presentation which it uses will become increasingly common in mainstream planning work. Already projects which do not themselves require a formal ES need the support of studies which follow more or less the same procedures. A significant proportion of ESs submitted under the Planning Acts are, in any case, voluntary: demonstrating the acceptance of developers and clients that environmental issues must be addressed. Planners will continue to be concerned with issues currently outside the normal scope of EIA, but gradually these will be drawn into the EIA process so that the present areas of overlap will be replaced by continuing integration. In particular, socio-economic effects will be dealt with in more detail, enabling a more effective focusing of the growth versus conservation debate than occurs at present. In short, EIA will cease to become a separate science, although it will remain one of the many branches of planning expertise.

In this integrated future, where an assessment of the environmental effects of a scheme is a fundamental part of all planning submissions, there will be a need for team leaders with feet in several camps. They will need some understanding of the cost implications of raft foundations, as well as the risk of heavy metals leaching into the aquifer. They must be able to visualise the changes to a historic landscape from road construction, as well as being aware of the social stress suffered in areas of high unemployment.

Priorities will change from time to time, but the team leader must above all be able to weigh the human costs and benefits of a project against its effects on the natural environment. To date, only a planner is able to do that. If the planners fail to achieve more effective leadership in environmental teams, it is the decision-making process that will suffer.

Notes and references

1 Quoted in Cullingworth, J B (1993) *Town and Country Planning in Britain*. London: Routledge, p 2.

2 Lichfield, N (1992) Planning and EIA: the integration of environmental assessment into development planning. Part 1: Some principles, *Project Appraisal*, Vol. 7, No. 2, 58–66.

3 Clarke, B D, K Chapman, R Bissel, P Walthern and M Barrett (1981) *Manual for the Assessment of Major Development Proposals*. London: HMSO.

4 Department of Transport (1993) *Design Manual for Roads and Bridges*. Volume II: *Environmental Assessment*. London: HMSO.

5 There is, of course, the more recent DoE (1994a) *Guide on Preparing Environmental Statements for Planning Projects (Consultation Draft)*. London: HMSO; DoE (1994b) *Evaluation of Environmental Information for Planning Projects: A Good Practice Guide*. London: HMSO.

6 DoE (1989) *Environmental Assessment: A Guide to the Procedures*. London: HMSO.

7 Lichfield, N, P Kette and M Whitbread (1975) *Evaluation in the Planning Process*. Oxford: Pergamon.

8 Roberts, M (1974) *Town Planning Techniques*. London: Hutchinson.

9 RTPI (1991) *The Education of Planners*. London: RTPI.

10 DoE (1994b) *op. cit.*

11 Lee, N and R Colley (1991) Reviewing the quality of environmental statements: review methods and findings, *Town Planning Review*, Vol. 62, No. 2, 239–248.

12 S54a, Town and Country Planning Act 1990.

13 DoE (1990) PPG1: *General Policy and Principles*. London: HMSO.

14 Lichfield, N *et al.*, *op. cit.*

15 Institute of Environmental Assessment (1993) *The Digest of Environmental Statements*. London: Sweet & Maxwell (looseleaf).

16 DoE (1991) *Policy Appraisal and the Environment*. London: HMSO.

17 Information for Industry (1994) *Environment Business Directory*. London: James Benn.

18 ENDS (1994) *Directory of Environmental Consultants*. London: Environmental Data Services.

CHAPTER 3

SCOPING AND PUBLIC PARTICIPATION

Andrew McNab

Introduction

This chapter considers practical experience of scoping and public participation in relation to four similar holiday village developments for which ESs were prepared by Cobham Resource Consultants (CRC). The statements were prepared in 1988 for a site in the Cotswold Water Park in Gloucestershire, in 1991 for a site near Market Weighton in Humberside, and in 1993 for a site near Penrith in Cumbria. Each planning application was approved. A fourth statement for a site near Carthorpe in North Yorkshire was prepared in 1990 but never submitted.

Each statement was prepared on behalf of the same clients: Lakewoods Ltd. The company is a joint venture between the Granada Group plc and John Laing plc which was formed specifically to build and operate holiday villages.

The statements were assembled and co-ordinated by CRC using inputs from Lakewoods consortium of consultants which included:

- Fitch and Company, architects;
- Ove Arup and Partners, engineers;
- Ede Griffiths Associates, landscape architects;
- Alan Boreham Associates, highway engineers.

Political and public relations issues were dealt with by GJW Government Relations and Dorman PR.

In this chapter we discuss the evolving approach to scoping and public participation from the 1988 statement, which was one of the first ESs to be prepared, to the 1993 statement, by which time a specific approach had been adopted and honed. The account is intended to be frank and honest and to describe the reasons for the adopted approach. No claims are made that the adopted approach is the correct one nor, indeed, that it will always be appropriate. Rather the intention is to give an insight into the actions of a developer and its consultants, an aspect of environmental assessment which has attracted little academic attention.

The first part of the chapter describes the nature of the holiday village concept, site requirements, the planning context and the environmental issues associated with holiday villages. An account is then given of the first environmental assessment in Gloucestershire with particular reference to scoping and public participation. The account looks at the guidance available in 1988, the constraints imposed by the developer, the approach adopted, the response of statutory consultees and the approach to public participation. Attention is also drawn to the role of public relations consultants in planning and environmental assessment. This account is followed by an analysis of the lessons learned.

Brief reference is then made to the statement prepared for the site near Carthorpe in North Yorkshire, to the different approach to scoping and public participation and to the subsequent decision not to proceed to a planning application.

Subsequent accounts are given of the environmental assessments in Humberside and Cumbria wherein a distinctive approach can be discerned. The final sections include a summary of the rationale for the approach and its effectiveness and a personal and professional reflection on the role of scoping and public participation in environmental assessment.

The holiday village concept

The holiday villages considered here are a product of Continental Europe. In the Netherlands, Belgium and Germany, firms like Center Parcs and Sun Parks International have successfully developed a new holiday product. The basic concept involves the provision of high quality self-catering accommodation in a quiet, usually afforested setting, with a very wide range of indoor and outdoor recreational facilities. The target consumer is the family group seeking a short break holiday.

The concept neatly meets a number of consumer demands. First and foremost it is about providing family holidays in a countryside setting. It provides a holiday that can be enjoyed regardless of the weather because of the extensive provision of indoor recreational and leisure facilities. It provides a range of sporting and recreational activities, usually including swimming, tennis, badminton, cycling, bowls and boating, which can be enjoyed by those of differing skills and provide opportunities for participation by different age groups. Such facilities can also meet the demand for more active and healthy holidays. The villages provide an attractive countryside setting which is eminently marketable. It is also a safe environment, enclosed by security fencing and policed by security staff. Finally the villages are deliberately designed to provide short break holidays of three to four nights. The short break market remains the most buoyant sector of UK tourism[1].

European experience has defined the commercially appropriate scale for a holiday village. Basically, a large number of self-catering units (600–700) are needed to facilitate the heavy investment in indoor leisure facilities. This commercial formula has been represented architecturally in a large village centre building, normally including a state-of-the-art fun pool, restaurants, shops, disco etc., a separate sports building, and individual self-catering units often linked as terraces or groups.

The concept tends to dictate locational and site requirements. As the villages are intended to cater for short break holidays, it is considered that guests will be drawn from a two to three hour travel time catchment. Commercial considerations therefore suggest a location with the maximum possible catchment population within this travel time. In the UK this tends to emphasise sites in the southeast and Midlands and rule out sites in the southwest, the north, west Wales and Scotland. Similarly, sites need to be highly accessible in terms of the road network, ideally immediately accessible from a motorway. The scale of the development demands a relatively large site; in the case of Lakewoods the four sites ranged from 150 to 270 ha. The site must also be attractive or capable of being made attractive.

Center Parcs was the first company to enter the holiday village market in the UK. They currently have three operational villages at Sherwood Forest in Nottinghamshire, Elveden Forest in Suffolk and Longleat in Wiltshire. Rank have also entered the market with a proposal for a village near Folkestone in Kent.

The problem that Center Parcs, Lakewoods and Rank face in planning terms is that holiday villages constitute a new and large scale development which requires a countryside setting. No Structure or Local Plan has made provision for such developments which are contrary to traditional policies of countryside protection. As a consequence of this, environmental assessment gains an increased importance as it provides the major source of information on the nature and impacts of a new sort of development.

The environmental impacts of holiday villages

Initially it is worth considering why each holiday village proposal since 1988 has been accompanied by an ES. Holiday villages are clearly not Annex I projects where there is a mandatory requirement for assessment. As an Annex II project, there is therefore scope for discussion between the developer and the local planning authority as to the requirement for an assessment. In that holiday villages constitute a relatively benign form of development, certainly compared with a power station or an airport, it might be expected that the need for assessment might be challenged. However, this was certainly not the case in relation to Lakewoods where CRC advised and Lakewoods agreed, in each instance, voluntarily to prepare a statement. We considered this was sensible because of the scale of the proposed developments, their location in the countryside, the novelty of the development and the desirability of presenting factual evidence in a succinct and comprehensible form.

Traditionally scoping an environmental assessment begins with the list of environmental parameters listed in Schedule 3 of the Town and Country Planning (Assessment of Environmental Effects) Regulations 1988[2]. In principle, it is clear that a holiday village, as a new development in the countryside, has the potential to create a significant impact on flora, fauna, the landscape, material assets and the cultural heritage. Thus much effort came to be expended on ecological surveys, archaeological surveys, and landscape and visual impact assessment. The principal impacts on water are likely to relate to discharges to existing water courses in the form of run-off or waste water. Subsidiary impacts may relate to hydrological considerations, including the impact on the water table and drinking water aquifers. Generally this area attracted less public concern than the more traditional conservation issues related to flora, fauna and landscape.

The impact on human beings is a rather all-embracing topic, the meaning of which was subject to some debate at the time of the first statement. Our initial considerations related to a disparate grouping of issues including employment, impact on local services (shops, pubs etc.) and noise. This segmented and partial approach attracted some criticism and it is clear that we failed to embrace the emotional response to the development encompassed in references to 'new towns', 'lager louts', 'disco dancing' and the destruction of peace and quiet. Noise is, in fact, not a significant impact whilst the impacts on employment are very positive and the impacts for local services are potentially beneficial. Perhaps the most controversial area, however, was traffic and the environmental impacts of traffic. The large number of traffic movements, which arise partly from the fact that guests arrive and leave on two fixed days of each week, provoked most debate.

Impacts on soil need not be significant, and a holiday village may be regarded as a reversible development, i.e. the nature of the buildings is such that they could actually be removed. Similarly the impacts on climate are not significant.

A holiday village in the Cotswold Water Park

The assessment process[3]

In July 1988, CRC was approached by Fitch and Company to provide planning advice to a company who were proposing a tourism and recreational facility in the Cotswold Water Park. By the time of our involvement the site had been selected and the village had been designed. Clearly the site met the commercial criteria: it had some 22 million people within the travel time catchment, good access to the M4, it was large enough and capable of being made attractive. A rapid initial review of planning and environmental factors suggested that there were strong arguments in favour of the development. The Cotswold Water Park was conceived in the late 1960s as a regional facility for water sport and recreation following extensive extraction of sands and gravels. The site comprised a series of pits formed from gravel extraction and variously designated in the Local Plan for tourism accommodation, water based recreation and nature conservation. Access to the site could be gained without passing through any adjacent villages and the proposed landscape works could effectively rehabilitate the site. A County Council planner had been described as 'receptive to the proposal'.

However, there were a number of immediately apparent environmental problems. The whole of the Cotswold Water Park was described as of potential grade 1 SSSI status in the Nature Conservation Review because of its importance for wintering wildfowl. Part of the site was rather unusually designated for the establishment of a National Nature Reserve. The site is also crossed by the infant River Thames, raising pollution concerns, and by the then proposed Thames National Trail.

CRC's appointment as planning consultants almost coincided with the introduction of environmental assessment and the news had to be broken to Lakewoods that an ES was likely to be needed with the planning application. Our advice was based on the scale of the development, the ecological sensitivity of the area and the specific reference in Schedule 2 to holiday villages. Lakewoods readily agreed 'voluntarily' to submit an ES.

The company management had two overwhelming and interlinked requirements for all their consultants. The first related to the extreme commercial confidentiality of the project. This was a proposal by two major public companies to enter a new market and involved an option to purchase a large site. Lakewoods required the project to remain confidential as long as possible. Related to this, Lakewoods wanted to lodge a planning application as soon as possible, their initial target being October 1988.

At the time, and more so in retrospect, it was a daunting task. It was made all the more difficult by the absence of examples of ESs and by the absence of advice. In Autumn 1988 there were simply the Regulations and Circular 15/88; the 'Blue Book', although promised in the Circular, had not appeared[4]. Both the Regulations and the Circular are strongly procedural in tone and content and provide little guidance to the developer. The words 'scoping and public participation' do not appear. Nevertheless, CRC recommended, and Lakewoods agreed to, a programme of confidential officer discussions to establish the scope of the proposed assessment. The organisations selected for consultation included the planning authorities, statutory consultees and other interested bodies and embraced:

- Cotswold District Council;
- Gloucestershire County Council (Highways and Planning);
- Wiltshire County Council (Highways);
- the Nature Conservancy Council (now English Nature);
- the Royal Society for the Protection of Birds (RSPB);
- the Wildfowl Trust (now the Wildfowl and Wetlands Trust);

- the Cotswold Water Park Project Officer;
- the Countryside Commission Thames Path Project Officer;
- Thames Water Authority (now the National Rivers Authority and Thames Water).

The consultations were used both to gather information and to define the scope of the assessment. Following the consultations, a brief scoping document was prepared and sent to the local planning authority for comment. The Council responded, suggesting a number of additional areas for study.

During this process, public relations consultants were appointed to deal with the non-technical aspects of the consultations, i.e. press, political and community relations. The consultants were again constrained by issues of commercial confidentiality, but resolved to undertake a local community audit to identify opinion leaders. The intention was to try and establish a local liaison committee through which information might be provided to local people. However, initial contacts almost immediately led to information about the proposed development coming to the attention of Parish Councillors. Lakewoods subsequently agreed to their request to brief the Parish Council and to an open meeting.

The meeting was acrimonious. The introduction by the Chairman was tendentious and opposed to the development. The developers and their consultants could not answer all the questions because, whilst the village had been designed, the environmental assessment was continuing and a number of issues, such as the means of sewerage disposal, remained to be agreed. Much reliance was placed on the yet-to-be-published ES as a definitive account of the environmental impacts of the proposed development.

Shortly after the public meeting, an outline planning application was lodged with an ES. It was at this point that a substantial programme of consultations and public involvement was initiated. The local planning authority convened a working party to consider the ES in detail and to identify areas of concern and points of difference between the developers and other parties. The developers also set in train an elaborate programme of public consultation. An exhibition, incorporating a large scale model of the proposed development, was prepared and open for view weekly on-site, when representatives of Lakewoods and their consultants were available to answer questions. Presentations were made to the County and District Councils and to the five adjacent Parish Councils. Open days were held at the site with conducted tours and evening visits were specially arranged for individual groups such as the Council for the Protection of Rural England (CPRE). Copies of the ES and the non-technical summary were made available free to all.

Whilst the scope of the statement stood up relatively well, quite a significant number of points arose from these consultations which required further clarification. A number of amendments were also made to aspects of the design following the consultations. The location of the main access was altered and a subsidiary service access was deleted. This change was made at the request of local people in order to reduce potential conflict between local traffic and visitor traffic. The highway authority, which had agreed the original plan, agreed to the amended proposal. However, the change actually moved the access closer to some houses in the nearest village and this provoked further criticism. Lakewoods also agreed to delete an open air amphitheatre shown in the grounds of the holiday village because of concerns over possible noise.

Other issues were raised in public consultations such as the policing of the site, access for emergency fire vehicles, and the use of function suites at the hotel. Many of these were detailed points which were not relevant to the outline planning process. However, Lakewoods and its consultants prepared responses to all queries.

Subsequently, over Christmas 1988, a supplement to the ES was produced setting out further information on a number of issues. This was formally submitted to the local planning authority and, again, made freely available to all. This information was supplemented by a series of local newsletters, produced by the public relations consultants with inputs from the planning and environmental team, and distributed to all local households.

The decision

The proposal was eventually called in by the Secretary of State for the Environment and was the subject of a marathon public inquiry. Lakewoods was supported by the local planning authority (Cotswold District Council) and Gloucestershire County Council. The opposition consisted, unusually, of the adjacent local authorities (North Wiltshire District Council, Wiltshire County Council), neither of which authority had jurisdiction over any part of the site, the local parish councils and the opposition group. No statutory consultee opposed the development. The opposition thus won the initial political battle, having the application called in, but Lakewoods won all the technical arguments. Following further delay, the application was finally approved.

Reflections on the assessment process

The general approach to environmental assessment was consistent with the concept of assessment as a process in which the statement represents the developer's view of environmental impacts at a particular point in time. The statement certainly served to promote debate and to spotlight areas where there were environmental concerns. Alterations were made to the design in response to consultations and other issues raised were followed up and reported upon. In essence, therefore, the process of environmental assessment worked as it should work.

With hindsight, the approach to scoping and participation was heavily constrained by issues of commercial confidentiality and a tight timetable related to a new company entering a new market. The issue of commercial confidentiality is perhaps somewhat unusual, but the commercial need to meet tight timetables is common.

As a consequence of these constraints, the approach taken to scoping was to involve only the local planning authority, statutory consultees and those non-governmental organisations with a known interest in the site. This approach proved relatively successful in that these organisations responded and the scope of the statement attracted little adverse comment.

Thus, the desirability of involving the officials from the local planning authority and statutory consultees at an early stage was firmly underlined. Such contact, however, is most appropriate following an initial site appraisal and sketch design. For a proposal of the scale and cost of a holiday village, investors need some assurance before committing large sums of money to design. Equally, local authorities and statutory consultees are likely, at the very least, to be extremely cautious about large scale proposals. To approach consultees to discuss a site, in principle, without initial site surveys and sketch design is likely to be counter-productive and unhelpful. The initial response of consultees will be very significant in determining the future actions of developers, as noted below in relation to the North Yorkshire site.

For the reasons set out, it was decided not to involve the public in scoping. It was always intended to organise a programme of public consultation following the lodging of the planning application. However, despite the best efforts to keep the proposal confidential, it was leaked prior to this stage. The subsequent public meeting, from the developer's viewpoint, was a public relations disaster and stimulated the formation of an organised opposition to the proposal. The elaborate consultation process which followed patently failed to alter the views of this opposition group. However, a petition in favour of the development was successful in attracting substantially more signatures than the petition against the development.

A number of very clear conclusions were drawn from this experience of public consultation. First, the decision not to involve the public in scoping was confirmed. The view of the developers and the consultants was that scoping could be successfully carried out via confidential consultations with the local planning authority, statutory consultees and those non-governmental institutions with a direct interest in the site or its surroundings. It was concluded that the best point at which to initiate public consultation was after the preparation and publication of the ES. At this point, people had basic facts with which to debate and dispute, whilst the developers and their consultants had given sufficient consideration to the development to be able to respond effectively to most questions and queries.

A second major conclusion was that the process of public consultation should be managed. From the developer's viewpoint the consultation process has three aims, the first being to explain the nature of the development and its likely effects. Any large scale development brings with it rumour and misconception which has to be dispelled. The second aim is to check conclusions reached in the environmental assessment and to receive local insights into the proposed development and its likely effects. At each site, Lakewoods and its consultants learned some further valuable information from the consultation process. Thirdly, the developer wants to build popular and political support for the proposal. Two lessons were learned from the Cotswold Water Park experience: the importance of the political process and the need to expend time and effort in building support rather than trying to assuage opposition. Planning decisions are political decisions and at the end of the day success or failure depends upon the attitude of individual Councillors. In addition to winning the technical argument, developers must win the political argument. In the Cotswold Water Park case much effort was spent in trying to change the views of vehement opponents of the scheme who were intransigent and not enough time on garnering the support of the often more reticent but nevertheless important supporters of the scheme.

A holiday village in North Yorkshire – the assessment process[5]

The delay in obtaining consent for the village in the Cotswold Water Park, following the call-in of the application, required that another site be brought forward as soon as possible. The second site which attracted Lakewoods attention was at Camp Hill Plantation, near Carthorpe, close to the A1 in North Yorkshire. This is an area of coniferous plantation with clearings adjacent to a small country house set in parkland.

The approach to scoping and public participation at this site was quite different from that at the Cotswold Water Park. This different approach was stimulated first by the lessons learned, but principally by the different attitude of the planning authorities (Hambleton District Council and North Yorkshire County Council). In the Cotswold Water Park, officers at both the County and District Councils were guardedly positive in response to initial consultations about the proposed development. The proposal had some support from the adopted Local Plan which showed the site as suitable for recreational use and holiday accommodation. The reaction of the officers, together with the advice of their consultants, led Lakewoods to conclude that there was a reasonable chance of obtaining planning consent and gave them the necessary reassurance to proceed.

Initial discussions with Hambleton District Council and North Yorkshire County Council were much less positive. Officers at the District Council were initially hostile, but subsequently advised that, given the absence of any supporting development plan allocation, they considered that they would have no alternative but to ask the Secretary of State to call in the application. Alternatively, Lakewoods could seek to promote the site through the development plan process. Officers were unable to offer a view on how the independent Councillors of Hambleton might respond to the proposal. County Council officers also suggested that there was no adequate policy basis in the Structure Plan against which to evaluate the proposal other than the general statement that North Yorkshire was an area of restraint.

Neither piece of advice was what Lakewoods wanted to hear. Having experienced the costs and time of one public inquiry they had no desire to plunge into another, whilst the time required to progress the proposal through the development plan system was also incompatible with the need to enter the market as soon as possible. In these circumstances, Lakewoods decided to commence an environmental assessment and then, prior to a decision on whether or not to submit an application, to 'go public'.

Contact was then made with each of the local authorities, statutory consultees and other interested parties to discuss the scope of the ES. In this case, the consultees included:

- the Department of the Environment;
- the Department of Employment;
- the Department of Trade and Industry;
- the English Tourist Board;
- Hambleton District Council;
- North Yorkshire County Council;
- the Rural Development Commission;
- Yorkshire and Humberside Tourist Board;
- the Forestry Commission (who had grant aided the plantation);
- Yorkshire Wildlife Trust;
- the Nature Conservancy Council.

It will be noted that consultation was here extended to government departments and economic development agencies. The involvement of government departments reflected first the entry of the government relations company (GJW) as a consultant to Lakewoods and the need to try and seek a national view given the likelihood of a request for call-in. The involvement of the Yorkshire Wildlife Trust was also to prove very significant. Following 'confidential' consultations the Trust chose to issue, without consultation, a very critical press release on the proposed development. This action was to lead Lakewoods and its consultants subsequently to treat the voluntary sector, especially the voluntary wildlife sector, with great caution.

A brief formal scoping document was then prepared and circulated to all consultees. Work proceeded on a draft ES. It was decided that once this statement was completed in draft the proposal should be made public with an invitation extended to the District Council to visit the site, a press conference and an open weekend at which members of the general public could view an exhibition on site and be given a conducted tour.

The programme was almost thrown off course when Hambleton District Council Planning Committee, somewhat surprisingly, nearly resolved not to visit the site. A motion was put, and only narrowly defeated, that members should not visit the site until such time as a planning application was received. Ultimately, it was agreed to visit provided no refreshments were offered...

The weekend visits were exceptionally well attended and provided an opportunity for individuals to discuss the project on a one to one basis with representatives of Lakewoods. In terms of the developer's three requirements for public consultation, described above, the programme was successful in disseminating information about the development and in checking the assessment against local perceptions. However, it failed to build political support and the officers adhered to their view that they would recommend a call-in. As the first application languished with the Secretary of State, still awaiting a decision, the need to obtain a site with consent became ever more pressing.

A holiday village in East Yorkshire

The assessment process[6]

By 1990 Lakewoods' site selection process had become quite sophisticated. A set of environmental and planning site selection criteria had been devised to supplement the commercial criteria. These principles were built in to an environmental charter which included the following commitments:

- avoidance of National Parks, Areas of Outstanding Natural Beauty and Green Belts, and conservation of all Sites of Special Scientific Interest;
- consideration of sites in areas requiring economic development such as Assisted Areas and Rural Development Areas;
- selection of sites which do not conflict with planning policies and offer scope for meeting overall planning objectives;
- avoidance of sites where development would lead to a substantial reduction in public access;
- selection of sites where access can be realised with minimal impact on local communities.

At weekly meetings up to five or ten sites were evaluated against these criteria. Thus, in 1991 a site was identified at Southcliffe near Market Weighton in the Borough of East Yorkshire (North Humberside). The site comprised a large area (273 ha) of open, arable farmland on the Humber levels, much of which had been 'set-aside' and was not actively cultivated. There was a small area of woodland and some very small remnant areas of heathland. The site lies within three miles of junction 38 on the M62.

As with the Cotswold Water Park site, initial consultations with local authority officers were relatively encouraging. Accordingly it was resolved to proceed rapidly to the preparation of an ES. Consultations were held with the relevant local authorities and statutory consultees. As the site lay close to the boundary of two District Councils (East Yorkshire and Boothferry), contact was made with officers of both authorities in an effort to overcome the problems experienced in the Cotswold Water Park. Indeed, the next nearest District, Beverley, was also contacted at an early stage. Generally, each of the consultees responded relatively quickly and helpfully to the inquiry about scoping. A brief scoping document was then prepared and circulated to all those consulted. Response to this document was fairly limited.

Whilst the ES was being prepared, a consultation programme was also being formulated. This was elaborately planned so that news of the development should be released first to the relevant local authorities, then to the press, then to the general public by means of a local exhibition and subsequently to Parish Councils, other local authorities and local interest groups. The rationale of this approach was to ensure that full and adequate information was released rapidly in order to avoid misinformation and rumours. The initial release to the local authorities reflected the recognition that these were the decision makers and that they should be given the courtesy of a first sight of the proposals. Despite extensive officer consultations and political 'soundings', news of the development did not break in the press until after the first presentation to the County Council.

It is worth noting one significant political difference between the Southcliffe site and the Camp Hill site. In relation to the former, both East Yorkshire Borough Council and Humberside County Council had clear political groupings, a clear ruling group and acknowledged leaders. Political soundings were thus facilitated and the developers could have some confidence that views expressed by leaders would be reflected by other ruling group members. This was not the case at Camp Hill, where a Council principally composed of independents had no very clear political grouping or leadership.

The public exhibition held in Market Weighton worked well. Again, despite something of a crush, it was possible to hold one to one conversations about particular issues. Again certain interesting local information was collated related, for example, to field accesses and possible archaeological remains. As a vehicle for communicating information and enabling discussion, a well-manned exhibition has considerable merits compared with a public meeting.

Despite the emergence of an effective pressure group and the decision of another neighbouring Council (Beverley) to oppose the development, the proposal was granted consent some 16 weeks after submission of the application and ES.

Reflections on the assessment process

From the viewpoint of the developer and their consultants the process of assessment worked well. The statement provided a clear and succinct summary of the likely impacts of the development which attracted little adverse comment. There was certainly no suggestion that the statement was inadequate in its scope. One major addition was agreed with the local planning authority and the Countryside Commission. This was a computer generated visualisation of the development at 5, 10 and 20 years after construction. This was a reasonable request given the relatively open nature of the site and its proximity to the high ground of the Yorkshire Wolds. The assessment of the visual impacts of the development were very dependent upon the success of the landscape proposals. In the event, the resulting visualisation was claimed both to indicate how well the development could be accommodated in the landscape and how obtrusive it might be.

The general satisfaction with the development proposal is perhaps best exemplified by the fact that the Parish Meeting in Southcliffe did not object to the proposal.

A holiday village in Cumbria

The assessment process

The fourth and final statement was prepared for a site at Whinfell Forest near Penrith in Cumbria. This was perhaps the most attractive of all the sites, comprising principally relatively mature plantation woodland on an undulating site in the Eden Valley with spectacular outward views to the North Pennines and the Lake District. Precisely the same process was used as in East Yorkshire. Initial confidential consultations with officers evinced interest in the proposal and the developers committed themselves to preparing a draft statement. The District and County Councils and statutory consultees were consulted on the scope of the statement. By this time the consultancy team and the developers had a clear understanding of those issues which were of most concern. Traffic and road safety issues were dominant in all the proposals and particularly in Cumbria, despite the decision to use an access direct to the principal road network (A66) rather than minor roads. The relative proximity of the site to the Lake District National Park and its comparatively unspoiled and quiet character were recognised as likely to create controversy.

Following publication of the statement a comprehensive programme of public exhibitions was staged both close to the site and in the adjacent market town of Penrith. Further detailed consultations were held with statutory bodies such as the Department of Transport and with voluntary bodies including the Friends of the Lake District.

The application progressed relatively smoothly. In accord with the above analysis, the developers were most concerned as to the attitudes of the Department of Transport in relation to the trunk road access and the Lake District Special Planning Board in respect of the potential impacts on the National Park. Neither body objected to the proposal and outline consent was duly granted.

Reflections on the assessment process

The principal opposition to the development derived strength from the Cumbria Trust for Nature Conservation and the Friends of the Lake District who both declared their opposition. The Trust was particularly critical and took exception to the fact that it was not consulted at an early stage. This was an explicit decision and it arose from the fact that Lakewoods feared, on the basis of its experience in Yorkshire, that a voluntary organisation, with members living in the vicinity of the site, would be likely to 'leak' the proposal. Although part of the site had been identified by the Trust as of local nature conservation interest, it was considered that the consultants' in-house ecologists could assess its significance without recourse to Trust records. Indeed, the thoroughness of the ecological survey was not challenged by the Trust.

Clearly, no conclusion can be reached as to whether the Trust would have leaked the proposals. However, despite their dissatisfaction at not being consulted at an early stage, hindsight does not suggest that the environmental assessment suffered as a result.

In relation to the Friends of the Lake District, again an explicit decision was taken not to consult them until the statement had been prepared. It was expected that the Friends would oppose the development in principle and that little would be gained by early consultation. This rather bleak conclusion was based upon our experience of the CPRE. In the early stages of the project we engaged in dialogue with the CPRE at national level, seeking to understand their stance on holiday villages and inviting them to identify locational principles. Nationally, CPRE officers indicated that they were not opposed to holiday villages and endorsed the locational principles adopted by Lakewoods, particularly the decision not to seek sites in National Parks and AONBs. However, local branches of the CPRE opposed each and every Lakewoods proposal and indeed every other holiday village proposal. Even, as in the Cotswold Water Park, where CPRE members were shown around the site and professed themselves surprised at its dereliction, implacable opposition followed. In such circumstances the rationale for involving similar groups in scoping exercises must be questioned.

Conclusions

This conclusion sets out to

- explain why Lakewoods adopted their particular approach to scoping and public consultation;
- assess the effectiveness of this approach;
- offer some personal reflections on the process of scoping, public participation and environmental assessment in the planning process.

The rationale for the approach

Lakewoods chose to undertake scoping exercises for each ES, but chose only to involve local authorities, statutory consultees and other interested parties. Lakewoods consciously chose not to involve the public in scoping primarily for reasons of confidentiality, political consciousness and timing. Each of these reasons may be examined in turn.

First, Lakewoods was greatly concerned with commercial confidentiality, perhaps unduly concerned. Confidentiality will not always be such a major concern, but many developers will not want prematurely to publicise their interest in a particular site, the nature of their proposed development or the fact that they are about to embark on a new business venture. Commercial concerns may include fears about the changes in the value of the land, about the impacts on share values, or about the impact on commercial rivals. This may not properly be a planning concern but it will profoundly influence the actions of major public companies. In that environmental assessment is principally concerned with large scale projects with significant impacts, commercial considerations will be important in many cases. It is difficult to see how a concern for commercial confidentiality can easily be reconciled with early disclosure of plans as part of public consultation in relation to scoping.

Secondly there is the issue of political consciousness or sensitivity. It has been said many times, but it cannot too often be repeated, that planning is a political process, although there are two components to any planning decision: technical and political. Developers must demonstrate to the local planning authority, statutory consultees and other technical consultees that their proposal is in accord with the policy context and will cause no demonstrable harm to features of acknowledged interest. But winning the technical argument is not enough. In the case of the Cotswold Water Park village, no planning officer ever recommended members to oppose the development and no statutory consultee opposed the development. Technically therefore the proposal, as demonstrated by the Inspector's decision, was acceptable. And yet it was called in and the subject of a nine week public inquiry. The political nature of planning is thus underlined.

There are different approaches to winning the political argument. Lakewoods approach, born of early disappointments, was to target political decision makers from the outset and to seek to win their support at an early stage. Politicians were deliberately accorded a privileged status in the consultation process. They were offered early and privileged information. It might be argued that such a status accords with concepts of representative democracy. More prosaically, it was argued that if a member of the public was to ring his local Councillor to complain about a proposed Lakewoods holiday village, the Councillor ought to know what was proposed.

Quite simply, early revelation of a proposed development through public consultation on scoping would deny the possibility of this approach and provide opposition groups with greater time and ammunition to mount their case.

The third consideration was one of time. A scoping process of the type used by Lakewoods, involving confidential consultations with officers of the local authorities, statutory consultees and other interested parties, can be controlled by the developer and is relatively quick and cost-effective. To organise a public consultation process on scoping will inevitably extend the time and cost of the exercise. Whilst it may be claimed that such consultation will save time and money later, there is little empirical evidence to suggest this is the case.

The effectiveness of the approach

It cannot be denied that Lakewoods measure of success is the number of planning consents they received and the speed with which they were achieved. However, professionally and technically the issue to be addressed is whether the scoping exercise succeeded and whether delaying public consultation had positive or negative impacts.

In relation to the first statement, the painstaking consideration of the text, chapter by chapter, by a working party of technical officers did identify areas on which further data were desirable. Such data were subsequently provided in an annex to the statement. It may be that fuller consultation at the scoping stage might have identified such issues.

Thereafter, there was almost no suggestion that the statements were incomplete or that critical information had been omitted. It may reasonably be argued, therefore, that the scoping exercises worked. If local authorities, statutory consultees and other interested bodies actively participate in the scoping exercise, then technical consultations alone should be sufficient. It is in the developer's interest to ensure that the scoping exercise is adequately carried out because otherwise there will be delay at a later stage.

Turning to the issue of public consultation or participation, Lakewoods conducted quite elaborate consultation exercises but only after the statements were published. It was argued that, notwithstanding the issues of confidentiality, political consciousness and timing, by delaying public consultation until after the initial assessment was completed, Lakewoods and their consultants were able to impart genuine information and to say what effects they thought the development would have and why.

Each proposed holiday village led to the formation of an opposition group and each was opposed by the CPRE. Would the involvement of the general public at scoping have avoided the formation of these opposition groups or won over the CPRE? I think not. It is in the nature of large scale development proposals that they provoke opposition. No amount of involvement or consultation will win over those implacably opposed to a development. This was a critical lesson learned at the Cotswold Water Park. Immense amounts of time and effort were spent in discussing the proposal with the local Parish Councils and the residents group but to no avail. No reassurance, no factual statements, no mitigating measures, no elements of planning gain would assuage their vehement opposition. The discussions became a war of attrition, especially in the context of the public inquiry, from which very little that was positive arose. I would argue that had the public been involved in scoping this war of attrition would simply have started earlier and gone on longer.

Professional conclusions

I believe environmental assessment is a valuable tool for creating environmentally sensitive, even sustainable, development. As a planner working in the private sector, environmental assessment has, at a stroke, given me a place in the design team. Assessment gives local authorities, statutory consultees, interested bodies and the general public a factual statement on which to debate and dispute. It is particularly important that local planning authorities should actively participate in the process, in scoping, in contributing data and in assessing the findings.

Much of the professional debate revolves around the nature of the assessment process and the status of the ES. On the one hand assessment may be seen as a process in which all should participate; which involves the whole community in the design process and in which the statement merely becomes the statutory document required at the time the planning application is submitted. On the other hand assessment may be seen as a process in which the statement forms a critical milestone, the point at which the developer unveils his plans and gives his account of their likely environmental impacts. Discussion and debate ensue.

Both models, it seems to me, are valid. The first may be seen as an ideal where a public spirited developer has the time, resources and ability to initiate a wide ranging programme of participation. It requires all participants to take a lively and rational interest in the proposal and preferably not to take up an entrenched position at the outset. It would seem most suited to public sector projects, projects initiated by the not-for-profit sector and proposals which are unlikely to provoke much opposition in principle. I am concerned that relatively few projects requiring assessment will fulfil the last criterion.

The second model is more suited to the private sector developer wrestling with the problems of commercial confidentiality and time constraints. Its acceptability appears to be endorsed by the latest draft guidelines on environmental assessment published by the DoE which, whilst emphasising the value of scoping and the need for early consultation with the local planning authority and statutory consultees, acknowledge the possible need for confidentiality. The guidance on public participation is similarly cautious, balancing the desirability and potential benefits of early disclosure with commercial concerns. However, the draft EU recommendations to make scoping statutory, whilst welcome and sensible in principle, may, on the basis of the above experience, cause some concern in relation to timing and commercial confidentiality.

Notes and references

1 English Tourist Board (1991) *Planning for Success: a Tourism Strategy for England 1991–1995*. London: ETB.
2 The Schedule 3 list is set out on page 16 of the Introduction to this book.
3 A holiday village in the Cotswold Water Park. Environmental Statement. Abingdon: Cobham Resource Consultants, 1988.
4 DoE (1988) Circular 15/88: *Town and Country Planning (Assessment of Environmental Effects) Regulations 1988*. London: HMSO; DoE (1989) *Environmental Assessment: A Guide to the Procedures*. London: HMSO.
5 Lakewoods holiday village: Camp Hill Estate, North Yorkshire. Environmental Statement. Abingdon: Cobham Resource Consultants, 1990.
6 Lakewoods holiday village: South Farm, Market Weighton, East Yorkshire. Environmental Statement. Abingdon: Cobham Resource Consultants, 1991.

CHAPTER 4

PLANNING AUTHORITY REVIEW

Richard Read

Introduction

Although EIA has been with us for 20 years or more, its introduction into the UK planning system in 1988 came into effect with little preparation. Perhaps many of us accepted too readily the Government's assertion that it would involve only a few cases a year and the process for planning authorities was just a bolt-on procedure to development control. As Peter Bulleid has discussed in Chapter 1, experience has taught us that the Government underestimated the number of EIAs by a large margin. On the other hand procedurally they seem, to a large degree, to have got it right. Most projects that are covered by the Regulations[1] are incorporated into planning administration and integrate well into development control case work.

Having said that, EIA has introduced issues to development control that otherwise would not have occurred. For instance, the idea of comprehensively investigating all environmental issues and not just traditional planning matters and the investigation of 'alternatives' have now become much more accepted practice. Also it must be admitted that the discipline of handling EIA has gradually introduced valuable concepts and procedures for considering the impact of projects into development control generally.

In Hampshire over 30 EIA cases have been dealt with by the planning authorities directly. These have included projects on mineral extraction (six); urban developments (nine); roads/infrastructure (six); landfill (eight); and waste processing plant (three). The majority of the cases have fallen to the County Council to process. Accordingly, a certain degree of expertise has developed within the County Planning Department by handling such projects. This chapter describes the practices developed by case officers in the Department to handle all the information generated by ESs. For clarity the procedure is referred to as 'planning authority review' or the 'review process' or simply 'the review'. These optional phrases are meant to include the examination of all the information generated by an EIA case that a planning authority needs to consider before making a decision to grant planning permission or otherwise. The review process is wider than the review of ESs, often referred to as 'ES review'. ESs are only the beginning of the review process for planning authorities and much additional information has to be considered before a case can be determined.

In the latter part of the chapter we consider the review process involved with a proposal for a household waste incinerator in Portsmouth. The case provided some important lessons that the routine EIA cases do not normally illustrate. It cannot be claimed that the experience of Hampshire County Council is all embracing. No doubt experience elsewhere can provide equally valid and different lessons but it is hoped that the matters described in this chapter are helpful to practitioners.

Administrative arrangements

A case can be made that the processing of cases involving EIA should not significantly differ from that of any other major applications that normally pass through the following administrative stages:

- registration of documents;
- publicity;
- carrying out of consultations;
- reviewing of environmental information;
- reporting and decision making.

Accordingly, planning authorities have well-established procedures into which the review can easily be integrated. However, there are some administrative measures of particular relevance to EIA cases that are worth considering.

The first of these is quite mundane and relates to the amount of documentation that is involved in an EIA case. It is quite common for the ES to run to three volumes and when the authority is perhaps asking the advice of 10 to 20 consultees the volume of paper generated can be staggering. This often creates major logistics and storage problems for normally overcrowded planning offices. The planning authority has the option to make use of the Regulations and ask the applicant to send copies of the ES directly to the consultees. However, there is some reluctance in making use of this option. Some planning officers consider that this results in a loss of control over the review process, with the applicant virtually becoming the case administrator.

Apart from normal case files, the ES and the responses from statutory consultees, there are also often large numbers of letters of objection – not infrequently hundreds – with petitions signed by thousands. Then there are supplementary submissions by the applicant, counter submissions from pressure groups (and their consultants) and so on. After all this, the issues associated with the original statement are all but forgotten. Indeed from the point of view of the review process, the subsequent documents are of greater significance than the ES itself.

The second point concerns the responsibility for the review process. Experience suggests that a case officer with experience in development control, at a senior level, is best suited to the task. Because of the wide ranging and often controversial nature of projects involving EIA it is important that there is one person who takes on the pivotal role of steering the case in all its aspects. There is a need for liaison between different specialists, be it internal to the authority or external, and close contact with the applicant. Similarly it is essential that the case officer is involved with all the discussions to prevent the process going off at tangents. Full regard must be taken of the interrelationships between all the elements of a project's impacts to prevent a particular specialist or interest group hijacking the process and hence the work programme. The task of the case officer is described in the Government *Good Practice Guide* for evaluating environmental information[2] and can be summarised thus:

- the management of consultations;
- familiarisation of all aspects of the documentation;
- evaluation of information from all sources;
- liaison with the applicant, consultees and the public;
- compiling report(s).

An experienced case officer is largely familiar with all these tasks, but some additional training in EIA is desirable, although not essential. The latter point may have to be borne in mind when considering the costs of training in periods of budgetary prudence. However, the one day workshops organised by various institutions like Oxford Brookes University can be considered as cost-effective alternatives.

Many planning authorities that receive ES or other major cases on a regular basis organise 'standing panels' of officers from various disciplines drawn from within the planning department and outside. The purpose of these panels is to develop a body of experts on the subject of review to facilitate processing of cases. Where such panels have not formally been constituted there often is a body of officers frequently involved in such cases who in effect function as a core of expertise from which the case officer can draw advice. An alternative or supplement to this approach is to engage external reviewers specifically to examine the ES. The purpose of this is to provide the planning authority with advice as to the scope and adequacy of an ES, and suggest areas of further investigation. In Hampshire, the Institute of Environmental Assessment has been engaged on occasion for this purpose. The practice does have the value of providing a set of references for further investigation. Otherwise, authorities can elect to do this task within their own resources. The employment of an external reviewer might be an advantage when a case is particularly controversial. In order to improve the credibility of the statement the authority may wish to demonstrate that it has been independently examined.

The final point to address about administration is programming of work.

Because of the complexity of applications involving EIA and the various parties involved a planning authority has to organise some sort of work programme. Failure to do this will inevitably lead to 'drift' in the process with perhaps the development of the attitude that 'the work will get done when it is done'! In these days when public authorities are under scrutiny for their performance it is essential that planning cases are subject to the discipline of a timetable. It should also be remembered that an application subject to EIA is meant to be processed, according to the Regulations, within 16 weeks. Furthermore, the applicant has often paid a large fee and may be impatient for a decision!

Publicity and public involvement

A major purpose of EIA is that all environmental aspects of a project should be placed before the public and, by implication, involve the community in decision making. The legislation[3] provides for the publicity of planning applications accompanied by ES by means of press advertisements and site notices and/or neighbour publicity. However, the legislative requirements are very much a minimum requirement and other procedures are often engaged as part of the review process.

It has to be acknowledged that the statutory time limits of 21 days for comment on an application are woefully inadequate. Given the amount of documentation involved with an ES it is unreasonable to expect experts, let alone 'lay people', to give a reasoned response to what are often complex projects. It is the practice in Hampshire to accept comments up to the day the case is being considered by the committee responsible for determining it. Indeed, the Council even has a policy which permits interested parties to address the committee direct. It is normal practice for controversial cases to be referred to a panel of committee members for a site visit. Frequently at these meetings the public attend and are invited to make comments.

Often the applicant is encouraged to prepare a small exhibition of the proposals so that interested parties have the opportunity to examine the project in more detail and opinions can be exchanged. This practice gives the developer the chance to experience how local people feel about the proposal. How far this may cause a change in the details of the project is another matter.

Another area of publicity is the public meeting and it is probably the least productive. The experience of the proposed household waste incinerator for Portsmouth, a case outlined at the end of the chapter, explains why. In this instance a whole series of meetings were arranged in the Portsmouth area, but the results were disastrous. The public meeting appears not to be the right forum for the exchange of information or opinion. It might function well as a community safety valve whereby the public can vent their frustrations with the authority and as such make a meaningful contribution to local democracy. But as a contribution to environmental decision making it is often unhelpful.

Having been critical about public meetings the final area of publicity that can be considered is perhaps even more radical. It is becoming more usual with planning cases for them to be placed before community forums of local people and other interested parties. This approach has been carried out successfully in Hampshire and elsewhere for dealing with unfriendly operations such as mineral and landfill sites. Admittedly this has been done more often to monitor permissions but it is now being used by the County Council as part of the review process. Over the next two or three years the County Council anticipates receiving proposals for waste processing plant and given the experience of the Portsmouth incinerator project it is accepted that a proactive approach is required to deal with public concerns. The view is taken that the earlier the community is involved in planning matters the better chance a project has of eventually being implemented. However, it has to be admitted that this approach cannot be taken lightly. The resource implications of servicing forums are considerable and indeed risky, as the debate may go in unexpected directions. Also, importantly, such a process cannot be hurried. Once commenced this form of public participation must be permitted to run its course or risk being charged with being little more than a cosmetic exercise.

On the other hand projects involving EIA frequently encounter community resistance and unless procedures are developed for engaging the public in environmental decision making the planning authority review process will become increasingly fraught.

Screening and consultations

Planning authorities have well-established procedures for consulting certain statutory bodies like the highway authority, English Nature etc. In fact under the legislation some of these consultations are mandatory. Accordingly, incorporating the comments of these bodies into the review process is now really very routine.

It is normal that before initiating consultations the case officer will submit the ES and application to a screening process to ensure that:

- the documentation meets legal requirements so it can be formally registered;
- the ES is basically adequate;
- the proposal is checked against the development plan (this can identify issues for later consideration and establish whether the project is a 'departure'[4]);
- a comprehensive list of consultees is identified.

Unless this basic groundwork is done there is a chance the review will encounter later problems quite probably involving retracing the process, to the annoyance of the applicant or the frustration of the case officer and probably both. There is nothing more exasperating to all involved in the review process than having to retrieve matters that should have been dealt with earlier. Indeed cases have been known to reach an appeal to the Secretary of State before it has been noticed that some simple procedure has been missed. Alternatively, the case officer may have to request, in a piecemeal fashion, further information that should have been identified at the beginning of the process. So the lesson is – make sure case screening procedures are in place and applied!

The case officer identifies a significant number of issues through consultations. Experience reveals that notwithstanding the quality and scope of an ES unanticipated issues emerge from consultees. There are a number of reasons for this. Firstly, consultees are often unaware of the full details of a project during preliminary consultation and are therefore not able to give full advice to an applicant before the submission of the application. Secondly, there may be different judgements as to the weight that should be given to impacts and the interrelationship of impacts can bring issues hitherto underrated to the fore.

The handling of these new issues is important as this is where disputes over the facts of impacts are often founded. There are no established techniques, procedures or framework to guide the case officer through these situations. The case officer's experience and basic professional skills are needed to identify the new issues and debate the matter with the relevant parties to hopefully a resolution. It is essential that the case officer critically examines the comments of consultees and in effect tests their strength. If the comments pass through this stage it may be necessary to initiate negotiations between the applicant and consultee. In many instances the matter may be resolved by agreement over the facts and/or mitigation measures. On the other hand these issues may remain as an outstanding matter to be resolved in the final evaluation of the review process.

Sometimes consultees cannot (or will not) provide the advice a planning authority needs. This situation happened over the Portsmouth incinerator case. Her Majesty's Inspectorate of Pollution (HMIP) would only provide perfunctory advice on the problem of atmospheric emissions, leaving the planning authority with many unanswered questions arising out of the ES. In these circumstances it is open to a planning authority to contract consultants to make good the deficiency in advice. The environmental consultancy business has burgeoned with the growth of EIA and, judging from what happened over the controversy generated by the Portsmouth incinerator case, no wonder! The case involved a consultant for the developer in preparing the ES; one for the City Council to examine the ES (although they were not the determining planning authority); and a consultant for the County Council to examine pollution and noise issues as this advice was considered deficient by the respective control agencies. Although there is no doubt that all concerned gave sound professional advice, indeed the County's consultant resolved some critical matters, the outsider may have doubted the credibility of the process when seeing such warring expert opinion!

Evaluation of environmental information

The evaluation of the environmental information is the most challenging aspect of a case officer's work in connection with the review process. It is at this stage that the case officer has to pull together and evaluate all the information relevant to the case. This includes the information provided by the developer (and consultants, where appropriate), the views of consultees, public comment, policy statements etc. Then the case officer has to make a judgement as to the acceptability of the project and report (invariably to elected members when a case involves EIA) for a decision by the planning authority.

This part of the review calls on basic core skills that any experienced case officer will possess. Such officers have been doing tasks of this nature for many years and the collective experience of these professionals accounts for more than all the guidance on impact techniques and evaluation provided by manuals and textbooks. At the end of the process judgements have to be made, which to a lesser or greater degree, are subjective as only a proportion of the issues involved are amenable to objective analysis. The case officer has to balance environmental topics that are fundamentally different and, depending on the individual assessor, they can be accorded differing priorities. It is the old problem of comparing apples and pears and there is no right answer to this conundrum. But it is a problem that case officers have to address daily and make recommendations which can withstand critical examination, by their political masters, the public and other interested parties.

What is involved in the information evaluation? The Government's advice[5] provides a framework that a case officer might employ and most planning authorities in effect follow a similar framework. It might not be so explicit and tidily organised as suggested by the Government, but practice has evolved techniques that have stood the test of time. The approach adopted by Hampshire's County Planning Department is to order the information in the following way:

- establish details of the site and surroundings including the references to basic planning constraints, e.g. SSSI, AONB etc., that affect the land or could be affected by the proposal;
- establish the final details of the proposal or project including any justification the applicant may have made, especially concerning the need for the development;

- identify the relevant development plan and other material planning policies;
- summarise the impacts as identified in the ES;
- summarise comments from the consultees, e.g. the National Rivers Authority, the District Council etc.

By putting the information into this structure the case officer in effect establishes the facts and issues relevant to the case, thus providing a context for an evaluation of the project. The evaluation then follows the following framework:

- highlighting issues critical to the decision;
- testing the principle of the project against policy;
- adjudicating the significance of the critical impacts taking into account possible mitigation;
- examining the impacts against policy criteria and the views of the consultees and expert opinions;
- addressing non-critical issues (which can either be resolved by use of planning conditions attached to the permission or discounted as of no significance);
- making an overall judgement as to the acceptability of the project.

The framework as described belies the fact that the methodology is effectively iterative. Information frequently arrives on the case officer's desk in an untidy order. Critical comments may be late and cause re-evaluation of some issues. This in turn may require further negotiations with the applicant, and redesign of part of the project or the introduction of additional mitigation measures, further consultation, further re-evaluation and so on. This is how the evaluation of environmental information works out in practice, all quite disorganised and reactive. However, this does not dismiss the value of adopting a framework as a reference guide for the case officer.

The identification and evaluation of critical issues are the most difficult aspects of the case officer's tasks as it is where very fine judgements are exercised in balancing intangibles. Some issues, e.g. noise impacts, are sometimes easily dealt with, as they can be measured as fact against recognised criteria. Others such as visual impacts are more difficult to judge and it may be necessary to balance community and/or professional perceptions of an adverse impact against the realisation of other policy objectives. In the case of the Portsmouth incinerator the issue came down to the problem of an over-large building versus the provision of the facility to deal with long term waste management needs in Hampshire. Cases often filter down to such fine matters of balance that are only capable of being resolved politically. Accordingly, the report to the elected members of the planning authority is a very significant part of the review process.

Reporting

The case officer's report should be a reflection of the review process. It is written in the name of the chief officer or manager of the planning authority – the County Planning Officer in Hampshire. The report provides the decision maker, invariably a committee, with key facts and opinions and identifies the issues. It is important that elected members are advised of the logic of the arguments involved and are aware of how issues are being balanced by their professional advisers. In Hampshire reports are structured thus:

- executive summary;
- background to the case;
- site and surroundings;
- proposal's details;
- development plan;
- summary of the environmental impacts (as identified in the statement);
- consultees' comments;
- public comment;
- views of the District Council(s);
- County Planning Officer's comments;
- recommendation.

The recommendation at the end of the report is the final judgement made by the County Planning Officer. However, it might be complicated by some residual matters. The chief amongst these is the use of 'planning conditions' to deal with mitigation measures arising out of the review process. The conditions will reflect the mitigation offered by the applicant or recommended by the Planning Officer to make a project acceptable. Conditions may require additional landscaping to address visual impact concerns of the neighbouring occupiers of land. Because of the wide ranging nature of mitigation measures, the use of conditions may not be entirely appropriate as they are highly proscribed by planning legislation. Government advice[6] sets out the rules clearly and there are two areas where an EIA case could fall foul of them.

The first is that the proposed mitigation, e.g. a highway improvement, cannot be regulated by planning conditions. In these circumstances the planning authority may need to make recourse to the use of legally binding agreements with the applicant to ensure the required works are carried out. The use of such agreements is fairly routine[7]. The second concerns the area of mitigation that is more properly administered by another agency, e.g. the National Rivers Authority. This is a little problematic as certain matters may be left hanging which may not be entirely satisfactory if the concern is controversial. In these circumstances the planning authority can only trust that the matter will be satisfactorily dealt with at the appropriate stage. This situation is particularly problematic with pollution problems where there is overlap between control regimes. The matter is addressed in recent Government advice on the relationship between planning and pollution control[8], but it remains to be seen whether the advice provided works out in practice.

Overall, the report is purposely designed to separate facts, either verifiable or reported, from professional judgement. This allows elected members the opportunity to argue their own priorities in the final balance of the issues. This final stage of the review process is most critical. No matter how completely executed the previous stages of the review are, there are frequently matters that have no absolute technical answer. Officers of the planning authority can give advice based on judgement and planning policy, but in controversial cases these matters can only be resolved politically. Accordingly, much of the review process is to expose those environmental impacts that cannot be addressed by technical solutions or require a decision between competing policy objectives. In the end the review process is a political one!

Household waste incinerator, Portsmouth

The household waste incinerator proposal in Portsmouth, or 'the Burner' as it became popularly known, illustrates a number of issues involved with planning authority review. These include amongst others:

- the credibility of the ES;
- the reliability of advice from consultees, particularly with regard to non-traditional planning issues such as pollution;
- disputes over policy;
- the involvement of the public;
- political issues.

The origins of the project were complex. It is sufficient to say that the proposal was conceived to address the well-recognised problem in the County of a shortage of landfill capacity. The situation was judged to be exacerbated by the enforced redundancy of a series of municipal incinerators which at the end of 1996 would not meet EC emission standards. The solution to the problem was realised by the County Council, as a waste disposal authority, entering into an undertaking with a private contractor to design, build and operate a large incinerator in Portsmouth. The undertaking was subject to the contractor obtaining planning permission independently from the County Council as a planning authority. The contractor submitted a planning application accompanied by an ES for the project in 1991.

The plant was designed to handle two-thirds of the household waste arising in the County and was to be built on a site of 3 ha comprising a redundant waste incinerator and vacant land in an industrial area in Portsmouth. It featured a building 200 metres in length, 45 metres wide and

38 metres high to include all the processes associated with incineration of household refuse. It also included a stack 85 metres high. The plant was designed to produce 34 MW of electricity as a by-product from the incineration of 400,000 tonnes of waste each year. The residue from the process was estimated at 95,000 tonnes of ash and its operation would have generated some 500+ lorries per day. It was recognised that the plant had a potential to emit to the atmosphere a whole range of polluting gases but these would be treated by a variety of control devices and procedures.

The ES submitted with the application ran to three volumes, comprising summary, main statement and technical appendices. It outlined the policy background to the project, described the development, examined alternative sites, technologies and waste management options and examined the existing environmental situation. The main impacts identified were:

- construction noise and vibration – controlled to acceptable levels;
- noise/vibration (operational) – no adverse effects;
- reduction in pressure on landfill resources – benefit;
- compliance with County Council waste management policy – benefit;
- traffic – marginal increases in lorry movements, some minor road improvements proposed;
- air quality – no significant impact, all emissions within EC guidelines, ground level contamination 1% to 2% above existing concentrations;
- visual impact – identified as a negative impact owing to the large scale nature of the building.

The ES was a source of difficulties almost from its publication. It took four months to prepare after the project's announcement. During this time the contractor and his environmental consultant had long discussions including 'scoping' debates with the planning authority. Notwithstanding this, the Council's planners were uneasy about the statement as there appeared to be a lack of rigour in the analysis of some of the impacts. There also appeared to be a lack of coherence in the impact assessment methodologies that was not helped by diffident editorial control on the documents, and the issue of alternatives and waste management options was covered very thinly. Finally, it quickly emerged that some factual information was in error!

In accordance with standard procedure the planning authority arranged for the documents to be the subject of wide ranging consultations. The planning authority also decided to engage consultants to advise on the matters of noise and air pollution. Some consultees were very critical of the project, particularly with regard to the issue of incineration in principle, the adequacy of pollution control, the concept of concentrating on one plant, the impact of the proposal on other waste management objectives and the size of the plant. The authority's consultants recommended that certain aspects of the noise (and vibration) and air pollution impacts be further investigated. It should also be noted that the response from HMIP, a mandatory consultee, was not comprehensive.

Arising from the consultant's advice and the reaction of some consultees, along with the concerns raised by the public, the applicant was 'directed' under the appropriate planning legislation to supply further information. A supplementary statement was requested to address the following matters:

- noise and vibration impacts;
- verification on emissions;
- visual assessment;
- visibility of the plume from the stack;
- the locations for fly ash disposal.

A supplementary statement was subsequently submitted with amendments to the application that included a reduction in the height of the building from 38 metres to 33 metres and additional air pollution control facilities. The amendments with the supplementary statement were publicised and additional consultations carried out. In the meantime the Government decided to call in the application for determination by the Secretary of State because of the policy issues raised by the project.

It was always recognised by the County Council that the proposal would be controversial and that it would be a case of great public interest. A series of exhibitions and meetings were organised to explain the proposal. Considerable effort was made to involve the public. Despite these efforts the reaction was negative.

The local newspaper began a campaign with the slogan 'Ban the Burner' before the application and ES were published. A local pressure group developed and the letters of objection arrived even before the facts were known. One person went to considerable efforts in submitting alternative photomontages to that illustrated in the statement. Their credibility was enhanced when it was discovered that the applicant had made errors in their own documentation on the visual impact of the proposed building!

Not surprisingly the public meetings were rowdy, with certain individuals dominating proceedings and baiting the applicant and Council officials. Within this cauldron of emotion, rational debate took a back seat and it was impossible for anyone to present the complex issues involved, let alone debate them. Notwithstanding this, taking the public involvement campaign as a totality it did bring forward issues on which the applicant was required to provide further information. However, the reaction to the project arising out of the supplementary statement was no more muted than the original.

A further dimension of the project was that it became a victim of local political issues. Different political parties were in control of the City and County Councils. The prospect of Local Government Review and the City Council's ambitions to become a unitary authority had commenced. There was also a degree of traditional rivalry between the City and the County. The case then ran into national election politics in 1992 and even threatened to become a local election issue.

Given the circumstances, conditions were not ideal for evaluating the information in an objective fashion and preparing a technical report to sum up the review process. However, this was done in July 1992. The report noted the impacts raised in the ESs, the views of the public and the advice of consultees and the Council's own consultants. It concluded that despite the controversy of so many issues related to the project the judgement was that the project and its impacts were acceptable. Reservations about the visual impact of the scheme were noted but the benefits and circumstances of the project outweighed the one adverse impact.

Notwithstanding this advice, the Council rejected the recommendation and declined to support the application. The Council decided that although the principle of an incinerator was acceptable the scheme was too large and that the way forward for the County was to dispose of its waste through a network of smaller incinerators.

Many lessons can be learnt from the case. The first is that the credibility of the statement was stretched from the very beginning. Significant flaws were found by the public – the photomontages were probably the most embarrassing – but there were many other minor errors. Additionally, some issues such as fly ash disposals were beset with serious errors or omission. Apart from this it became apparent that the methodologies for evaluating air pollution and noise impacts were vulnerable to criticism. These matters should not have jeopardised the project as deficiencies in information can be remedied. Indeed, most ESs require further clarification and submissions of further information. In most circumstances this is integrated successfully into the review. Unfortunately, with the Portsmouth case the errors, omissions and indeed the style of the documents did not do justice to the project and its implications.

Second, inadequate advice from statutory consultees means that alternative sources have to be found. It was always recognised with the Portsmouth case that air pollution would be a critical issue and consultants were hired to deal with this. However, the HMIP's attitude was that the air pollution issue would be a matter to be addressed when the applicant applied for authorisation under the Environmental Protection Act 1990. This might be very neat in bureaucratic terms but is not satisfactory for dealing with queries arising out of a planning application. Although the County obtained alternative advice, not all planning authorities are in this position and a failure in the provision of advice can endanger the satisfactory conclusion of the review process.

The third point is that the current EIA regime cannot cope with policy vacuums very easily. The Portsmouth incinerator project arose out of proposals in the Hampshire Waste Management Plan and as such was well conceived. However, it was readily apparent during the review process that the Plan provided an inadequate context for the project. Waste management policies were, and still are, evolving and the project appeared out of sympathy with ideas on recycling. Moreover the debate on incineration had at that time only just begun and the statement failed to address this matter satisfactorily. When an individual project raises unresolved policy issues it is very difficult to retrieve the situation within the review process. It is one thing to expect alternative sites or processes to be investigated but to cover alternative policy options is another matter, well beyond the scope of project assessment.

The involvement of the public was critical in the case and although the use of public meetings and exhibitions is commendable it is readily apparent that this approach is inadequate for controversial cases.

Finally, if the review process becomes tangled with political issues these will inevitably colour what eventually is decided. Most planning cases are not directly politically driven and so this consideration is not always critical, but even so the decisions are eventually made by politicians and this fact should not be forgotten. However, political issues do not exist in isolation and the question does arise whether in the absence of the other factors the outcome may have been different.

Some conclusions

The planning authority review of environmental information in EIA cases is not dissimilar to that used in handling any major planning application. The EIA cases that Hampshire has had to deal with as a planning authority are only a proportion of equally controversial and complicated 'normal' planning applications. Each authority has its own practices, but the differences are within a similar framework. All authorities depend, to some degree, on consultation arrangements with specialist agencies. All authorities have methodologies for examining environmental information, making judgements between competing policy objectives and reporting. Finally, all planning authorities are political organisations and this fact cannot be separated from the review process. So often the fate of EIA cases depends on quite fine judgements that do not have a technical basis. It is the political process that has to complete a planning authority's review.

Notes and references

1 Town and Country Planning (Assessment of Environmental Effects) Regulations 1988; Town and Country Planning (Assessment of Environmental Effects) (Amendment) Regulations 1994.
2 DoE (1994a) *Evaluation of Environmental Information for Planning Projects: A Good Practice Guide*. London: HMSO.
3 Town and Country Planning (General Procedures) Order 1995.
4 A 'departure' is a form of development which is considered by the planning authority to be contrary to the provisions of the development plan. Departure applications have to be advertised as such and the relevant Secretary of State has to be informed and can 'call in' the application for determination.

5 DoE (1994a) *op. cit.*

6 DoE (1985) Circular 1/85: *Use of Conditions in Planning Permissions.* London: HMSO.

7 Legal agreements between developers and local authorities take many forms but are normally used to secure some form of mitigation requirement that cannot be secured by planning conditions. The most widely used are known as 'planning obligations' which are secured under the terms of S106 of the Town and Country Planning Act 1990 (as amended by the Planning and Compensation Act 1991). Advice on their use is set out in DoE (1991) Circular 16/91: *Planning and Compensation Act 1991: Planning Obligations.* London: HMSO.

8 DoE (1994b) PPG23: *Planning and Pollution Control.* London: HMSO.

CHAPTER 5

CONSULTATION AND THE CONFLICT OF INTERESTS IN THE EIA PROCESS

Joe Weston

Introduction

Consultation is a vital part of the EIA process and is at the heart of the 1985 EEC Directive. Article 6 of that Directive specifically requires the implementation of public participation and consultation procedures before decisions are made on EIA projects. This requirement goes back to the early days of EIA, particularly in the USA. The whole concept of EIA sprang, in part, from a general disenchantment with environmental decision-making processes which excluded the public. It was very often the public who suffered most from bad planning when people had to live with the consequences of decisions over which they had little or no influence. EIA was seen by many of its advocates as a means of making public participation and consultation central to environmental decision making[1].

In the UK participation and consultation have long been an important part of both development control and strategic and local development plan making. Unsurprisingly, given the nature of the UK planning system, consultation has been defined by the courts as follows:

> in any context the essence of consultation is the communication of a genuine invitation to give advice and a genuine consideration of advice ... to achieve consultation sufficient information must be supplied by the consulting party to the consulted party to enable it to tender helpful advice. Sufficient time must be given by the consulting to the consulted party to enable it to do that, and sufficient time must be available for such advice to be considered by the consulting party. Sufficient, in that context, does not mean ample, but at least enough to enable the relevant purpose to be fulfilled[2].

In EIA terms, consultation is the means through which the synthesis of environmental information can take place and the wider interpretation of potential impacts can be established. Consultation, particularly prior to the submission of a planning application, is also essential for the success of the scoping exercise. Through consultation the main focus for the EIA can be established and agreed by all parties which can save time and resources otherwise needlessly spent on immaterial impacts. The participation of statutory consultees, other local or national bodies and local residents provides the iterative requirements of EIA, in that the results of consultation should be integrated into the assessment and where necessary design changes made to the project. That of course will depend on a number of factors including the balance to be struck between the requirements of consultees, the environmental costs of not complying with their wishes and the financial costs of incorporating all the changes they suggest. Each party in the EIA process has individual priorities, perspectives and demands. Yet consultation in the UK is not, or rarely, carried out on the EIA process and is not the collection of comments and the incorporation of the responses to consultation into the project and the ES. The principal consultations in the UK planning process take place after the ES has been produced and a planning application lodged. It is, of course, possible under Regulation 22, and advised by the DoE, for the developer to consult with certain statutory bodies, such as Environmental Agency and the Countryside Commission, prior to the submission of a planning application and the completion of the ES, and this was suggested as a mandatory requirement of the revised Directive[3]. This does happen on occasion but for the most part the statutory consultees rarely know that a project proposal exists until the application is received by the local planning authority and they are notified and formally consulted[4]. Developers may feel that prior consultation with such bodies weakens their position in the competition between interests that the planning process has become and yet, as recognised by the DoE in its guidance, such early consultation can save the developer valuable time and money as it can often reduce the need for costly redesign and amendment after submission[5].

As a result, consultation is in reality principally about debate between the different interests in the environment and how those interests are taken into consideration by the decision makers. Essentially this is the means by which interests are identified by the planning process and, according to the weight, the materiality, of those interests, the planning balance is struck. Within the context of EIA, of course, consultation is also the main means through which the 'competent authority' collects 'environmental information' which is not contained within the ES.

The competition of interests is not simply between the developer and the consultees. It can also be a conflict between consultees, with the developer stuck in the middle hardly able to satisfy all parties and the 'competent authority' left to establish a planning balance where no such balance can be struck. This conflict, for conflict is very often what it is, takes place within a complex web of interconnected agencies, public bodies and interest groups which come together within the formal arena of the planning process to protect or promote their particular interest in the environment or, sometimes, just to cover their backs. This chapter examines these fascinating and complicated relationships through two case studies. The first deals with a rather unique, if telling, case in Oxfordshire while the second raises issues which go far beyond the process of consultation and EIA. Through the case studies presented here we can identify some of the weaknesses of the consultation and public participation process. Yet, at the same time, we can recognise how difficult it is, given the organisational structure of statutory consultees and local government and the complex conflicting interests that organisations, groups and individuals have in the environment, to satisfy everyone.

Project Witch

Background

The Atomic Energy Authority's (AEA) Research Establishment, Harwell, is located to the west of the A34 about 16 kilometres south of Oxford. It is in fact closer to the village of Chilton than to Harwell from which it gets its name and which lies 3 to 4 kilometres to the north. The site is part of an extensive old RAF base which was used during the Second World War as a bomber and glider base. Indeed some of the first men to land in France on D-Day took off from the base, a fact commemorated on a memorial stone at the end of what was once the main runway. The Harwell Research Establishment is within the Vale of White Horse District of Oxfordshire.

On the southern edge of the old airfield the RAF built a bomb store, approximately 3.6 ha of land housing small concrete buildings which were blast protected by earth banks both around the buildings and around the perimeter of the site. In addition to the munitions stored there, between 1938 and 1946 the site was also used for the storage and disposal of the chemical cleaning materials used to degrease weapons and machinery[6].

After the war the site became the base for Britain's research into the peaceful use of nuclear energy and it was at Harwell that much of the technology for the UK's nuclear power programme was developed. The AEA also used the old bomb store and continued the practice of disposing of cleaning agents and other chemicals on the site, and they also stored low level radioactive waste there until it was made ready for final disposal at sea. The chemicals disposed of consisted mainly of chloroform, carbon tetrachloride, trichloroethylene and tetrachloroethylene together with smaller amounts of benzene, toluene and xylene[7]. During the 1970s the AEA also disposed of solvents in pits at a licensed waste disposal site on the western edge of the Harwell complex, approximately 1.25 kilometres northeast of the southern storage site; indeed from 1973 they disposed of chemicals in these pits as a commercial service to schools, colleges and hospitals[8]. In the southern storage site, the old bomb store, approximately 4 tons of solvents were disposed of in all, while the western storage site received up to 20 tons. In both cases the method of disposal was simple. The chemicals were poured into holes in the ground.

The western storage site is within the Research Establishment's security perimeter wire, while the southern storage site is separated from the main part of the laboratory and is immediately adjacent, on its eastern boundary, to Chilton Primary School. A few hundred metres northeast of the site is a short row of houses known as Severn Road, which are all that remain of a residential area which included 75 prefabricated houses built to accommodate AEA staff in the 1950s. That area of land, a little over 14 ha in all, was allocated for redevelopment by the Vale of White Horse District Council in its Draft Rural Areas Local Plan in 1988 and will eventually accommodate some 275 new dwellings[9]. A bridle road runs close to the southern boundary of the southern storage site and this provides access to Upper Farm which is about 200 metres to the west of the site. The land beyond the bridle road has planning consent for a golf course. Beyond the primary school to the east is a converted pub, two dwellings and Chilton Garden Centre which is immediately adjacent to the A34.

The problem

In the late 1980s, above background levels of chlorinated hydrocarbons were detected in boreholes used by Thames Water to supply drinking water at Blewbury and Upton, some four miles east of the AEA site[10]. In early 1990 the NRA commenced a programme of research to discover the source of this pollution and began taking borehole samples from a wide area around the villages of Blewbury, Upton, Chilton and Harwell. From this research they concluded that the source of this pollution could be the AEA's waste storage sites[11].

Confidential discussion then took place between the NRA and the AEA after which the AEA agreed to carry out their own research and if necessary implement action to deal with the pollution. That research included extensive borehole testing and took 18 months to complete at a cost of half a million pounds[12].

The NRA, charged with the protection of the water environment, had the power to prosecute those responsible for causing pollution. It would perhaps have been very difficult for them to prove, beyond reasonable doubt, that the AEA were responsible for the pollution of drinking water sources so distant from the waste disposal sites. The AEA's press officer Mr Nick Hance was reported as saying that Harwell did not accept liability for the contamination to the public water supply at Blewbury, although he conceded that it was a possibility that could not be completely discounted[13].

The Vale of White Horse District Council's Chief Environmental Health Officer was extremely concerned by the actions of both the AEA and the NRA. In September 1992 he reported to his members:

I find it surprising that an organisation with the international standing of AEA continued in the 1970s to dispose of chemicals by this method and particularly when much of the waste was being imported from other commercial users. I am also surprised that the NRA have not invoked their legal powers knowing that high levels of pollution of the aquifer have taken place[14].

The AEA were in the process of structural change at this time, commencing the difficult transition from public government agency to a commercially oriented research organisation. This possibly made them highly sensitive to the public's perception of their activities and, despite the absence of any public threat from the NRA, the AEA began borehole investigations. These eventually confirmed the suspicions of the NRA and the local authority and indicated that solvents were entering the aquifer from both the western and the southern storage sites. These investigations also suggested that material from the western storage site had not as yet spread beyond the boundary of the AEA's site whereas the solvents from the southern storage site had spread much further[15].

The southern storage site had been used intermittently for nearly 40 years for the disposal of chlorinated solvents which had been poured into earth pits that had eventually been filled in with soil. Beneath those pits was fractured chalk and with rain infiltration the chemicals had been washed through the chalk to the aquifer below, eventually forming a plume of contamination flowing generally southeast off the site towards the village of Chilton and Blewbury beyond[16].

The proposal

The AEA embarked on a search to find a solution to this problem. After consultations with the NRA, other UK environmental consultancies and overseas agencies – particularly in the USA where similar problems had been encountered – the AEA concluded that there was now nothing they could realistically do to clean up the aquifer and that it would remain polluted for possibly hundreds of years until all the solvents that had reached it were washed out. Yet there was a process available which they could use to prevent any additional solvents reaching the water table.

Basically the AEA's preferred system would pump water from the aquifer immediately downstream of the source of pollution, pass that water through some form of filter system and then re-inject the water upstream of the source. In this way a closed loop is created so that no new water enters the aquifer upstream of the extraction point. This also creates a local zone of hydraulic depression which attracts the pollutants and prevents them moving off site. The plant would operate until all the pollutants were removed from the source and when the monitoring of the extracted water no longer indicated any evidence of the pollutants being present.

The AEA proposed to use this system on both the storage sites but with variations between the two. On the southern storage site the water was to be pumped up to the top of a 9 metre high air stripping tower from where it would cascade down through a system of baffles, allowing the solvents to evaporate to air; the water would then be pumped back to the aquifer. Because of higher concentrations of solvents, and the presence of pesticides and other liquid wastes, at the western storage site AEA considered it necessary to install two carbon filters after the stripping tower to remove any remaining contaminants. In both cases the water would be returned to the aquifer at 'better than drinking water standard'[17]. The process is basically a contaminated water containment exercise; it was not an attempt to clean up the aquifer[18]. In all, with ancillary pipework, pumps and operating plant the proposals would require permanent foundations covering 100 square metres for the southern storage site and 120 square metres for the western site[19].

These were significant, if not massive, pieces of equipment. Without doubt they constituted developments which would require planning permission and a Waste Management Licence. Both sets of authorisations would eventually be dealt with by the County Council as Waste Regulation Authority and, because the development dealt with waste material, 'county matters' planning applications. These regulatory requirements brought the issue to the County Council for the first time as until then only the District Council had been involved. The Vale of White Horse's Planning Department had been aware of the issue for two reasons: firstly because an application for one of the containment plants had been received by them before a change in the planning legislation had made them 'county matters' and secondly, and more significantly, because the planners were in negotiation with the AEA's planning agents over the allocated housing site adjacent to the southern storage site.

These negotiations slowly became entwined with the issues surrounding the contamination of the aquifer when it was also discovered that the southern storage site had been used to store radioactive material and for the disposal of beryllium, a potentially carcinogenic material used for cladding in the nuclear industry. The level and number of contaminants at the southern storage site came as somewhat of a surprise to the Vale's planners. They had, after all, allocated the adjacent land for a significant housing development, the largest single housing allocation in the district. After long and detailed negotiations with the AEA, during which the beryllium had never been mentioned, the Vale were suddenly confronted with the prospect of being responsible for the granting of planning permission for a major residential development next to a site with unknown quantities of beryllium, chemical wastes and even the possibility of residual radioactive material.

The Vale's planners were not unreasonably concerned to ensure that, at the very least, the installation of the groundwater containment plant at the southern storage site would not disturb this beryllium and would not adversely affect the proposed new housing development. The Vale's Environmental Health Department shared these concerns but were also responsible for the safety of the existing residents at Severn Road, other nearby residents, the pupils and staff at Chilton Primary School and, of course, those people drawing drinking water directly from the contaminated aquifer.

The southern storage site is effectively screened by the large earth embankments that surround it. Over the years these have become colonised by trees, shrubs and hedgerow and apart from the perimeter security fence with its warning notices there is no hint to passers-by, or the unaware local resident, that the site has been used for waste disposal. Inside the site the RAF's brick and concrete bomb stores have been demolished and all that is left is the road network which connected them and which now runs between the large man-made, now overgrown, earth embankments that are the disposal pits. The proposed pollution containment plant was to be located in the centre of the site and only the very top of the 9 metre high stripping tower would be visible beyond the site perimeter.

The scale and complexity of the problem could not be hidden so easily and all the parties involved, the Vale, the County Council, the NRA and the AEA, recognised that the full implications of the proposal would have to be investigated. The AEA withdrew the planning applications for the groundwater containment plant so that they could provide more information to take account of the additional issues now being raised. The two new applications, one for each of the waste sites, would now be dealt with by the County Council and the Vale of White Horse would be restricted to the role of consultee.

The need for EIA

The planning applications were for rather unique plant to deal with a rather unique problem. The processes involved were not 'prescribed' for which separate authorisation would be required from either HMIP or the local authority under the terms of the Environmental Protection Act 1990. The plant, equipment or processes were not treating, disposing or creating controlled wastes and could not easily be seen to fall within the scope of the Town and Country Planning (Assessment of Environmental Effects) Regulations 1988. Yet the County Council took the view that a full EIA would be required and the AEA did not challenge this view and agreed to carry out an EIA; they submitted an ES with each of the two planning applications.

Paragraph 20 of Appendix B of Circular 15/88 states that should a developer 'volunteer' an environmental assessment and state that the ES constitutes an ES for the purposes of the Regulations, the application should be treated as an application to which the Regulations apply. As the AEA's ESs state at the very beginning that they are written in accordance with Schedule 3 of the Regulations the County Council could treat the projects as ones to which the Regulations apply[20]. This meant that these were now applications governed by the 1988 Regulations and the requirements of those Regulations would need to be met in full including the consultation process. This is significant in terms of both this case study and the role of EIA generally. Without the submission of the ESs in this case the level of information on which the consultees were to make their comments would have been scant. Even after providing the level of detail necessary for an acceptable ES the AEA were subject to strong criticism that even the information that had been provided was insufficient. Yet more significant still is that under the terms of the Regulations no formal EIA was required. Even though the process involved the release of relatively large amounts of solvents to the atmosphere adjacent to a primary school and had the potential to disturb and possibly release even more harmful pollutants, the terms of the UK Regulations did not consider there to be the potential for 'significant environmental effects'.

The planning process

The two planning applications were made to Oxfordshire County Council and, as a statutory consultee on planning and environmental health matters, the Vale of White Horse District Council which was given 28 days to respond to the applications and accompanying ESs. The latter had, of course, in effect already had much longer for they had known about the problem and the proposed solution for some time, longer indeed than the County Council. In addition to the District Council the other consultees were:

● the National Rivers Authority;
● Thames Water;
● the Parish Councils of Chilton, East Hendred and West Hendred;
● the County Engineer (Highways);
● the County Engineer (Waste Disposal);
● the Health and Safety Executive;
● the Nuclear Installations Inspectorate;
● Her Majesty's Inspectorate of Pollution;
● the Countryside Commission;
● English Nature.

The ESs covered the possibility of the project disturbing and spreading other waste material disposed of at the two sites. The disposal areas on the western site were well documented and trial trenches had been dug on the southern site, where there were few if any records, to ensure that the proposed site of the plant was not near waste disposal sites. The ES for the southern storage site deals with the possibility of the operation of the plant leading to other wastes becoming 'mobile' in just over a page. It was argued that the other wastes, like the beryllium, had not been mobile over the preceding 20 to 40 years and that the solubility of beryllium is very low – 'Thus no significant migration would be expected'[21]. The ES covered the possibility of disturbance to residual radionuclides with similar brevity and stated that radionuclides in the water and soil were at background or near background levels[22]. Furthermore the existence of these other wastes and the possibility of their disturbance were not the only issues to be considered.

The Vale's Environmental Health Department were concerned at the outset that the release of solvents to the atmosphere through the stripping towers was an unproved technique and that some of the compounds to be released were to be banned from release, under the terms of the Montreal Protocol, during the lifetime of the plant[23]. The environmental health officers also took the view that it was against the principle of the integrated pollution control system introduced under the Environmental Protection Act 1990 to remove a pollutant from one environmental medium and release it to another. Despite the fact that the groundwater containment plants and the process were not prescribed by the Act the officers felt that as a matter of environmental principles this position should be upheld. Also, as a matter of principle, the Vale's environmental health officers were concerned that some of the solvents to be released were known ozone depleters and contribute to global warming[24].

The AEA is an internationally recognised and respected research organisation which leads the field in very many areas other than nuclear research. The District Council's officers did not have the same level of expertise and could not compete in this field with the same authority and took the view that they needed the help and support of an equally respected consultancy: particularly essential should the whole matter finish with an appeal before a DoE Inspector. When it came to it few consultants were willing to stand before an Inspector and say that they disagreed with the AEA. In the end the Council found only one: the Department of Trade and Industry's own Warren Springs Laboratory based then at Stevenage.

The use of consultants was certain to result in further delay and hence an inability to meet the County Council's 28 day deadline. To safeguard its position the Vale's Planning Department lodged what it thought to be a 'holding objection' with the County Council[25]. However, the planning application for the southern storage site's plant was considered by the County Council's Minerals Working Party on 7 September 1992. The Working Party was recommended to approve the application by the Director of Planning and Property Services. His report acknowledged most of the Vale's concerns but he concluded that:

> On balance, I consider that planning permission should be granted. The proposed development deals with a pollution problem that must be addressed, and conditions can be imposed to ensure that its operation does not have any adverse environmental side effects[26].

The Working Party did not, however, accept this advice and deferred determination of the application to provide an opportunity for the Vale of White Horse to substantiate its objection and to allow the applications for both sets of plant to be considered together. The western storage site application had been submitted some time after the southern site application and had yet to complete its consultation process. It is interesting to note that the County Council's Director of Planning was willing to recommend that planning permission should be granted on the basis of the information provided by the ES, the statutory consultees and other interested parties. Unlike the Vale he did not consider it necessary to employ external consultants to assess or review the ES. There were, at that stage, no objections to the scheme from the NRA, Thames Water, the Health and Safety Executive or HMIP[27]. Later the County received the following comment from the NRA in respect of the applications:

> Attention is drawn to the importance of the application with regard to NRA's responsibility to maintain and improve the groundwater quality. The proposal results from NRA requirements, and is the first step to prevent further deterioration of the groundwater prior to a more expensive clean up programme. The problem was first identified in early 1990 and series of delays have ensued. The further the pollution spreads, the lower the chance of significant improvements using clean up techniques. Groundwater of unacceptable quality identified at a number of locations in the area and public water supply at Blewbury affected[28].

This is not so much a comment on an application as a position statement and an attempt to apportion blame for the delay in implementing the Project Witch proposals. There is clear pressure here from the NRA for the County to pass the application without further delay.

Planning considerations

The Vale's planning and environmental health officers also recognised the importance of Project Witch and yet were willing to stand up against the AEA, the NRA and the County Council. The reason for this is both the issue of principles discussed above and the contents of the ESs, the conclusions of which were:

> The overall conclusion is that the environmental impact of the plant is on balance a positive one. The plant will prevent the worsening of a serious pollution situation, whilst the impact on the environment of the plant itself is small. The plant has been designed in accordance with the 'Best Available Techniques Not Entailing Excessive Costs' (BATNEEC) criteria and is the most technically and economically appropriate solution to the problem[29].

There are a number of interesting issues arising from this statement. Firstly the ES states that the plant is the most technically and economically appropriate *solution to the problem*. As stated earlier, and recognised by the AEA, the plant would not solve the pollution problem, it would simply prevent it getting any worse. Furthermore, in employing the air stripping method, which would release the solvents from the water into the air, they were creating a second form of pollution rather than stopping one.

The second major issue is the use of BATNEEC as the basis for an assessment of the plant. BATNEEC is the basis for an authorisation of a prescribed process under the Environmental Protection Act 1990. BATNEEC is a control test for specific environmental legislation and has no planning function whatsoever. It should of course be remembered that the case under discussion here took place before the Gateshead case and the publication of PPG23 with its advice on the relationship between planning and pollution control. Yet, even allowing for the lack of clear planning guidance available at the time, the reliance on BATNEEC as a measure of planning merits was misguided.

The test for planning is in many ways far more stringent than is required for either an authorisation or a prosecution under the Environmental Protection Act. The test for planning is whether or not the development under consideration will cause a loss of public or private amenity. Loss of amenity is far more difficult to assess than is compliance with emission levels or preventing a statutory nuisance, yet, as a threshold, a loss of amenity can occur long before a failure to comply with the Environmental Protection Act can be proved. Not only is the use of BATNEEC as a justification inappropriate for an ES, which is after all a planning tool, it is misleading as it suggests that satisfying BATNEEC is the only hurdle a development of this nature needs to cross. The use of a technical term such as BATNEEC can confuse and seriously mislead the public and other consultative bodies and does not help the EIA participation process.

There is another environmental test which could have been applied in this case. The local environmental pressure group Blewbury Environmental Research Group argued, in their submissions to the County Council, that the standard to be applied should have been best practicable environmental option (BPEO). By inference the Vale's view that it was wrong to transfer pollutants from one environmental medium to another, and their stated belief that cost was not an appropriate test in this case as the 'concept of the polluter pays is appropriate', is a reliance on BPEO as the right approach for this proposal[30].

The distinction between the two standards is fine and yet significant. In their Twelfth Report the influential Royal Commission on Environmental Pollution defined BPEO as:

> the outcome of a systematic consultative and decision making procedure which emphasises the protection of the environment across land, air and water. The BPEO procedure establishes, for a given set of objectives, the option that provides the most benefit or least damage to the environment as a whole, at acceptable cost, in the long as well as the short term[31].

BPEO like BATNEEC is a test, an assessment, and yet unlike BATNEEC the emphasis of BPEO is on the protection of all environmental media. Section 7(7) of the Environmental Protection Act 1990 introduces BPEO into the BATNEEC test where a prescribed process releases pollution into more than one medium. However, BPEO can clearly have a role of its own in requiring a consideration of the environment as a single and interconnected element[32]. Cost remains a consideration under BPEO but unlike BATNEEC it is not central to the assessment and the emphasis on 'least damage to the environment ... in the long as well as the short term' would have, in this case, dealt with the Vale's concern that the solvents being emitted would be banned during the lifetime of the decontamination process.

The AEA's ESs for Project Witch did examine alternative methods of dealing with the problem and narrowed the choice down to air stripping and carbon absorption. The ES for the southern storage site, for example, states that both methods could produce the same results but found that 'Air stripping has significant cost advantages over carbon absorption, particularly in respect of operating costs'[33]. Against this cost advantage was the disadvantage of releasing pollutants to the atmosphere through air stripping. The AEA considered that the level of emissions at the southern storage site would be so low (20,000 times below the maximum levels for occupational exposure to the chemicals involved) that the fitting of carbon filters would not be warranted[34]. This is not a BPEO assessment as it places the cost before the principle that the decision-making process should emphasise: 'the protection of the environment across land, air and water'.

Representations

The Vale of White Horse's officers sent the ESs for both sites to Warren Springs for review and asked that they specifically address the principle of the release of the solvents to air. Their concern was that although the AEA had calculated what the emissions would be, they had no real way of knowing if those levels would be higher and if so whether they would cause odour or health problems for the children at the school or the people in the nearby houses. The environmental health officers also doubted the accuracy of the emissions plume analysis models used in the ES to assess odour and health impacts. While Warren Springs agreed with the AEA that the emission levels were likely to be low they also agreed with the District Council's Chief Environmental Health Officer that although the process was not 'prescribed' the principles of integrated pollution control should be adopted[35]. This was a unique project which was not covered by normal pollution control requirements and because of this there were no published guidance notes on what would be acceptable levels of discharge. The Council's attempts to seek such guidance were unsuccessful as even HMIP were unable, or unwilling, to help. Because of this it is not surprising that the Vale's officers decided that the best course of action would be to apply the 'precautionary principle', a national environmental policy principle, to this case.

Project Witch came before the Vale's Planning and Development Committee on 28 September 1992 when they received a full report from both the Director of Development and Leisure and the Chief Environmental Health Officer. Appendix 2 of the report was a letter from the County's Assistant Chief Planning Officer which asked the Vale to provide its comments by October 16th so that they could be incorporated into a report to the County's Environmental Committee which would meet to discuss the two applications on November 4th[36]. The Vale's meeting of September 28th would be the last opportunity for the Planning Committee to discuss the project before that date and yet by that time they had not received the full response from Warren Springs. The County's Planning Officer asked that the Vale's comments on the applications cover the following points:

(i) if you are challenging information in the applicant's environmental statement and/or proposing different standards could you please give the basis of the challenge and the standards (including an indication of by whom they are accepted) on which you are relying to propose alternatives;

(ii) whether your Council, through the Environmental Health Officer, would wish to be responsible for monitoring air emissions;

(iii) an undertaking that if this Council refuses planning permission for technical reasons put forward by your Environmental Health Officer and/or consultants your Council would be prepared to defend those reasons at any public inquiry[37].

The report before the Vale's planners made clear that the officers were far from being able to provide the detailed information required by the County. They had met with representatives of AEA on September 8th and had asked for additional information. They required a detailed cost–benefit analysis for fitting filters to the stripping towers to prevent emissions to air; more detailed assessment of the hydrological effects of the plant on the immediate area; and an assessment of the cumulative effects of the two air emission plumes. By the time the planning meeting took place this information had yet to be received and analysed. With uncertainties remaining and without all the necessary information, guidance and advice, the Vale's officers favoured the precautionary principle viewpoint and argued:

The Southern Storage Site is adjacent to Chilton Primary School and close to existing houses and the allocated housing site where there is a proposal for 275 new houses. Given these circumstances, and the uncertainties relating to the operation of the plant described in the Chief Environmental Health Officer's report, it would seem prudent to have failsafe mechanisms built into the system to prevent emissions if the relevant standards are exceeded. Alternatively the plant should be a fully contained system as described in the Chief Environmental Health Officer's report. It has been the Environmental Health Officer's view throughout that the safest and most practical way of ensuring that no problems arise is to fit filters to remove the solvents before they reach the air. It has been argued that this would be possible at a later date if monitoring indicated that standards were being exceeded. However, at the meeting of September 8th a representative of Harwell stated that it would be 'engineeringly impractical' to put in filters at a later stage. Therefore it would appear reasonable to require filters to be fitted from the outset[38].

Their recommendation was that the County be informed that the Vale was of the view that planning permission should be granted subject to a requirement that filters should be fitted to both plants to prevent emissions to the atmosphere. They further recommended that should the County reject that view it should require emission limits at a pre-agreed standard and in the event of emissions exceeding that standard filters should be fitted at that stage. The Committee 'echoed' the officers' concerns and accepted their recommendation with the additional safeguard that the Director of Development and Leisure, in consultation with the Chairman of the Committee, be delegated authority to amend the Council's comments to the County after receipt and analysis of the 'further information' and the views of their consultants Warren Springs[39].

The response from Warren Springs supported much of what the environmental health officers had been arguing and it highlighted some of the deficiencies of the ES such as the lack of consideration of synergistic effects and the interaction of the plumes from each site. In the light of these concerns it was Warren Springs' opinion that:

atmospheric release of contaminants should either:

a) not be permitted; or

b) be subjected to rigid control such that a stated concentration is not exceeded[40].

On 9 October 1992 the District Council wrote to the County to inform them of their views on the proposals. They demanded firstly that the western storage site plant be a totally contained water treatment system with no emissions to air; and secondly that the air stripping tower on the southern storage site be fitted with a carbon filter to reduce emissions to air.

The County Council also received representations from the affected Parish Councils, two local residents, the local CPRE branch, Blewbury Environmental Research Group, an environmental campaigner from Banbury, the NRA, Thames Water, the Countryside Commission, English Nature, HMIP and the Health and Safety Executive. Of the national bodies charged with environmental protection only the NRA made any detailed comments and these, as reported above, were little more than an explanation of their position and a complaint about the delays in implementation. English Nature simply wanted to ensure that any screen planting was of indigenous species while the Countryside Commission and the Health and Safety Executive had no objections to either scheme. HMIP also had no objections and made no comments on the proposals; this lack of any detailed comment from HMIP is principally because the process was not 'prescribed' under the terms of the Environmental Protection Act and therefore not one for which HMIP are responsible. Indeed HMIP had written to the AEA in October 1991 making just this point but adding that if the process had been 'prescribed' they would not have permitted the transference of a prescribed substance from one environmental medium to another[41].

Given the unique nature of the project, the issues of principle raised and the concerns of the District Council, supported by Warren Springs, it is perhaps, at the very least, disappointing that the body with prime responsibility for the protection of the environment did not feel able to become more deeply involved with a consultation process which is specifically designed to ensure such bodies provide advice on areas of their expertise. Yet the Vale were not completely alone in raising concerns about the air stripping process: West and East Hendred Parish Councils felt that filters were a better option as did the Blewbury Environment Research Group. All these, and other, observations were reported to the Environment Committee of Oxfordshire County Council on 4 November 1992.

Determination

There was pressure on the County's planning officers to approve the application as it stood; the NRA were particularly concerned about the delay. The AEA had bought the plant even before they had lodged the planning applications and were eager to install it. To take up the District's requirement would mean further delay and further cost. Furthermore the AEA were claiming that they had set themselves 'the most stringent standards available'[42].

On this occasion the Director of Planning and Property Services took a slightly more cautious view than he had on September 7th:

> On balance, I consider that planning permission should be granted. The proposed development deals with a pollution problem that must be addressed. Conditions should be imposed to meet the recommendations of the District Council as Environmental Health Authority and so far as possible to ensure that the operations do not have any adverse environmental side effects[43].

Both applications were recommended for approval subject to 'planning conditions that the plants include suitable filtration systems of a type to be approved by DPPS to remove solvents from the water and any water vapour'[44]. Some members of the Committee were not satisfied by this and wanted further clarification on emission limits following the comments of the District Council. In order to satisfy their concerns it was necessary for the County to itself instruct outside consultants to check the proposed emission levels.

Eventually planning permission was granted by the County on 7 January 1993, subject to conditions which required that details of a 'system to filtrate all solvents from the groundwater have been submitted to and agreed by the local planning authority in writing and the agreed system has been fitted to the plant'[45]. In agreeing the 'system' the plant for the western storage site became in effect fully enclosed with no air stripping and the southern storage site had emission limits imposed which if exceeded would trigger a requirement for filters to be fitted to the air stream.

Project Witch was fully operational a few months after the planning permissions were issued and the system is being constantly monitored.

Project Witch and EIA: some thoughts

There is always a danger of reading too much into case studies. They are of course all unique and yet there are important issues raised by individual cases which can have important implications throughout planning and the consultation process. Project Witch was interesting in that it was a project for which an EIA was not required by the Regulations and in the end the debate rested more upon environmental principles than on the details supplied by the ES. Yet there was from the beginning the risk that the project would create 'significant environmental effects'.

Even if the ES was not the central determining factor in this case there are still some important conclusions which can be drawn. Firstly, of all the statutory consultees involved, only the Vale of White Horse District Council fully pushed for the adoption of the precautionary principle and the principle of the polluter pays. These are both basic environmental principles of the Government's policy, *This Common Inheritance*, and the EU's Fifth Action Programme on the Environment[46], and yet the major environmental agencies responsible for their implementation, the NRA and HMIP, failed to demand their use in this case.

Both HMIP and the NRA appeared only to be concerned with their strict statutory requirements. As Project Witch was not a prescribed process HMIP were apparently not concerned that pollutants, some of them ozone depleters and carcinogenic, were proposed for release directly into the atmosphere next to a primary school. The NRA, on the other hand, seemed only concerned with the delay being caused by the debate over this release. Their responsibility to protect the water environment seemed to be the limit of their concern. Had HMIP responded fully and constructively to the consultation process they may have been able to supply the Vale's officers with the reassurance or emission standards they needed to be able to comment quickly. That reassurance could have prevented the delay the NRA were hoping to avoid.

The other important feature of consultation raised here is the relationship between the District Council and County Council. Unlike the other major statutory consultees the Vale's officers had to consult democratically elected members before it could make its comments to the County. The debate and the information it was considering were therefore open to public inspection and to an extent controlled by the committee cycle. The County Council set the timescale for comment and yet it was the Vale's officers who were leading the debate. Significantly, as planning authority in this case, the County could have refused to accept the Vale's recommendations and granted planning permission for the plant as originally proposed by the

AEA. It was only the County's elected members who prevented this and at that time some of those members were also members of the Planning Committee of the Vale of White Horse District Council.

This last point is central to one of the themes of this book which is that the 'environmental information' must be taken into consideration by the 'competent authority', and yet it can be set against other considerations which may override it. In the next case this issue is returned to. Yet like Project Witch the second case considered in this chapter raises other important issues on consultation within EIA and its relationship to the planning process.

Llanystumdwy abattoir

Background

Dwyfor District Council granted itself outline planning permission for a 'food business park', including the provision of an abattoir, in November 1993. The site for the park is about 1.5 kilometres west of Llanystumdwy close to the A497 between Criccieth, 5 kilometres to the east, and Pwllheli to the west. This green field site is not within the Snowdonia National Park or within an AONB; it is, however, within 100 metres of the river Dwyfach which then joins the river Dwyfor, a class 1a designated river and indeed one of Britain's most important sea trout rivers[47].

The Council had purchased the site after a search of the District for a suitable location for a food park which would promote 'sustainable industrial development', be close to the trunk road network and be 'compatible with local agricultural industry and other rural enterprises'[48]. Central to the whole concept of the food park was the abattoir which would provide a slaughtering facility for locally reared cattle, sheep and pigs and provide local farmers with an alternative to transporting livestock to abattoirs further afield. The whole food park, which would include a meat processing plant, would employ about 200 people with 75 (37.5%) of these working in the abattoir itself[49].

The need for EIA

An abattoir is a class 7(f) Schedule 2 project requiring an EIA where there are likely to be 'significant environmental effects'[50]. Yet no EIA was carried out at the outline planning stage for the food park, the Council having decided that no EIA was necessary at that stage. This decision was made notwithstanding that:

- the food park application, as a whole, was contrary to the policies of the development plan, and had to be advertised as such with notification sent to the Secretary of State for Wales;

- the abattoir was not only a significant part of the proposal but was central to the whole concept of the food park;
- there was no existing sewage treatment system on the site, and the development clearly had the potential to give rise to significant environmental effects on the nearby sensitive river system and have significant landscape effects in this part of scenic North Wales.

Circular 15/88 (Welsh Office Circular 23/88) states at paragraph 35: 'Environmental assessment techniques will be of greatest benefit to developers and decision-making authorities if they are applied early in the planning stages of a project'[51]. In this case the developer and the decision-making authority were one and the same, and as the requirement for EIA of Schedule 2 projects is discretionary, the Council were not in breach of the law or the regulations in not carrying out an EIA. However, when the Planning Committee considered the outline application for the 'food business park with an abattoir' it accepted that there was need for an EIA for the abattoir[52]. Presumably they accepted that the project could give rise to significant environmental effects. Yet they did not heed the advice of the Government which makes clear that where an EIA is required it should take place at an early stage and involve early consultation. The DoE and Welsh Office publication *Environmental Assessment: A Guide to the Procedures* (1989) is very clear on when an EIA should take place. Paragraph 21 states:

> Ideally, EA should start at the stage of site selection and (where relevant) process selection, so that the environmental merits of practicable alternatives can be properly considered.

It goes on to state at paragraph 33:

> Where an application is in outline, the planning authority will still need to have sufficient information on a project's likely effects to enable them to judge whether the development should take place or not[53].

In granting themselves outline planning permission before they had carried out an EIA of the project, the Council had established all the locational features of the project and alternative sites could not then be properly or comprehensively assessed. While the Council recognised the need to carry out an EIA, they failed to also recognise that the correct time to carry out that assessment was at the outline stage. This has implications for the consultation process in that the slightly more rigorous notification and publicity arrangements for EIA projects did not take place until after the principle of the development had been established through the granting of an outline planning permission.

This is not to suggest that the Council failed to consult adequately in respect of an outline planning application. In posting site notices and by publicity through newspaper notices they followed the requirements of the 1988 General Development Order. They also notified, by letter, some local residents of the proposal, although there was some kind of administrative error which prevented all residents considered most affected from receiving a letter, an error which the Local Government Ombudsman considered later to be a 'technical' maladministration which did not result in any real injustice[54].

The response to the proposal from the statutory consultees was generally favourable and there were only two letters of objection from residents at this stage. The planning committee referred the application to 'full council' which, as there had been no strong objections to the park, decided to refer it back to the planning committee after it had been considered by the Secretary of State for Wales as a departure from the development plan. The Secretary of State did not call in the application and the application was approved on 18 November 1993[55].

More applications

On the same day that Dwyfor District Council granted itself outline planning permission for the food business park it made reserved matters application for road and other on-site infrastructure works. This application was subject to normal planning consultation procedures and was granted permission on 16 December 1993; contractors began work on site on 10 January 1994[56]. This was some six months before the detailed application for the abattoir itself was lodged with its accompanying ES. Once again, many of the decisions which would result in environmental impacts had been made before the EIA had been carried out. This point is made only too clear in a *Daily Post* report of 16 February 1994 where the Council's Chief Executive is quoted as saying:

> The public must by now accept the fact that planning permission has been granted for this site and that we did conduct our consultations responsibly, fairly and widely.

> The Welsh Office were given an opportunity to intervene, but declined.

> Planning permission has been given, the land has been bought, agreements have been signed for certain site works and, as far as the council is concerned, this development is going ahead[57].

This then was a demand by the Council that the public accept a development for which no EIA had yet taken place and for which the Council had already accepted that an EIA was necessary. The consultation process had obviously not provided the reassurances and participatory legitimacy to the scheme which it is designed to do. In fact many people were claiming that it was not until the work began on site clearance and road construction in January and February 1994 that they either knew of the project or realised the full implications of the recently granted planning permission[58]. Public meetings were organised to debate the project and a protest group, the Llanystumdwy Abattoir Action Group, was formed; it claimed in an April 1994 newsletter that 372 local residents (63% of the Llanystumdwy electorate) now objected to the proposal[59].

The abattoir and the ES

The abattoir and effluent treatment works applications were submitted on 3 June 1994 together with an ES which had been produced by consultants instructed by the Council. Consultations were carried out in accordance with the Regulations including site notices, advertisements in local newspapers and individual letters to local residents.

The proposed abattoir would have a footprint area of 1800 square metres and the total site area including hardstanding, effluent treatment and other plant would be 18,000 square metres. The building would have an eaves height of 6 metres and a ridge height of 10 metres. The building would be visible from the A497 and adjoining fields[60]. The ES covered the construction and operation of the abattoir together with a new effluent treatment plant and its main conclusions are summarised as follows:

> The most significant effect of the abattoir on the environment would arise from the visual impact of the building in the landscape. Secondly, the operation of the plant and the by-products and waste created would have effects on air and water quality and would create some environmental noise. The third major effect of the abattoir would be on the socio-economic profile of Dwyfor by providing about 75 full-time job opportunities by April 1997, together with another 40 to 50 supporting jobs in the community[61].

These effects were to be mitigated, where necessary, through design and landscaping measures and:

> Rigorous attention would need to be given at all times by the operators of the plant to all processes, and particularly those concerned with noise,. emissions to the atmosphere and effluent treatment, so that the abattoir does not give rise to unacceptable pollution of air, land or water courses within or adjacent to the food park site[62].

The consideration of the abattoir application took place after the ruling in the Gateshead case[63] which dealt with the relationship between planning and pollution control. Although PPG23: *Planning and Pollution Control* or equivalent advice was not published by the Welsh Office, the Gateshead case was relevant and it made clear that planning should not attempt to control those matters that are the subject of controls by other agencies. In effect where a discharge of a pollutant is the subject of control by one of the pollution control agencies it is not a material planning consideration. This particular policy has important implications for both control mechanisms and yet, significant as it may be to the operation of both systems, it is unlikely to be fully understood or appreciated by the public at large. The fact that a planning authority does not have control over some aspects of a development may not affect the public's perception of its role in the decision-making process. Where the development is being proposed by the same council that is determining the application the distinction between all these control systems may seem even more irrelevant to those being consulted.

Consultations and consultees

The processed effluent would be discharged from the proposed abattoir to the river Dwyfach. These discharges are controlled and regulated by the NRA and require prior authorisation. The ES states at paragraph 4.56:

> Pollutants reaching the river Dwyfach would have an extremely serious effect whether they are organic materials which would cause oxygen deficiency in the water, or chemicals which would result in the poisoning of animals and plants.... The result would be very damaging biologically in a river of this quality[64].

The ES goes on to report:

> The abattoir is not likely to have deleterious ecological effects providing that the effluent treatment is carried out strictly as specified by the NRA[65].

Local anglers were concerned about the risk to the rivers and lodged objections with the NRA in the hope of forcing an inquiry into the discharge authorisation[66]. By October 1994, the NRA were prepared to give consent for the discharge application, which caused grave concern to the now growing army of objectors to the scheme. In October a public meeting was called to discuss the project and a leaflet circulated at the meeting said of the proposed discharge consent:

> Possibly as many as 300 objectors to the discharge proposals are expecting copies of full details of the consent in the week beginning 3rd October. The main shortcomings in the way the NRA is dealing with the application are that it has no direct flow measurements for the Dwyfach, it is not proposing to set limits on a number of abattoir pollutants usually monitored (eg: fats/oils/grease) and there is apparently not going to be a ban on discharge when river flow goes below a certain level. Very low flow occurs in the summer months when abattoirs are at their busiest[67].

The NRA had now joined the Council as the focus of local opposition to the abattoir. The problem for the objectors in such cases is that the NRA's authorisation process is a technical assessment rather than the more political assessment carried out by planners and is far less susceptible to lobbying. The consultation process had in this case, as it does in many such cases, become a political campaign with the objectors targeting every avenue open to them to defeat the Council's scheme. The process had moved from consultation to confrontation and the NRA, rather than simply responding to a consultation exercise, were being increasingly seen as the only official body that could now stop the project.

The ES became the focus for this campaign, a tool used by both sides to strengthen their case. The developer, the Council, used its findings to help justify decisions that had already been made. The opponents of the project teased out the weaknesses in the ES to strengthen their case. They carried out a review of the ES and produced a detailed critique of every aspect of the document from the locational justification to the treatment of effluent. Some of their criticisms were telling. For example, on waste treatment they made much of the fact that the environmental consultants had not been given full details of matters such as carcass throughput and the amount of solid and liquid wastes produced. They complained that the ES was full of vague assumptions that did not relate to the experience of the operation of other abattoirs[68]. Some of the Action Group's more detailed criticisms were as follows:

> The job argument depends on the commercial viability of the abattoir. As no evidence has been given to support the latter, and there is plenty of evidence to the contrary, the jobs argument is mere speculation. The abattoir at Llanidloes has a far higher throughput than the one projected here yet it employs only 40 people. The figure of 75 for this abattoir looks suspiciously high!

> Why were baseline noise measurements not made at the five nearest residences and why were the measurements not carried out to the appropriate British Standards?

> 'Occasionally animals are also kept overnight ... in adjoining fields.' Which fields are referred to – there appears to be no provision for this on the site unless the food park is extended eastwards or the existing land to the west is not used for buildings. If the latter is the case, over what route and by what means will the animals be moved into the large pens[69]?

> The plans for the abattoir and the effluent treatment should be completed showing proper and far more thorough mitigation measures and resubmitted before they are considered by the planning committee. The public should then be given the statutory period to make representations on the revised plans and on the thoroughly reworked environmental statement, hopefully without having to wade through the gratuitous padding and pictures which have mainly cosmetic effect in the present one[70].

In all, the Action Group put more than 40 detailed questions about the content and findings of the ES to the Council. Unfortunately the Council made its formal planning decision before it provided the objectors with a response to these questions[71]. The Council also received more than 200 letters of objection which mirrored the Action Group's main concerns over location, visual amenity, river pollution, noise, need and over-capacity of abattoirs. Planning permission was granted by the full Council on 5 October 1994.

Llanystumdwy abattoir and EIA: some thoughts

The objectors were never reconciled to the need to locate the abattoir at Llanystumdwy. The ES set out a case for its location at the site and yet many of the locational requirements identified could have been true of very many sites. The ES states that the site was considered 'suitable for effluent treatment'[72]. This seems a strange statement in light of the need to first construct a treatment plant on the site with discharges to a class 1a river. The Action Group believed there were far more suitable alternative sites on existing industrial parks elsewhere in the District and never accepted that these had been thoroughly researched. The ES did deal with alternative sites but not in any great detail. The main criterion seemed to be effluent treatment and the Council based their choice on the NRA's advice that the Dwyfach and Dwyfor were suitable for discharge. The industrial estates favoured by the Action Group were dismissed on the grounds that the sewage systems in Pwllheli and Porthmadog were already beyond capacity and 'too urban in nature to meet the criteria for an abattoir'[73]. The need for a green field site is not justified in detail and it is difficult to understand why this abattoir could not be located in an industrial estate when others are.

The objectors also raised some convincing financial arguments against the proposals. With the food park being part funded by Welsh Office grants, perhaps local people's concerns would have been better served if the Secretary of State for Wales had used his powers to call in the application in the first place.

The difficulty for the producers of the ES was that the decision to locate the abattoir at Llanystumdwy had been taken before they had been appointed to carry out the EIA. There was at that stage no real point in a detailed examination of alternative sites as the Council had already discounted other sites. This had the effect of reducing the scope of both the EIA and the consultation exercise to on-site issues.

One of the major concerns of objectors in this case was that the Council were 'judge and jury in their own cause'[74]. They felt helpless in the face of this and this sense of helplessness was not exorcised by the statement of the Council's Chief Executive that the decision had already been made before the details of the abattoir and the ES had been fully considered. The Action Group formed to fight the proposals became frustrated and disillusioned with a system that allowed the planning process to operate in this way when, legally, the Council appeared to have done nothing wrong. With their questions on the ES unanswered and their faith in the planning process severely dented it is not surprising that the opponents of the abattoir changed the focus of their campaign to the sewage discharge authorisation process and the NRA. At the time of writing (January 1995) this authorisation remains unresolved with the Secretary of State for Wales still to decide whether or not he should call in the application. The Council have their planning permission and yet, without a discharge licence, they may even now find that their abattoir project falls.

Some conclusions

Consultation has always been seen as a crucial part in the iterative process of EIA. In these two cases the system has largely operated against the spirit of this process. In both cases detailed decisions had been made about the projects before the EIA and the consultation process had begun. Issues like project design (Project Witch) and site location (Llanystumdwy abattoir) had been determined long before consultees had a real opportunity to take part in the EIA process. The developers were then reluctant, or unable, to make the significant changes that the consultation process suggested were necessary and the ESs became less like documents for discussion than a focus for disagreement – ammunition or justification, whichever side of the debate you happen to be on.

The other important issue which flows from these two case studies is the role of the statutory consultees in the EIA process. By the time most readers look at this chapter both the NRA and HMIP will have been subsumed into the UK's new Environment Agency. Whether that agency will be more willing to look beyond its strict remit to play a more positive role in the EIA process is for future analysis and yet we can say here that it will largely depend upon the commitment of the agency and the resources made available to it. On the basis of the terms of reference of the agency, as set out in the draft Management Statement published with the 1995 Environment Bill, that commitment and those resources will be wanting[75].

Notes and references

1 Jorissen, J and R Coenen (1992) The EEC Directive on EIA and its implementation in the EC member states, in Colombo, A G (ed) *Environmental Impact Assessment*. Dordrecht: Kluwer Academic, p 7.

2 *Reg. v Secretary of State for Social Services, ex parte Association of Metropolitan Authorities*, [1986] 1WLR 1.

3 Fuller, K (1994) EIA Directive to be revised, *Environmental Assessment*, Vol. 2, No. 2.

4 Melton, J (1994) The role of statutory consultation in environmental assessment, MSc Dissertation on Environmental Impact Assessment and Management. Oxford Brookes University.

5 DoE (1989) *Environmental Assessment: A Guide to the Procedures*. London: HMSO.

6 AEA devoted to Harwell clean-up, *AEA Times*, July 1992.

7 Fellingham L (1994) The investigation and remediation of groundwater contamination at Harwell Laboratory, England. Paper presented to Superfund '93 Conference, Washington, DC, USA, December.

8 *AEA Times, op. cit.*

9 Vale of White Horse District Council (1993) *Local Plan: Draft for Consultation.* Abingdon: Vale of White Horse District Council.

10 Report of the Chief Environmental Health Officer, in Report of the Director of Development and Leisure to the Planning and Development Committee 28 September 1992: Groundwater Containment Plant, Harwell Laboratory, Southern and Western Storage Sites, CHI/12724/1-CM and EHE/7645/5-CM. Report No. 220/92, Appendix 3. Abingdon: Vale of White Horse District Council, 1992.

11 Fellingham, L, *op. cit.*

12 Harwell to clean up pollution, *Oxford Mail,* 21 May 1992.

13 *Ibid.*

14 Report No. 220/92, Appendix 3, *op. cit.*

15 *Ibid.*

16 AEA Engineering (1992) Environmental Impact Statement: Groundwater Remediation Plant, Southern Storage Site, Harwell Laboratory. Harwell: AEA Technology, p 9.

17 Groundwater Contamination Plants, Southern and Western Storage Areas, Harwell Laboratory, Application Numbers CHI/1274/1 and EHE/7645/5. Report by the Director of Planning and Property Services for the Environmental Committee, Oxfordshire County Council, Oxford, 4 November 1992.

18 *Ibid.*

19 *Ibid.*

20 DoE (1988) Circular 15/88: *Town and Country Planning (Assessment of Environmental Effects) Regulations 1988.* London: HMSO; AEA Engineering, *op. cit.* p 4.

21 AEA Engineering, *op. cit.* p 38.

22 *Ibid.* p 45.

23 Report No. 220/92, Appendix 3, *op. cit.*

24 *Ibid.*

25 Report of the Director of Development and Leisure to the Planning and Development Committee 7 September 1992: Groundwater Containment Plant, Harwell Laboratory, Southern and Western Storage Sites, CHI/12724/1-CM. Report No. 156/92. Abingdon: Vale of White Horse District Council, 1992.

26 Groundwater Contamination Plants, Southern and Western Storage Areas, Harwell Laboratory, Application Numbers CHI/1274/1 and EHE/7645/5. Report by the Director of Planning and Property Services for the Mineral Working Party, Oxfordshire County Council, Oxford, 7 September 1992.

27 *Ibid.*

28 Environmental Committee, Oxfordshire County Council, 4 November 1992, *op. cit.*

29 AEA Engineering, *op. cit.* p 8.

30 Report No. 220/92, Appendix 3, *op. cit.*

31 The Royal Commission on Environmental Pollution (1988) *Twelfth Report: Best Practicable Environmental Option,* Cm. 310. London: HMSO.

32 Ball, S and S Bell (1994) *Environmental Law.* London: Blackstone Press, p 257.

33 AEA Engineering, *op. cit.* p 20.

34 *Ibid.*

35 Minute A.119 of Meeting of Planning and Development Committee, Vale of White Horse District Council, 28 September 1992.

36 Report No. 220/92, Appendix 2, *op. cit.*

37 *Ibid.*

38 Report No. 220/92, *op. cit.*

39 Minute A.119, *op. cit.*

40 Letter to Assistant Chief Environmental Health Officer, Vale of White Horse District Council, from Warren Springs Laboratory, 25 September 1992.

41 Letter to AEA Environment and Energy from Her Majesty's Inspectorate of Pollution, 9 October 1991.

42 Environmental Committee, Oxfordshire County Council, 4 November 1992, *op. cit.*

43 *Ibid.*

44 *Ibid.*

45 Planning Application Decision Letters CHI/12724/1 and EHE/7645/5, Oxfordshire County Council, Oxford, 7 January 1993.

46 DoE (1990) *This Common Inheritance.* London: HMSO; Ball, S and S Bell, *op. cit.* p 64.

47 Cynefin Environmental Consultants Ltd (1994) Environmental Statement: Proposed Abattoir Parc Amaeth/Bwyd Dwyfor, Dwyfor Agri/Food Park, Bont Fechan, Llanystumdwy, Gwynedd. Menai Bridge: Cynefin Environmental, p 1.

48 *Ibid.* p 2.

49 *Ibid.* p 7.

50 Town and Country Planning (Assessment of Environmental Effects) Regulations 1988.

51 DoE and Welsh Office (1988) Circular 15/88 (Welsh Office Circular No. 23/88): *Town and Country Planning (Assessment of Environmental Effects) Regulations.* London: HMSO.

52 Cynefin Environmental, *op. cit.* p 4.

53 DoE (1989) *op. cit.*

54 Letter to Ms C. Williams from The Commission for Local Administration in Wales, 14 October 1993.

55 *Ibid.*

56 Llanystumdwy Abattoir Action Group (1994a) Proposed food industrial estate and abattoir near Bont Fechan, Llanystumdwy, Gwynedd: fourth edition of a report by objectors, 20 May 1994. Llanystumdwy: Llanystumdwy Abattoir Action Group.

57 Williams, E (1994) Development poses risk to river life, say anglers, *Daily Post,* 16 February.

58 Williams, E (1994) 'We weren't asked' rap over food park project, *Daily Post,* 9 February.

59 Llanystumdwy Abattoir Action Group (1994b), Dwyfor's industrial estate and abattoir for Llanystumdwy. Llanystumdwy: Llanystumdwy Abattoir Action Group, 4 April.

60 Cynefin Environmental, *op. cit.* p 35.

61 *Ibid.* p ii.

62 *Ibid.*

63 *Gateshead MBC v Secretary of State for the Environment and Northumbrian Water Group Plc,* [1994] 67 P&CR 179.

64 Cynefin Environmental, *op. cit.* p 34.

65 *Ibid.* p 65.

66 Williams, E (16 February 1994), *op. cit.*

67 Llanystumdwy Abattoir Action Group (1994c) Proposed Llanystumdwy abattoir/ meat factory and effluent plant: planning fact sheet. Llanystumdwy: Llanystumdwy Abattoir Action Group, 3 October.

68 Llanystumdwy Abattoir Action Group (1994d) Questions relating to Dwyfor's abattoir/meat plant for Llanystumdwy – the Environmental Statement. Llanystumdwy: Llanystumdwy Abattoir Action Group, July.

69 Llanystumdwy Abattoir Action Group (1994e) Dwyfor's proposed abattoir for Llanystumdwy: summary of an analysis of the Environmental Statement dated May 1994 from Cynefin Environmental Consultants. Llanystumdwy: Llanystumdwy Abattoir Action Group, 1 July.

70 Llanystumdwy Abattoir Action Group (1994d) *op. cit.*

71 Communication from member of Llanystumdwy Abattoir Action Group to the author.
72 Cynefin Environmental, *op. cit.* p 2.
73 *Ibid.* p 12.
74 Garney, M (1994) Fury over agripark decision, *Caernarfon Herald*, 11 February.
75 Environment Agency Bill published, *Environmental Law Monthly*, Vol. 3, No. 11, November 1994.

CHAPTER 6

EIA AND PUBLIC INQUIRIES

Joe Weston

Introduction

The principal aim of EIA is, as we have seen, to provide decision makers with comprehensive information about the likely impact of a development project on the environment. In the UK planning system those decision makers come in a variety of forms. At the top of the tree is the relevant Secretaries of State (Environment, Wales, Scotland and Northern Ireland[1]); below them are a host of Inspectors, sometimes called Reporters (Scotland); further down the list come Councillors, the elected members of district, county, unitary or metropolitan borough councils; and at the very bottom are chief or senior planning officers who deal with 'delegated decisions'. In terms of the number of decisions made, this pyramid is of course inverted, with by far the majority of planning decisions being made by planning officers granting permission for domestic house extensions and minor changes of use. As a rough guide we can say that the larger the project the higher up the pyramid of decision makers the decision is made. Yet this is not always true. The UK appeal system only operates when planning applications are refused; there is no third party appeal against a planning permission unless it is a legal challenge through the courts. Councillors are normally the highest up the decision-making pyramid that most planning applications reach. They only go higher, to an Inspector or Secretary of State, for two main reasons: firstly that the Councillors have refused planning permission and the developer has appealed against the decision and secondly if the relevant Secretary of State believes the application raises more than local issues and calls in the application for his/her determination[2].

The planning inspectors work for a semi-privatised agency, the Planning Inspectorate, and like planning officers have delegated powers from the relevant Secretary of State to make a decision on most appealed applications. In some cases the Secretary of State removes this delegated power and makes the decision himself/herself. The Inspector still hears all the evidence and writes a report which the Secretary of State then assesses and following that assessment makes the decision. In reality of course it is not often that the Secretary of State actually makes the decision even in these and call-in cases. More normally a very senior civil servant in the

Environment Department or Welsh or Scottish Office assesses the Inspector's report and makes a decision in the Secretary of State's name.

Planning inspectors, like Councillors, have a great deal of power and because they are fairly high up the decision-making pyramid their decisions have considerable influence. Appeal and call-in decisions are rather like the system of precedent that operates in the legal system and yet one Inspector's decision is not necessarily binding on another's or indeed on a local planning authority. In *North Wiltshire District Council v Secretary of State for the Environment*, Mann LJ considered the weight to be given to the decisions of other Inspectors dealing with similar cases:

> Consistency is self evidently important to both developers and development control authorities. But it is also important for the purpose of securing public confidence in the operation of the development control system. I do not suggest and it would be wrong to do so, that like cases *must* be decided alike. An Inspector must always exercise his own judgement. He is therefore free upon consideration to disagree with the judgement of another but before doing so he ought to have regard to the importance of consistency and to give his reasons for departure from the previous decision[3].

Inspectors' decisions are also important in the interpretation of Government planning policy and guidance, and local authorities and other Inspectors do look to public inquiry decisions to guide their deliberations. The importance attributed to decision letters, whether made by Inspectors or the Secretaries of State, is evidenced by the emphasis placed on them in journals like *The Journal of Planning and Environmental Law, The Planning Appeals Digest* and Compass' *Development Control Practice*. It would therefore seem important that a book about EIA, which claims to be practice based, includes an examination of the decisions made on projects covered by the 1988 Regulations by those decision makers with the most influence on the planning system.

Between the introduction of the EIA Regulations in 1988 and the beginning of 1995 over 2000 ESs were submitted under all the 20 sets of Regulations[4]. By far the largest proportion (70%) of these were submitted with planning applications falling within the Town and Country Planning Acts for England, Wales and Scotland. Of these the Oxford Brookes' *Directory of Environmental Impact Statements* identifies 104 that have been the subject of public inquiries for either call-in applications or appeals[5]. Much of this chapter is based upon an analysis of 54 of the decision letters from these inquiries – a 52% sample. The sample appeal cases range from pig units, through waste incineration plants and mineral extraction to new settlements. The sample includes cases determined by the Scottish and Welsh Offices as well as the Department of the Environment and the Planning Inspectorate[6]. The cases were analysed to assess which issues were discussed and which issues were considered by the Inspectors to be the most significant factor on which the final assessment of the case turned. A summary of the results of

Table 6.1 Percentage of cases per issue at EIA public inquiries

Issue	Discussed	Significant
National or local policy	75%	65%
Amenity	57%	9%
Noise	40%	9%
Risk	17%	7%
Flora and fauna	23%	13%
Soil	11%	3.5%
Water	13%	5.5%
Air	27%	7.5%
Landscape	74%	32%
Conservation area, listed building, archaeology	25%	11%
Traffic	77%	13%

this assessment is set out in Table 6.1 which provides the percentage of cases where each issue was discussed and the percentage of significance to the final decision.

The public inquiry comes at the very end of the development control process and has always provided an opportunity for planning applications to be scrutinised in far more detail than is the case with applications determined by planning authorities. Evidence is presented to Inspectors in the form of written proofs which are either read in full or summarised by expert witnesses. These witnesses and their proofs are then cross-examined and tested by the 'opposition's' advocates and the Inspector. Proofs of evidence have always been detailed and often extremely technical documents and this remains the case at inquiries into projects subject to the EIA Regulations. Proofs are produced for the inquiry by the developer's witnesses despite the fact that they have previously submitted an ES. Anecdotal evidence from professional planners suggests that an ES is treated little differently from the proofs of evidence presented at non-EIA inquiries, suggesting perhaps that the existence of an ES, and the EIA process behind it, adds little to the nature and conduct of planning appeals and inquiries.

Furthermore, as was argued in the Introduction to this book, the ES is not the limit of the 'environmental information' necessary to make a decision and the ES is often but one source of the necessary information. For example in a Cornish appeal into a proposed windfarm the Inspector considered all the 'environmental information' put before him and he said in his decision letter:

all topics covered by the Assessment are dealt with in greater detail in the evidence put to the inquiry, and are more closely linked to the scheme as it has been revised. I therefore consider that the Assessment, while still a material consideration, is of less weight than the evidence, and it will be treated accordingly[7].

At public inquiries the ES does not stand alone as a 'truth': it is simply treated as one piece of evidence relating to the assessment of environmental impacts among the accumulation of other, often conflicting, evidence. The ES is, after all, produced by the developer's 'experts', based upon their individual or collective experience and professional opinion. As such the ES is subjective and is little different from the proofs traditionally produced by expert witnesses for public inquiries. Like those proofs it is tested through cross-examination and the presentation of counter evidence by other, opposing, witnesses. It is perhaps significant that in those EIA cases which do not go before Inspectors at public inquiries the ES is not subjected to the same rigorous degree of examination and cross-examination. In those cases a consideration of the 'environmental information' is far more reliant on the quality of the ES and the ability of the competent authority to make an informed judgement on the detail of the information provided. This is perhaps of even more interest when we consider that only 6% of planning ESs have been subjected to the rigours of a full public inquiry.

Inspectors are greatly assisted by the skill of advocates and the thoroughness of cross-examination which can and does highlight the strengths and weaknesses of a project and its impact assessment. Debate over the assessment and the quality and adequacy of ESs took place in six of the 54 cases studied. Inspectors seem to accept the minimalist approach to ES quality sanctioned by Circular 15/88. This is illustrated by the Reporter's discussion of the evidence put before him at a Scottish Office appeal case dealing with a proposed quarry extension at Craigie[8]. The appellants' and the Kyle and Carrick District Council's witnesses had spent some time debating the quality and adequacy of the ES and the Reporter summarised the Council's case thus:

> The ES in question failed to achieve the objectives of EA. It contained a number of statements which were incorrect or contradictory, notably on lorry traffic. Many of the statements were incapable of verification due to the absence of information or data.

This opinion was supported by some of the statutory consultees and Reporter Gordon noted:

> The Countryside Commission for Scotland advised the planning authority that the ES had major shortcomings, and recommended that planning permission should not be granted until certain matters, including traffic, visual impact, hydrology, dust, noise, landscape and afteruse, had been adequately addressed. The ES was also criticised by the Nature Conservancy Council.

However, having heard all of this evidence the Reporter was forced to accept that the Regulations and the Circular make no quality requirements for an ES and he took the view:

> The ES has been strongly criticised by a number of parties. I agree with many of those criticisms. Few of the topics dealt with by the ES are covered in depth, and

the document does not demonstrate that a proper analysis of environmental impacts has been made. Some of the comments on output and traffic generation are confusing. The ES falls well short of 'best practice'.... Despite its shortcomings, the ES appears to me to comply broadly with the statutory requirements of the EA Regulations, and with the terms of the EC Directive from which the EA Regulations are derived.

In assessing all of the conflicting evidence before them Inspectors are likely to find, as in the Cornish case above, that other evidence is of more relevance than the ES and this may help to explain why in 53% of those cases examined the ES was not specifically referred to by the Secretaries of State or the Inspectors in their decision letters.

The appeal decision letters provided very little evidence that the environmental information set out in an ES is afforded more weight than when environmental issues are raised at non-EIA inquiries. The environmental factors listed in Schedule 3 of the Regulations are discussed as are other planning issues such as amenity, risk, need and policy. In fact in the majority of the cases examined (65%) either national or local land use polices were the determining issue identified by the Inspectors and the Secretaries of State. Many of the Schedule 3 environmental factors such as flora and fauna, landscape and air were also significant and yet these too are traditional planning matters which have long been the subject of debate at inquiries, even before the introduction of formal EIA in 1988. Other issues which are more directly related to the introduction of the Regulations are not, or are rarely, discussed under the headings given in Schedule 3. Climate was not an issue in a single case and cultural heritage and material assets, although discussed, were not debated under those headings. The headings which dominate the decision letters of the Inspectors and Secretaries of State are the traditional planning material considerations such as amenity, various forms of risk, traffic and need, although some factors such as flora and fauna, noise and landscape do tend to be discussed separately.

Amenity

The loss of public or private amenity is a crucial, and often overriding, planning consideration which does not easily fall within any single environmental factor listed in Schedule 3 of the 1988 Regulations. The threat to amenity, in one form or another, was an issue in most cases studied. As an undefined concept amenity was an issue in 57% of cases and yet a determining issue in only 9%. Amenity is itself a difficult concept and is rarely defined in legal texts or indeed legislation or regulation and yet it is an essential part of the planning assessment. It is understood by this author to mean 'that part of the environment we enjoy'. This simple definition accepts that the environment is made up of very many factors some of which we do not enjoy or derive value from. An inner city slum or a piece of derelict contaminated land are elements of the environment but they are not necessarily enjoyed or aesthetically valued and not seen as amenity. This understanding of the concept squarely relates the environment to people's perception of its aesthetic value and meaning; which in turn makes the impact of a development on amenity an impact upon the Schedule 3 environmental factor 'human beings'.

The impact of development on people is of course the main focus of any planning system. For all the discussion about the rational use and management of resources and the protection of the countryside 'for its own sake', planning is essentially about people. It is a societal decision to protect the countryside and it is carried out because people want and demand that protection. There would be no ecological catastrophe or earth threatening breakdown of nature if bats and badgers became extinct in the UK. It would be very sad if they did and very many people would feel that their lives had been diminished in some way. But that would be all. Fleischman (1969) convincingly argues that:

> Nature will not miss whooping cranes or condors or redwoods any more than it misses the millions of other vanished species. Conservation is based on human value systems. Its validation lies in the human situation and the human heart[9].

Similarly, it is often people who suffer most as a result of environmental damage, whether it be health problems resulting from pollution or a degraded built environment due to poor design or overdevelopment[10]. Even where a species of plant or animal deserves special protection because of its potential for the development of medicines, food or industrial uses, it still constitutes protection for the sake of people and not for any inherent right to survival. It is wholly legitimate to argue that all environmental impacts are essentially impacts on human beings in one form or another and that there is no real justification for this separate category in Schedule 3 of the Regulations. Yet Schedule 3 does not directly refer to any specific impacts, such as noise, odour, disturbance and visual impacts which all affect our enjoyment of the environment and hence our amenity and are therefore impacts upon human beings.

Because amenity is such a fundamental planning issue it should not be surprising that, on the evidence of the sample decision letters, the discussions of amenity issues by Inspectors and the Secretaries of State are not materially different from when those issues arise at non-EIA appeals. However, with issues such as noise and odour the detailed technical assessments in the ES tend to be the basis for the Inspector's own assessment. This is not to suggest that the conclusions of the ES will be accepted by an Inspector, often quite the opposite. In the 1990 decision letter for the proposed Flint By-pass the Inspector discussed the impact from traffic noise on visitors to Flint Castle which was close to the proposed route. The ES had accepted that noise was a 'disturbing factor' and yet Clwyd County Council, proposers of the route, considered noise acceptable. The Inspector however concluded:

I do not consider that acceptable standards for visitors could be achieved. Certainly I myself would not find my visit to the castle an enjoyable and relatively peaceful one with the level put forward. Moreover the anticipated noise levels from traffic would interfere with events which could be held there[11].

Here the issue of amenity can also be seen as an impact upon 'cultural heritage' as people are only having their amenity affected by visiting the historic castle and the noise and disturbance caused by the proposed road would affect their experience of that visit.

Noise is a common issue with EIA projects and was a major concern in 40% of the cases studied. The ES for such projects should, under the terms of Schedule 3 of the Regulations, set out the proposed means for mitigating noise impacts and these measures are also the subject of debate at inquiries. As with all planning considerations the Inspectors and the Secretaries of State have to assess whether those mitigation measures are sufficient to overcome objections to the proposed project. Sometimes this is a very fine balance and in some cases Inspectors, even in EIA cases, have very little real evidence to help them; after all the prediction of impacts is not an absolute and precise science as each case, each site and each set of circumstances are unique. The complexity of the balance that needs to be struck in such cases is illustrated in this extract from the Inspector's report following the public inquiry into a proposed sand and gravel extraction scheme at Higher Brockholes, Samlesbury, Preston, in Lancashire:

The background noise affecting the dwellings near the site is already higher than normal rural areas. I am satisfied that, with the mitigation measures proposed, the noise from normal sand and gravel winning and processing operations would not exceed those background levels. The noise from operations like the building and removal of the screen mounds nearest the river would be higher, but these operations would be short-lived and the noise could be kept within what most people would regard as tolerable for an operation of relatively short duration. There may be some occasions when the noise from the site makes out of doors teaching at Samlesbury C of E School very difficult, but in my opinion such instances would be rare. Overall I conclude that Samlesbury residents would not find the noise from the workings of the site to be intolerable[12].

There clearly remain a number of uncertainties and yet the Inspector had to make a recommendation and the Secretary of State, in this case, a decision.

This uncertainty is often dealt with by the imposition of conditions to the permission which in this case restricted hours of operation and set off-site noise limits. Yet even with such restrictions the acceptability or otherwise of increased noise is subjective.

Environmental impacts of many types are subjectively experienced and no more so than in the case of impacts upon public and private amenity; what is acceptable to some people may not be to others. This is clearly the case with odour impacts as was pointed out by Inspector Waldron in his decision letter following the twin appeals for two alternative proposals for pig breeding and finishing units at High House Farm, Parham, in Suffolk. Mr Waldron stated:

It was established at the inquiry that there is no quantitative measurement of odour intensity. Therefore determining whether or not smell from the proposed pig units would unacceptably affect the amenities of residents of High House has to be a subjective assessment[13].

In this case the Inspector was faced with conflicting information. The ES contained an odour plume analysis which suggested that odour would be detectable at the nearest dwelling from both proposed sites but that levels would not be so great as to warrant a refusal of either application. However, the Inspector also saw published guidance from the Agricultural Development Advice Service which suggested that few smell problems, in the form of complaints from residents, normally occur where large pig rearing units are more than 400 metres away from dwellings. Here the Inspector was faced with an impact which could only be subjectively assessed and was provided with two means of making that assessment: firstly predictions made from an analysis of wind and atmospheric conditions in the area, and secondly a simple rule of thumb which states that the further the source of the odour is from the receivers the better. The nearest dwelling, High House, was within the 400 metre 'highest risk sector' of one of the proposed sites. Inspector Waldon concluded that the site which was further away offered less threat to the amenity of the residents and as a result, on balance, opted to favour that site.

One uniquely 'human beings' and amenity impact which can be a material planning consideration is the fear that a development will adversely affect television reception. This was discussed in some detail at an appeal into a windfarm proposal for 15 turbines at Trysglwyn Fawr, near Amlwch, Anglesey[14]. The BBC had objected to the scheme and the Inspector heard evidence that there was a '10% probability of significant interference with the re-broadcasting link that crosses the site'. This matter was settled through the completion of a legal agreement between the developer, National Wind Power Ltd, and the BBC which required the appellant to provide remedial works should it prove necessary.

Clearly the boundaries of amenity are difficult to define and it is equally difficult to separate many of the environmental factors listed in Schedule 3 of the Regulations from amenity or the impact of projects on 'human beings'. This section has tried to indicate the wide range of 'human beings' impacts that are discussed at EIA inquiries. There are very many others that have not been discussed here, some of which will be dealt with below as we look at the other main issues discussed at EIA public inquiries and their relationship to the Schedule 3 environmental factors.

Risk

Risk, in one form or another, is an increasingly important feature of EIA inquiries and was a major issue in 17% of the appeal cases examined. Yet there remains debate as to how far the risk of accident, plant failure or human error can be taken into account in arriving at planning decisions.

Since the Gateshead case and the publication of PPG23: *Planning and Pollution Control* in the summer of 1994, the existence of a pollution control regime, the Environmental Protection Act (EPA) and Integrated Pollution Control (IPC), has been formally recognised as a material consideration in arriving at planning decisions[15]. However, the PPG has been widely criticised for failing to provide the promised and much needed clear definitive statement on the relationship between planning and pollution control[16]. In his article 'Thin green line on pollution' Roger Milne considers the question of risks as remaining a 'grey area' and this is clearly one of the main problems with the PPG[17]. Risk, as we have seen, has been a major issue in many of the appeal cases studied and despite the advice in PPG23 planning Inspectors and the courts will continue to grapple with the arguments on environmental risk.

Paragraph 3.2 of the PPG tells us that 'the sensitivity of the area, in particular as reflected in landscape, agricultural land quality, nature conservation or archaeological designations, if evidence suggests that there is a *risk* of such features being affected by pollution' is a material planning consideration. At paragraph 3.18 the PPG says 'The perception of risk should not be material to the consideration of the planning application unless the land-use consequences of such perceptions can be clearly demonstrated'[18]. These sections of the PPG seem to identify risk as a material consideration where that risk has land use implications. However, the PPG confuses matters by demanding that risk assessment should not be the role of the planners but should be part of the authorisation process of the relevant pollution control authority and that the planners should rely on that assessment when they determine planning applications. However, the pollution control authorities are under no obligation to offer this advice and, as we saw in the Project Witch case in Chapter 5, they can be reluctant to offer advice which is beyond their remit. Furthermore it is perhaps so clearly beyond their powers and duties to offer advice on the risk of a loss of amenity that they are unlikely to be equipped or willing to provide the type of advice the PPG seems to suggest they should.

This confusion over risk assessment is compounded by the PPG which seems to retain it as a planning matter when it states:

> there may be circumstances where a development that is likely to satisfy pollution control requirements may still be considered by the planning authority to present an unacceptable risk in planning terms, because of social, economic or environmental factors incorporated in that risk[19].

It is not clear what those 'environmental factors' could be and how the 'environment' is defined here. If it is defined in the same way as the term is used in the EPA – 'consists of all, or any of the following media, namely, the air, water and land; and the medium of air includes the air within buildings and the air within other natural or man-made structures above the ground'[20] – then risk of pollution remains an issue for planners when assessing the operation of a plant or process that has IPC or LAAC authorisation. Therefore the PPG does not have the effect of 'pushing planners further off the pollution control authorities' patch' as the *ENDS Report* of July 1994 would suggest[21]. Furthermore, the DoE's *Environmental Assessment: A Guide to the Procedures* published in 1989 makes clear that in cases where an accident could give rise to harmful effects to people and the environment the ES should include an indication of the preventative measures that will be adopted to reduce that risk. It does not go beyond stating that the inclusion of a risk assessment is anything more than 'desirable', yet it is an acknowledgement of the importance of risk assessment for potentially polluting industries[22].

Planners have always, of course, been responsible for this type of risk assessment. Indeed the crucial part of any planning assessment is the potential risk that a development will result in a loss of public or private amenity. That assessment is at the centre of the balance that planners have to strike between the benefits and disbenefits of any proposed development. Risk assessment, in its widest sense, is therefore not new to planners. In the remainder of this section we examine the treatment of risk at EIA public inquiries and the relevance of risk assessment to the Schedule 3 environmental factors.

Human beings

In one case the Inspector had to decide whether a proposed gravel works and landfill site would attract birds and increase the risk of bird-strike to a jet aircraft which took off from the adjacent runway. The site, at Rofford Hall near Chalgrove in Oxfordshire, was at the end of a runway used by Martin Baker, the manufacturers of ejector seats. The appellants' ES made the case that the landfill would not contain any 'waste attractive to birds' and that there were already a large number of birds in the area and on the field in question, particularly when it was being ploughed. The Inspector took the view that:

> it is very likely that more than 'the odd sandwich' would be deposited on site from skips that had been placed in a street, and the possibility of illegal tipping around the appeal site cannot be ruled out[23].

Here then a crucial 'human beings' issue: the safety of the public and the pilot should a development increase the risk of bird-strike. On this point the Inspector concluded:

> Overall I have to conclude on the information available to me that allowing the appeal would make the long established operation of the Martin Baker Company slightly, but appreciably, more hazardous than now. In so doing I bear in mind the present stance of the Ministry of Defence. Nevertheless, I have not been made

aware of any instance where workings of this kind have been allowed immediately adjoining an operational airfield, and I believe that the hazard here would not be negligible[24].

Water

Water was an issue in seven cases and here the discussion was predominantly about flood risk or other drainage issues. Only in the mineral extraction/ waste disposal cases was water quality or impact upon an aquifer of major importance.

In one very significant case, a proposal to create a regional waste disposal centre at Kirk Sandall near Doncaster, the Secretary of State dismissed the appeal because:

> the location of the proposals above an important unprotected aquifer so near the surface, provides sufficient reason to outweigh the argument concerning need and other benefits associated with the proposal[25].

In this case the potential impact on the aquifer was identified and the risks were minimised through proposed mitigation measures including multiple man-made barriers. However, the Secretary of State took the view that although barriers could be designed to contain all 'foreseeable spillages' there would always be a risk of failure and that due to the importance of the aquifer that risk, 'no matter how small', was unacceptable. It is clear that all the parties involved in the case accepted that the proposed waste disposal site was located above the 'most important aquifer in Northern England' which is 'unprotected by overlaying clays'. It was also agreed by the parties that even small quantities of certain chemicals 'could cause large-scale pollution and the resultant clean up operation would be an expensive, long term, project with no guarantee of success'[26].

Risk of pollution is fundamental to the decision here and this case also highlights another element of the risk assessment to be drawn from the EIA process. Risk here can be seen as not simply the environmental risks but also the developer's risk in continuing to promote a proposal, right through to appeal, when the EIA process has identified a significant and eventually determining potential impact.

Air

The Schedule 3 environmental parameter of 'air' was identified as an issue in 15 cases. Here 'air' covers a wide range of issues such as chemical and particulate emissions, dust and the amenity issue of odour generation discussed earlier. Here again is the problem of the interconnection between the Schedule 3 environmental factors and the difficulty of assigning impacts to any single environmental parameter. Risk of pollution is a threat to human health as well as of wider environmental concern. Health is of course a 'human beings' factor and risk to public health was discussed at some length at many inquiries, particularly those dealing with projects capable of producing gaseous and particulate emissions to air.

At a public inquiry into an animal waste incinerator in Hereford and Worcester the Inspector took the view that there was sufficient doubt of a pollution control authorisation being granted that a refusal of the application was warranted because 'the well-being of the local community may well be at risk from pollution'[27]. The nature of the risk, in that case, was also described by the Inspector:

> In this case, the nature of the feedstock, the constraints of existing air quality, the nature of all the technology to be utilised in the process and its ability to meet the requirements of HMIP, are matters which influence the assessment of the risk of pollution that might affect land uses or the social and economic well-being of the area. Neither the Environmental Statement nor the evidence at the inquiry gave that information with any clarity or certainty.

In another case, a chemical and thermal waste treatment centre at Howdon on Tyneside, residual uncertainty of impacts remaining after all the evidence had been considered was deemed to be a material consideration but one which could not, in that case, form the basis of a dismissal of the appeal on its own[28]. This was also the view held by the Secretary of State in his decision letter for the industrial waste incinerator proposals at Seal Sands, Billingham, Cleveland[29]. Based upon these cases, and there is nothing within PPG23 to suggest they should now have been determined differently, it would appear that the risk of pollution, particularly when there are other factors such as the relationship of the development to and the effect on a residential area or a particularly important environmental feature, can be attributed significant weight. Risk to the environment as a result of some form of plant failure should and must be a very important consideration as there is sufficient history of failures to plant and of major accidents to suggest that such risks can be anticipated.

Any assessment of the risk of plant failure and its implications for atmospheric pollution and public health will always need to be weighed against other factors such as need, policy and the ability of pollution control regimes to control and minimise that risk. In his report following the public inquiry into the proposed waste incinerator at Vulcan Street, Middlesborough, the Inspector concluded:

> it is not possible to seek conclusive proof of safety of a particular installation. A situation of no-risk is not attainable and the degree of risk has to be balanced against other aspects[30].

The degree of detail of any risk assessment contained within an ES will depend upon the sensitivity of the local environment to accidental releases or plant failure. In a Welsh Office case, a proposed gas and oil terminal at Point of Ayr, Talacre, Clwyd, the Inspector placed considerable weight on the fact that the Health and Safety Executive, which has a great deal of experience and expertise in risk assessment, had agreed with the modelling procedures and analysis of risk produced by the appellants[31]. The risk evaluation in that case was based upon a quantitative risk assessment which estimates the risk of death per population per year. Clearly such an assessment requires technical analysis of the type not uncommon to other spheres of EIA and where they are provided Inspectors find them helpful. In a second Welsh Office case, a chemical treatment facility proposed for Newport in Gwent, there had been no consideration of accidental releases of unscrubbed gases to the atmosphere in the ES[32]. As a result a great deal of time was taken up at the inquiry on this issue, with the results of a quantitative risk assessment being debated, only for the Inspector to conclude that the level of the risk of failure, and its likely impact, were acceptable. As the public and the local authority had not seen any detailed accident risk assessment prior to the inquiry the fear of that risk was an important issue which could not be removed in the often charged and adversarial atmosphere of a public inquiry. This the Inspector acknowledged when he stated:

> The public's perception of the hazards and risks remains. In my judgement, this is a factor which counts against the development. Nevertheless, bearing in mind actual evidence regarding foreseeable risks to health and all the circumstances surrounding this case, I find that opposition of the general public, expressed through various bodies and individuals as well as the LPA, is insufficient to override the acceptability of the proposals in terms of Development Plan Policies and the lack of demonstrable harm to the public or the environment[33].

Risk, in all its forms, is clearly a major feature of many EIA appeals and yet in very few cases is a fully structured evaluation of risks carried out and included within the ES. Where risk of pollution, and its consequential impact on health and the environment, is likely to be a concern of the public and therefore an issue for the determining authority or an appeal Inspector, the ES will unquestionably be an aid to the decision-making process if it includes a full environmental risk assessment.

Need and the planning balance

Whether it be public or private amenity, the risk of accidental failure of some kind or the impact of a project upon any of the Schedule 3 environmental factors, planning in the UK is and remains about striking a balance between the need for a project, however that need is defined, and the likely adverse impacts. The weight to be given to the competing issues in the balance often depends upon the value attributed to environmental features and in the UK this normally depends upon some form of national or local designation.

Flora and fauna

Flora and fauna were mentioned as issues in 23% of the cases examined. The protection of wildlife species and habitats has long been a planning concern in the UK and yet that protection almost exclusively depends upon some kind of special designation.

The importance of designations in the weight to be attributed to flora and fauna was at issue in a 1990 appeal into a proposed opencast coal mine at Hilton in County Durham. Here the Durham Wildlife Trust had expressed concern about the impact of the proposals on an area 'rich in wildlife'. The Inspector took the view that:

> Clearly the workings would cause massive disruption to the wildlife and to the ecological balance of the area and this would take a number of years to re-establish as flora and fauna recolonised the land. There is however no evidence that this agricultural landscape warrants special protection for its natural history interest and it has no specific policy safeguards[34].

Against this is the weight attributed to important wildlife designations. In the Flint By-pass proposals discussed above there was risk of serious damage to the Dee Estuary which is a Ramsar Convention site and a Special Protection Area. Here the Secretary of State for Wales, in accepting the Inspector's very strong criticisms of the Council's proposals, took the view that the status of the Dee Estuary:

> remain factors which increase the weight to be accorded to the issue of nature conservation within the Dee Estuary which is itself a material consideration in the determination of this application.... The Secretary of State accepts the Inspector's conclusion that the proposed by-pass would cause unacceptable harm to the natural habitat of the Dee Estuary, an interest of acknowledged importance, which would not be rendered acceptable by the proposed compensatory measures[35].

This last comment refers to a proposed mitigation measure of creating a new saltmarsh area to accommodate the birds displaced by the routing of the proposed road through the Ramsar site. The Inspector commented:

> it seems to me that there must be considerable doubt over whether such extreme measures could, even eventually, after a period of becoming established, adequately compensate for lost roosting and the like. Ignoring the impact such a scheme might itself have upon its environment, harm would still have been caused to the bird wildlife here through initial disturbance[36].

In that case the Nature Conservancy Council played a significant role in criticising the Council's ES and in presenting counter evidence to the inquiry. In much of this the Inspector appears to have favoured the evidence presented to him at the inquiry to the environmental information provided in the ES.

This debate between the impact of proposals and the mitigation measures offered was an issue at a number of the cases examined including the

Cotswold Water Park and the Centre Parcs proposal for Longleat[37]. It is a difficult balance to strike and once again Inspectors are in essence assessing differing levels of risk. This assessment is often reliant on the information provided in the ES and the other evidence making up the necessary 'environmental information'. In a landfill case at Stalybridge, Thameside, the Inspector had to decide whether the natural erosion of the ecological quality of a local authority designated wildlife site was sufficient reason to allow landfill operations which, once complete, would provide new habitat. In that case Inspector Burden concluded that:

> the ecological consequences of the appeal proposal are likely to be rather worse than the outcome if the site is left to its own devices. If left the scrub would eventually mature into woodland, probably not dissimilar to the adjoining mature woodland[38].

It is perhaps instructive that in all this, after the completion of an ES, the gathering of the other 'environmental information', the cross-examination of expert witnesses and the input of statutory consultees, Inspectors remain unable to state with confidence what environmental impacts are likely to occur. The decision letters remain full of statements such as 'likely to be' and 'probably not dissimilar'.

Soil

Soil was seldom an issue and when it was raised it was more usually related to agricultural land quality. The loss of good quality agricultural land is most often debated in proposals for mineral workings where that loss is set against the need for the particular mineral. For example, in his decision letter for the sand and gravel extraction proposal at Samlesbury, discussed above, Inspector Burden concluded:

> In my view the need for the sand and gravel deposits is very strong and I do not consider the loss of good quality agricultural land is serious enough to stand in the way of releasing the underlying mineral resource[39].

In that case it was estimated that the proposal would result in the loss of between 15 and 23 ha of grade 2 land and the Inspector conceded that 'Grade 2 land is certainly among the best and most versatile land to be found in Lancashire'.

In a Northumberland case the Inspector took completely the opposite view. Here the proposal was to excavate sand and gravel from beneath 30 ha of grade 2 agricultural land which makes up only 3% of land in the county. The site was not proposed to be infilled and would be lost to agriculture completely as a fishing and boating lake. Inspector Heijne concluded that this irreversible loss was unacceptable when set against national and local policies for the protection of the most versatile land and where the appellants had failed to demonstrate an overriding need for the minerals[40].

It would seem clear from this that an assessment of need, in these cases, is as important, if not more so, than an assessment of the impact of the proposal on the environmental medium of soil.

Landscape

Landscape protection and enhancement has always been a major feature, and a determining material consideration in the UK's planning system. Landscape is a distinct Schedule 3 factor and yet, as with virtually all of the Schedule 3 factors, landscape impacts are, essentially, impacts upon human beings as it is only human beings that put a value upon landscape. In essence, an adverse landscape impact will inevitably result in a loss of public or private amenity. As with flora and fauna the protection of landscape features is often achieved in the UK planning system through a range of landscape designations and these generally relate to their 'natural beauty', another strange notion in a nation like the UK where very little landscape can be truly termed 'natural'. Again the impact of projects upon those designations is weighed and balanced against the need for the development and the policies for protection.

In the EIA decision letters examined landscape was an issue in 74% of cases and a determining issue in 32%. Landscape would appear to be an issue in virtually all Schedule 1 and Schedule 2 projects, whether they be waste incinerators which require 35 metre high chimneys or opencast coal or other mineral proposals which often scar the landscape for a generation.

It is often argued by appellants that mineral workings are not permanent features and can be restored either to replace or improve the original landscape. At the Rofford Hall, Chalgrove, Oxfordshire, sand and gravel and waste disposal proposals discussed above, the Inspector seemed particularly taken by the argument of local people that the 15 year duration of the proposal, with its harmful effects on a 'handsome open landscape, where long vistas are only partly screened by mature native hardwood planting and occasional hedgerows', was equivalent to an 'entire childhood'[41].

What could more clearly illustrate the link between landscape as a Schedule 3 environmental factor and the impact of a project upon amenity and 'human beings' than this reference to the experience of that landscape change on an 'entire childhood'?

Landscape was a major determining issue in this case, even when set against a marginally demonstrated need for the minerals it was proposed to excavate. The site was not within a national landscape designation and had only been included within the draft Local Plan for local authority designation after objections to the plan from local residents. It would appear from this evidence that landscape protection does not hinge entirely upon designations.

In the joint inquiries for the proposed new settlements in the A45 corridor near Cambridge, the Inspector was of the view that landscape issues, including the impact of the sites on the setting of other settlements, was a determining issue in seven of the eight cases under examination[42]. Again not all of these sites were within even local authority landscape designations.

Conversely designations like Areas of Outstanding Natural Beauty (AONBs) are not presumptions against development. Mineral Policy Guidance Note 1 reminds developers and local authorities that minerals can only be worked where they occur and they often do occur in the most protected landscapes like AONBs and National Parks[43]. The 'need' to work the minerals in such cases will be set against the impact and often that need will override the designation.

Even where need is not demonstrated the general policy approach to AONBs, namely that it will normally be inconsistent with the aims of designation to permit the siting of major industrial or commercial development in AONBs, can be overridden where other circumstances and considerations suggest. In the case of the Centre Parcs proposals for Longleat in Wiltshire the Secretary of State took the view that:

> when weighed against the benefits of the scheme ... such as tree planting and its implications for employment in the area, the conflict with AONB and development plan policy is not so significant as to justify refusing planning permission[44].

Landscape is an area of planning, and therefore EIA, where at first glance there appears to be an overriding presumption in favour of protection. Yet there is a conflict between that presumption and the need for minerals, or even alternative sources of energy as in the case of windfarms. In EIA terms this conflict is most often resolved through mitigation measures such as tree planting and restoration.

Material assets and cultural heritage

Of all the Schedule 3 environmental features material assets and cultural heritage are perhaps the most difficult to define. They cover a whole host of areas and impacts including buildings, roads and transport infrastructure, traffic, archaeological features, historic and listed buildings, conservation areas and even perhaps cultural identity. As with all the other Schedule 3 environmental parameters most of these features have long been material planning considerations. For listed buildings and conservation areas the planning acts impose a duty to ensure that there is a consideration of the desirability to preserve or enhance their character or appearance. Again protection depends to a large extent upon designations. In the case of archaeology such designations are only available to the most important and significant sites which could leave the vast wealth of unreported and unknown archaeological features and artifacts unprotected. However, since the publication of PPG16: *Archaeology and Planning* such sites have been attributed far more weight in the assessment of planning applications[45].

At risk of labouring the point it should also be noted that impacts on all such environmental features are fundamentally impacts upon human beings.

The conservation of listed buildings, conservation areas and archaeological sites and their settings was debated in 25% of the cases studied. Traffic impacts were issues in 77% of public inquiry cases and significant, determining, issues in 13% of the cases. However, in no case were the issues assessed by Inspectors or Secretaries of State under the headings cultural heritage or material assets.

Despite archaeology's increased importance as a material planning consideration archaeological impacts rarely result in the dismissal of an appeal as the development under consideration can be the only way that a site investigation can be funded. PPG16 provides guidance on conditions which can be imposed on planning permissions to ensure that archaeological investigations are carried out either before or during the development. For example the Port Wakefield freight village proposal near Castleford, Yorkshire, was granted consent by the Secretary of State subject to just such a condition following the Inspector's conclusion:

> my view on the available evidence is that the features likely to be found should be recorded but that there is unlikely to be any need to preserve remains *in situ* or to prevent development of part of the appeal land[46].

Just as there is often a gap between the public's perceived risk from industrial pollution and the results of objective analysis so it is with traffic generation. There is always a difference between the level of traffic the public is willing to accept as safe and that which is deemed acceptable in strictly highway engineering terms. This point is brought home in this quote from the Inspector's report following the inquiry into the proposed chemical treatment works at Newport, Gwent:

> Whether that survey [the appellant's] is truly indicative of routine pedestrian movement and takes account of activity at the local schools, commercial and recreation centres was not demonstrated. However, even if the objectors' contention that Spitty Road/Ringland Way is subject to significant pedestrian flows, it seems to me that the 130 additional vehicles, over and above those already using the roads and junctions, would not be large enough to have significant effect on the accident potential of the route[47].

Here again is an issue for EIA in that the fears of local residents had not been allayed in any way by the contents of the ES. Had the developers consulted and involved the local residents at an early stage of the EIA process and produced a traffic survey which was acceptable to them, it is unlikely that more accurate information would have resulted in the proposal becoming any less objectionable to residents. Perhaps this is more clearly illustrated by the words of the Inspector in his report following the Cotswold Water Park inquiry:

It is not unusual for objections to be raised even to minor proposals, as there is frequently a hostile attitude to change, with preference expressed for the status quo. I do not doubt the sincerity of those persons objecting to the proposed development, but the objections must be of substance if they are to influence a decision.

I accept that concerns expressed by local residents are genuine, but in light of the element of agreement to highway capacities and proposed highway improvements, including the proposed upgrading of the A419 and its junction with the Spine Road, I find the concerns laboured and possibly presented as a means of providing a defence against change[48].

A 'material asset' considered at the inquiry into a clinical waste incinerator at Knowsley, Kirby, in Lancashire was the industrial park in which the proposed development would be located. The concern here was that the proposed incinerator would have a detrimental effect on the future of the park in that potential occupiers would not wish to locate adjacent to a potentially polluting industry[49]. The Secretary of State took the view that this issue was a material consideration but not one that, in the circumstances of the case, warranted a refusal on its own. This was also an issue in the Seal Sands, Cleveland, waste incinerator appeal. Here it was argued that the proposed incinerator, on land allocated in the development plan for B2 general industrial use, a use which includes waste incinerators, would adversely affect the 'image of Cleveland as an attractive place for cleaner and more labour-intensive industries'[50]. The Secretary of State accepted that this was a material planning consideration but did not believe it was germane in that case as the site was allocated for the use proposed. In a third case the Secretary of State took a wholly different view. This was the proposed integrated waste treatment centre, including treatment of sewage sludge by 'chemical and thermal means', at Howden in North Tyneside. Here the Secretary of State concluded that:

> Urban regeneration is a material planning consideration in determining this appeal.... The creation of a climate of confidence in which regeneration can take place and succeed is a key element in the Development Corporation's strategy ... the perception of the Integrated Treatment Centre in this location would be wholly negative.... The Secretary of State is persuaded that the presence of this plant, so close to housing and a key regeneration site, would have serious, albeit unquantifiable, effects on the regeneration of this part of North Tyneside. He agrees with the Inspector that this is a sound and clear-cut planning objection to these proposals[51].

These impacts were crucial to the decision and yet they are rarely discussed in an ES submitted with a planning application and only come to light through the evidence presented at a public inquiry. These socio-economic impacts of a project are not formally required by the EIA Regulations and Glasson (1994) argues that such matters tend to be too often neglected in EIA[52]. Economic impacts are often impacts upon 'material assets' and clearly need to be included within ESs where the impacts are likely to be significant and material to the planning decision.

Public inquiries and EIA

There are a number of main themes which have emerged from this review of inquiry decision letters. The first is the importance and relevance of risk assessment, in all its forms, to both the EIA and planning processes. Second, all the issues raised and debated at inquiries are part of an overall planning balance assessment which has long been the overriding and determining feature of the UK planning system. As Tromans (1991) so ably puts it:

> [although] the Regulations should ensure that environmental impacts are considered, they do not have the effect of increasing the weight to be given to such considerations, or shifting the balance between such considerations and other material considerations[53].

For the public inquiry process, at least, it would appear that the introduction of EIA has had little marked effect. By the time a project becomes the subject of a public inquiry the sides are drawn and the hearing becomes a focus for adversarial debate between opposing, expensive, experts directed and spurred on by advocates schooled in the art of cajoling witnesses into submission and contradiction. Such debates are seldom rational or in any other way related to the systematic, iterative and co-operative characteristics of good practice EIA. By the time the inquiry comes around, and all the investment has been made in expert witnesses and smooth talking barristers, it is far too late for all that.

Notes and references

1 This chapter, as with this book in general, does not deal with EIA in Northern Ireland where a completely different, highly centralised, planning system operates.

2 There is no room in a work of this kind to deal in detail with the full legal and organisational structures of the public inquiry and appeal system. For a comprehensive discussion of the system readers are recommended to refer to Carnwarth, R, B Hart, A Williams and His Honour Judge G Dolby (1990) *Planning Appeals and Inquiries*, 4th edn. London: Sweet & Maxwell.

3 *North Wiltshire District Council v Secretary of State for the Environment* [1992] P & CR 137.

4 Frost, R and A Frankish (1995) *Directory of Environmental Impact Statements July 1988–September 1994*. Oxford: School of Planning, Oxford Brookes University.

5 *Ibid.*

6 This chapter also draws on previous work by the author, published as Weston, J (1994) Assessment at the appeal cutting edge, *Planning* 1075.

7 Planning Inspectorate, T/APP/P0810/A/92/207638, 6 August 1993.

8 Scottish Office, P/PPA/SQ/336, 6 January 1992.

9 Fleischman, P (1969) Conservation, the biological fallacy, *Landscape*, Vol. 18, pp 23–27.

10 Weston, J (ed) (1986) *Red and Green: The New Politics of the Environment*. London: Pluto, p 2.

11 Welsh Office, SJG/LR/3/530/89, 17 September 1990.

12 DoE APP/C2300/A/91/190801, 11 June 1992.

13 Planning Inspectorate, APP/J3530/A/90/165751-174227, 2 December 1991.

14 Welsh Office, APP45-36, 10 December 1993.

15 *Gateshead M.B.C. v SOS and Northumbrian Water Group plc* [1994] 67 P & CR 179; DoE (1994) PPG23: *Planning and Pollution Control.* London: HMSO.

16 Weston, J and M Hudson, (1995) Planning and risk assessment, *Environmental Policy and Practice*, Vol. 4, No. 4.

17 Milne, R (1994) Thin green line on pollution, *Planning* 1077.

18 DoE (1994) *op. cit.*

19 *Ibid.*

20 Section 1(2) Environmental Protection Act 1990.

21 Guidance aims to clarify interface of planning and pollution controls, *ENDS Report*, July 1994.

22 DoE (1989) *Environmental Assessment: A Guide to the Procedures.* London: HMSO.

23 DoE, APP/U3100/A/90/17268, 15 April 1992.

24 *Ibid.*

25 DoE, APP/F4410/A/89/126733, 11 November 1991.

26 *Ibid.*

27 Planning Inspectorate, APP/F1800/1/93/222851, 21 January 1994.

28 DoE, APP/K9530/A/89/145489, 2 November 1992.

29 DoE, APP/V0700/A/89/137357, 2 November 1992.

30 DoE, APP/X9520/A/90/152522, 26 November 1992.

31 Welsh Office, P1/185, 11 February 1993.

32 Welsh Office, P34/919-P34/971, 4 February 1993.

33 *Ibid.*

34 DoE, APP/Y1300/A/89/125808, 22 May 1990.

35 Welsh Office, SJG/LR/3/530/89, 17 September 1990.

36 *Ibid.*

37 DOE, SW/P/5224/220/2, 16 August 1991; DoE, SW/P/5411/220/4, 4 August 1991.

38 DoE, APP/G4240/A/91/190553–556, 7 January 1993.

39 DoE, APP/C2300/A/91/190801, 11 June 1992.

40 DoE, APP/R2900/A/91/183605, 20 August 1992.

41 DoE, APP/U3100/A/90/17268, 15 April 1992.

42 DoE, E1/W0530/2/4/03, V0510/2/4/03, G0500/2/6/03, G0500/2/6/04, G0500/2/6/05, G0500/2/6/10, 5 March 1992.

43 DoE (1988) MPG1: *General Considerations and the Development Plan System.* London: HMSO.

44 DoE, SW/P/5411/220/4, 4 August 1991.

45 DoE (1990) PPG16: *Archaeology and Planning.* London: HMSO.

46 DoE, YH/5115/219/14, 28 September 1992.

47 Welsh Office, P34/919-P34/971, 4 February 1993.

48 DoE, SW/P/5224/220/2, 16 August 1991.

49 DoE, APP/V4305/A/91/191817, 15 June 1993.

50 DoE, APP/V0700/A/89/137357, 2 November 1992.

51 DoE, APP/K9530/A/89/145489, 2 November 1992.

52 Glasson, J (1994) EIA – only the tip of the iceberg?, *Town and Country Planning*, February, pp 42–45.

53 Tromans, S (1991) Town and country planning and environmental protection, *JPL*, Occasional Paper 18.

CHAPTER 7

EIA MONITORING AND AUDIT

Richard Frost

Introduction

Since the introduction of EIA regulations in the UK, most practice and published research has concentrated on the earlier stages of the process, up to the point of decision. This is partly because relatively few of the projects subject to EIA have gone ahead on the ground yet. However, it could also be due to how formal EIA activity has been adopted in the UK. Being incorporated into existing consent procedures, EIA's procedural nature has perhaps been overemphasised, and there has been less concern over both the EIA methods used and the substantive outcomes, projects on the ground. A preoccupation with the production and quality of ESs has also deflected attention from the real outcomes and much less attention has been given to what happens after a project is given consent, even though it is widely accepted that the full EIA process should include monitoring and audit so that some feedback can be achieved. It is almost as if those involved with EIA would rather concentrate on the procedures than dare to look at the end results. The development of strategic environmental assessment (SEA) could also contribute to a continuing neglect of EIA follow-up work.

In this chapter we attempt to examine the state of monitoring and audit activity in UK EIA practice. We focus mainly on projects dealt with under the Regulations, but briefly report on follow-up work for projects assessed before the Regulations came into effect. A careful definition of terms is provided, followed by a brief review of legislation. Reasons for undertaking follow-up are then put forward. Whilst EIA monitoring and audit are recognised as costly activities, the potential financial savings are also highlighted. Research into EIA follow-up is not a new field; however, there has been very little *recent* research. Past EIA audit research is critically reviewed. Recent original research findings are then presented, with the aid of case studies, although some of the findings are still preliminary. This is followed by a summary of recent project audit work carried out by consultancies. Based on this recent research and consultancy work some good practice approaches are provided together with examples. A section reflecting on wider implications considers how prediction bias may arise from contextual factors in the UK, and then looks at what bias means for the principle of EIA in the UK. The conclusion summarises key findings and draws together common issues.

Definitions

The meaning of the terms EIA monitoring and audit needs to be clarified. A characteristic of a growing field of practice such as EIA is that there is confusion over the meaning of terms. *Effects monitoring* in EIA can be defined as the repeated (or continuous) measurement and recording of selected parameters enabling the evaluation of the effects of a development. *Effects audit* requires a comparison of the effects predicted with those which occur after (or during) project implementation. The term 'effect' is usually more appropriate than the term 'impact' because, as Duinker (1989)[1] claims, impacts cannot be monitored and audited directly. Technically, an impact prediction is the difference between the projected trend after a project and the projected baseline trend without it (see Fig. 7.1, Pe – Pb). When it

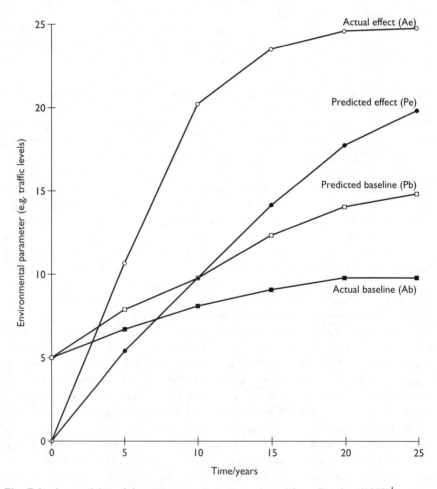

Fig. 7.1 Impossibility of direct impact monitoring, adapted from Duinker (1989)[1]

comes to follow-up, it is impossible to know exactly what that baseline trend would have been without any intervention in the environment by the project (e.g. instead of Pb it may have been Ab). For those ESs that do provide projected baseline trends it would be an interesting exercise to examine their accuracy if the project did not go ahead.

Effects monitoring is an integral part of effects auditing; however, they should not be used interchangeably. In general terms, auditing is more of a discrete one-off activity, involving a comparison with original objectives. This chapter relates mainly to project EIA audit which involves examining the full range of effects arising from a project. It also means considering unpredicted effects together with those that were predicted but did not occur. Tomlinson and Atkinson (1987)[2] have identified several other types of EIA audits and this chapter relates to two of them. Implementation audits ensure that projects and mitigation measures are carried out and managed in the way in which they were proposed in the ES. Predictive technique audits aim to establish the accuracy and utility of the methods used by comparing real consequences with those predicted.

It should be acknowledged that less formalised types of follow-up may also exist, providing some feedback into EIA practice. For example, when considering an application, planning officers may carry out site visits to similar projects that are in operation, to get some indication of the likely future effects.

Legislative context

The requirement for monitoring and audit was included in the original draft of Directive 85/337/EEC; however, during the lengthy consultation period it was dropped from the final version. Although once again the merits of post-hoc monitoring reports were considered during the consultation period, monitoring requirements have not been included in the recently agreed amendments to the Directive[3]. It should be noted that there has been little consideration over whether there should be a minimum requirement for monitoring proposals at the ES stage. The UNECE Espoo Convention on EIA in a transboundary context makes a specific provision for monitoring and audit[4]. This enables the parties concerned (at the request of any of the parties) to determine whether and how an EIA audit should be carried out, specifically concerning the transboundary effects, together with any mitigation agreed as necessary. The EIA Directive may have to be amended still further to accommodate the requirements of this new convention.

Due to the absence of any measures for follow-up in the Directive, there is no requirement relating to it in any of the UK EIA Regulations. The DoE guidance on EIA procedures[5] does not even refer to monitoring or audit. Disappointingly recent guidance to developers on the preparation of ESs also does not mention monitoring or audit proposals[6].

The Government argues that a wealth of recent environmental legislation, some of which requires monitoring, makes further regulation for these costly EIA tasks unnecessary. Principal among these are requirements under the Environmental Protection Act 1990 for integrated pollution control (IPC) and Waste Management Licensing. Under these requirements conditions applied to consents often require emissions monitoring. Similarly licences to abstract and discharge into water bodies may require monitoring under the Water Resources Act 1991. However, these piecemeal requirements are no real substitute for effective EIA follow-up. Monitoring requirements normally only relate to direct emissions from the facility, rather than off-site effects. The scope of any monitoring is similarly restricted, normally being focused on a few key environmental receptors rather than the whole range of effects from a project, or their interactions. This monitoring activity also only relates to the operational stages of a project, rather than including construction and decommissioning.

Under planning legislation, conditions requiring monitoring may be attached to planning permissions. However, Circular 1/85[7] establishes the following five tests of validity for conditions: (i) relevant to planning; (ii) relevant to the development; (iii) reasonableness; (iv) certainty; and (v) enforceability. As well as meeting these tests any conditions should not duplicate powers to require monitoring under other legislation such as IPC. Planning agreements (S106s or S50s) including provisions for monitoring may also be arranged. With the agreement of all relevant land holders these are a means of enabling off-site monitoring. Although not binding legislation, the EEC eco-audit and management scheme[8] and British Standard 7750[9] are also relevant to EIA follow-up, particularly the EEC scheme as this requires site-specific reporting. However, environmental management auditing takes several years to set up and normally only relates to the operational phase of the project life cycle.

EEC Directive 90/313 on the freedom of access to information on the environment was transposed into UK legislation at the end of 1992[10]. Again this relates to operational projects; however, it may help facilitate EIA monitoring and audit on a voluntary basis.

Reasons for EIA monitoring and audit

The requirement for follow-up checks could lead to an improvement in the environmental design of projects even before these designs leave the drawing board. However, the main reason for carrying out monitoring and audit is because it can facilitate extension of the environmental design process beyond the point of development consent. In some cases this continuous design may need to be more substantial than 'fine tuning'. At present project EIA is failing to take into account wider sustainability issues. Effects monitoring in EIA can play a part in indicating when local critical environmental thresholds and capacity limits are being approached. In some cases it may detect unanticipated effects at an early stage. In addition, predictive techniques audits can enable the calibration of EIA methods and the testing of mitigation measure effectiveness.

These are all good reasons based on the need to protect the environment. However, developers and government have also to take into account other considerations, such as the need to avoid costs and help promote the development industry. The additional costs of EIA have always been of great concern. This is partly because there is a risk that the project may not gain development consent, and also because pre-development costs may incur high levels of interest. In the UK the DoE argues that regulation to require post EIA analysis would impose unacceptable costs on developers and lead to overlaps with other regulations. Long-term commitments to monitoring are undoubtedly costly; however, the potential financial benefits are seldom emphasised. Compared with up-front EIA costs there is less risk involved and the monitoring may be financed out of returns from the project. Effects monitoring may actually reduce costs by avoiding the need for unexpected mitigation at a later stage. In some cases establishing that effects have not arisen can remove the need for costly mitigation measures altogether. EIA audits involving project operational stages may reduce costs by helping to identify excessive waste of materials and energy. Finally, EIA monitoring can help establish liability for pollution, thereby avoiding costly litigation and helping to keep down rising insurance premiums.

Discussion about best practice EIA rarely addresses the relative resourcing of EIA tasks. It could be argued that resources should be reallocated from providing extensive baseline analyses (and in some cases sophisticated predictions) towards better monitoring and management of effects. Agreed amendments to the Directive include a limited provision for improved scoping of EIAs. Scoping and monitoring requirements are not unrelated in that a more focused EIA may enable more resources to be devoted to follow-up.

One other important reason why developers should invest in EIA follow-up work is that the findings can be used to support any similar applications in the future. This explains why larger more active developers have been more involved in EIA monitoring and audit.

Past EIA audit research

There has been very little recent research into EIA follow-up or mitigation in the UK. This is partly because relatively few projects have been operational for a long enough period, given that an adequate time series is needed so that a project's effects can be evaluated and that many mitigation measures are 'time dependent'. However, it should be noted that most of the EIA Regulations have now been in effect for a full seven years, and so this lack of research cannot be entirely attributed to project phasing limitations.

In 1980 a team at CEMP (Aberdeen University) set out to investigate the feasibility of carrying out EIA audits for a range of projects[11]. After a broad scale survey, four projects were selected for detailed audits: Sullom Voe and Flotta oil terminals, Cow Green reservoir and the Redcar steelworks. A key finding was that only about 10% of all the predictions taken together could be audited. Between 50% and 60% of the predictions of each project were found to be accurate; however, no general bias in predictions was found. The reasons for the low number of predictions that could be audited included vague ES predictions, alterations to the project design during later stages of the EIA process, and a lack of appropriate time series monitoring data. It was found that in most cases monitoring activity was not geared towards effects monitoring. Significantly, only a very few effects occurred which were not included in ESs. The research showed that it is difficult to carry out EIA audits unless monitoring and auditing requirements have been considered during the early stages of the EIA.

The work may have provided more valuable results if a larger number of projects had been examined. Due to the remit of the agency funding the research, only effects on the natural and physical environment were examined, and so the audits were not full project EIA audits. Reports of the research findings failed to clarify the exact criteria used to establish prediction accuracy. The research was limited because it did not attempt to explore the reasons for the levels of prediction accuracy determined. In addition, the research methodology can be criticised because it did not address the following difficult problem with EIA audit research: the ease with which predictions can be audited may be automatically related to the accuracy of the predictions. A systematic review of the quality of predictions in ESs could be carried out to establish whether there is any correlation between more clearly stated predictions and observed accuracy. However a more intractable problem could remain in that developers producing ESs with the most accurate predictions may be the same developers who carry out the most effects monitoring.

In a major study, researchers at Northwestern University, USA, audited forecasts in 29 representative ESs submitted in the USA during the mid-1970s[12]. A content analysis of the ES predictions revealed that most (86%) were imprecise in one way or another. It was therefore thought safer to use the term 'forecast' rather than 'prediction'. The researchers were able to find monitoring data to test about 15% of these forecasts. Only about 50% of the forecasts were found to be either close or at least within the range of a vague forecast. However, very few forecasts were found to be clearly inaccurate, and there were almost no unanticipated effects. These findings are generally consistent with the earlier CEMP study findings in the UK.

Work in Australia has been carried out on all the testable predictions in ESs submitted during the late 1970s[13]. The accuracy of each prediction was standardised by expressing it as a ratio of the actual effects to the predicted effects, so that a comparison could be made across different types of predictions. It was found that for any testable prediction the accuracy was about 44%, meaning that the observed effect coincided with the predicted effect by only that amount on average. It was also found that the more severe the effect, the less accurate were the predictions. Emissions predictions were found to be more accurate than environmental quality predictions.

Recent EIA monitoring and audit research

Project description audits

Project description audits are a form of EIA implementation audit which aims to establish whether projects in ESs are implemented in the way they were proposed. It should be noted that the CEMP study had found that in many cases predictions were rendered inauditable because of later alterations to project design. Research has recently been carried out into the degree of alterations to project design occurring after the submission of the ES[14]. A representative sample of 30 ES projects was examined. It was found that 15 out of the 30 underwent some form of design alteration post ES and Table 7.1 provides a summary of these. The key finding was that in about half the altered cases no further EIA work was undertaken and for a third of them there was very little further consultation on the redesign. Environmentally beneficial alterations tended to be made despite a poor ES, rather than in response to one of better quality. Other recent research has also found that about half of the projects examined underwent alterations after ES submission[15].

Design changes to the Corby CCGT power station in Northamptonshire provide an example of substantial alterations. Figure 7.2(a) shows the site layout in the ES for the outline application, while Fig. 7.2(b) shows the layout that was finally approved by the LPA (at the reserved matters stage). The two plans in each figure are at the same scale and orientation so that a direct comparison can be made. It can be seen that the main changes relate to a change of cooling system and the site access. The change in cooling system arose because of inadequate consultation at an early stage of the EIA. The ES justified the choice of location partly because of proximity to Eyebrook Reservoir, which it was proposed would be used as a source of cooling water. However, this reservoir was in fact an SSSI, but this had not been established because initial consultation had been made with the wrong regional branch of the Nature Conservancy Council (NCC). Once aware of this the NCC objected to the

Table 7.1 Project alterations after ES submission from a sample of 30 projects[14]

	Type of project	Main alterations
1	Corby CCGT power station, Northamptonshire	Change from water to air cooling process. Redesign of site planning
2	Killingholme A CCGT power station, Humberside	Rephasing and redesign of turbine modules. Redesign of site planning
3	Isle of Grain CCGT power station, Kent	Rephasing of turbines with increased capacity. Changes to site planning
4	Ling Hall quarry, Warwickshire	Major changes to landform and land use in restoration scheme, involving increased extraction and infilling
5	Doddington Crossing quarry, Northamptonshire	Redesignation of some of the land uses in restoration scheme from recreation to agriculture
6	Symon opencast coal mine, Shropshire	Redesignation of some of the land uses in restoration scheme from agriculture to recreation
7	Delabole windfarm, Cornwall	Change to number of turbine blades
8	Llandinam windfarm, Powys	Resiting of turbines at same location
9	Coca-Cola plant, Brackmills, Northamptonshire	Change to warehousing system with major reduction in building height. Reduction in water requirements. Rephasing, involving part development as a distribution depot
10	Cowley Rover works redevelopment, Oxford	Major highway modifications. Rephasing
11	A39 Wadebridge By-pass, Cornwall	Increase in bridge height over Camel estuary
12	Blackwater Valley route (centre section), Surrey	Rerouting of accommodating road to protect meadow habitats
13	Cotswold Water Park holiday village, Gloucestershire	Redesignation and management of lakes to protect ecology. Major resiting of lodges
14	Coleshill sewage incinerator, Birmingham	Decrease in stack height
15	Botley hazardous waste transfer station, Hampshire	Major reduction in range and quantity of wastes to be stored

application until an additional assessment had been carried out on the ecological effects of abstraction, primarily on waterfowl. The consultants undertook this assessment and a separate document was made available in May 1989, which concluded that the effects would not be significant. However, this did not reassure the NCC and in effect an impasse was reached. Finally the developer proposed a change of process from water cooling to air cooling. The LPA were formally notified about the effects of the design change by way of a letter. The LPA agreed to the alteration, and the project was granted outline consent.

The change in site access arose at the reserved matter stage. This was

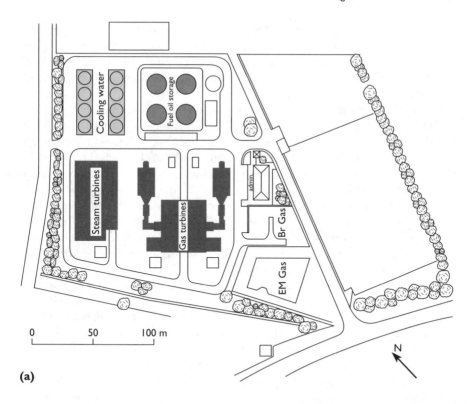

(a)

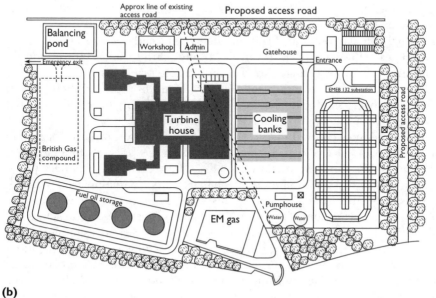

(b)

Fig. 7.2 Corby CCGT power station: (a) site plan in ES (adapted), September 1988; (b) site plan given consent

because the LPA wanted the option of using the through site road to service adjoining land owned by the local authority to the north of the site. This led to the major change in site layout for the power station, which was approved without any formal reassessment of environmental effects or further consultation being carried out.

Proposals for sand and gravel extraction followed by landfill at Ling Hall Airfield, near Rugby in Warwickshire, illustrates another example of a post ES alteration. The existing use was agricultural, but the site had been an airfield and the tarmac runways remained in place. The alterations made after the ES was submitted relate to the proposed restoration and landscaping schemes. It was stated in the ES that the runways would be retained, with landfilling around them (see Fig. 7.3(a)). The basic objective of the restoration strategy put forward in the ES was to enhance opportunities for informal recreation through the provision of a municipal nine hole golf course and a nature conservation area with fishing lakes, and the runways would facilitate access onto the site.

The LPA had been consulted prior to the submission of the ES; however, after a fuller consideration of the proposals they advised the applicants that the runways should be removed to create a more sympathetic final landform and allow more extraction and landfilling (see Fig. 7.3(b)). To achieve this the nature conservation area had to be reduced in size and the fishing lakes proposal had to be abandoned. After a further period of time the applicants also dropped the proposal for the golf course. Comparison of Figs 7.3(a) and 7.3(b) shows that the overall restoration strategy was changed from recreational use to agricultural use. No formal environmental assessment work was carried out on the potential effects (both positive and negative) of these alterations. Local consultees who had been involved during earlier stages were not re-consulted over the changes to the restoration proposals or the possible effects of increased working followed by landfill. Some of these effects may have been significant issues, such as noise from the removal of the runways and an increase in vehicle movements.

It is sometimes claimed that, relative to other sections, project description in ESs is of a reliably high quality; however, these research findings show that many ESs can have a short shelf-life. Many practising planners would acknowledge that post-submission changes are commonplace. What is surprising is that the EIA Regulations have been drawn up without any mechanisms for dealing with this, particularly as earlier research such as the CEMP study[16] highlighted this as an issue. This is a good example of EIA practice suffering from its introduction into existing consent procedures. The lack of transparency during the later stages of the EIA process is in some cases a cause for suspicions to be raised, and this is not helped by the tendency within LPAs to think in terms of amended applications rather than altered applications. Changes to the Regulations, such as a requirement for the submission of an addendum (as distinct from further information),

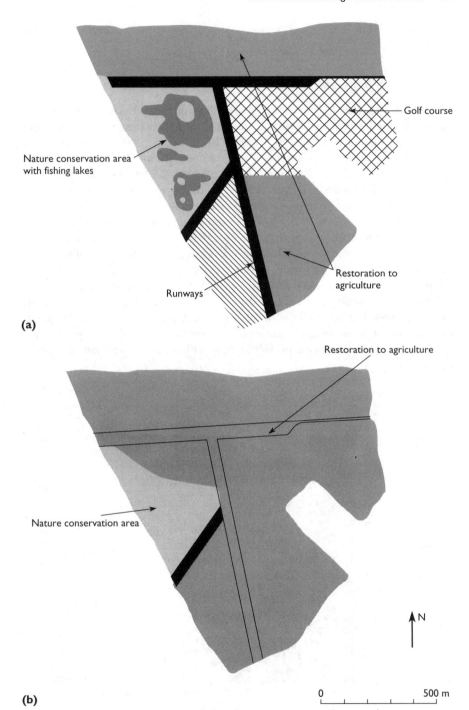

Fig. 7.3 (a) Ling Hall quarry restoration scheme in ES (adapted), March 1990; (b) Ling Hall quarry restoration scheme given consent, August 1990

would consolidate existing EIA practice and foster greater certainty in the planning system.

Monitoring proposals in ESs

A contents analysis of a representative sample of almost 700 ESs and summaries of ESs (taken from the Institute of Environmental Assessment's *Digest of Environmental Statements*[17]) has been carried out to establish the extent of monitoring proposals made within them. It was found that approximately 30% of ESs included at least one reference to further monitoring. The analysis revealed (Fig. 7.4) that proposals to monitor effects are far from comprehensive, with only a few cases of proposals to monitor over a range of effects. The type of monitoring stated was found to be heavily dependent on the type of project. For example landfill monitoring proposals are skewed towards leachate, landfill gas and water quality, rather than other issues such as traffic, noise or ecology. There was also a tendency for particular consultancies to produce ESs with more monitoring proposals than others. This perhaps reflects their ability to carry out later monitoring work themselves. The analysis has also revealed (Fig. 7.5) that water quality monitoring (a form of environmental monitoring) was the most frequent proposal, being even more prevalent than either air or aqueous emissions monitoring.

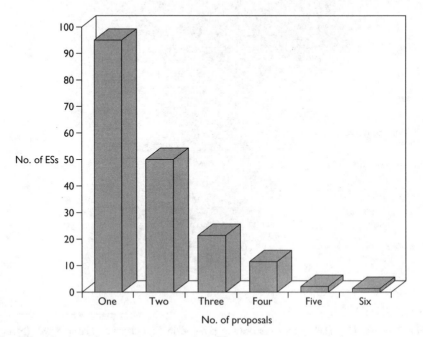

Fig. 7.4 Number of monitoring proposals in ESs

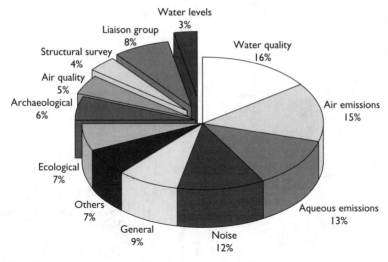

Fig. 7.5 Types of monitoring in ESs

Monitoring arrangements in practice

Further research has recently been carried out to compare monitoring proposals in ESs to monitoring arrangements actually set up. Selecting those ESs with monitoring proposals where the project had started, a broadly representative sample of 17 projects was selected. Contact was made with the relevant LPAs to establish any monitoring arrangements for each project. Although the findings are only preliminary the key overall finding was that ESs tend to understate rather than overstate the actual monitoring arrangements set up (see Fig. 7.6). This understatement works out at approximately 30%. Perhaps surprisingly, there were very few cases where monitoring proposals actually came to nothing. In general, for any given project the monitoring arrangements in practice cover a wider range of environmental effects than those covered by the monitoring proposals in the ES. There are some examples of very extensive monitoring arrangements such as those for the Second Severn Crossing, the Cardiff Bay Barrage and the Calder Valley sewage incinerator.

The main reason why ESs tend to understate the monitoring arrangements set up is because much of this monitoring is required either under planning conditions (or agreements) or because of later licensing conditions, such as those applied under IPC. It should be noted however that this research has not established whether or not this monitoring is appropriate for EIA monitoring and audit or of an adequate standard. In fact in some cases monitoring may not even be carried out, as LPAs have applied conditions requiring monitoring data to be supplied only if problems arise.

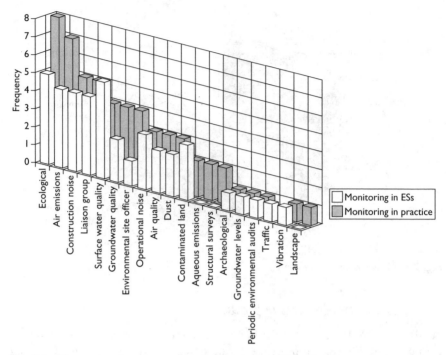

Fig. 7.6 Comparison between monitoring proposals in ESs and arrangements in practice

Audits of visual impact and mitigation

Recent research into the adequacy of visual effects assessment involved both audits for project effects and the implementation of mitigation measures[18]. Although the findings are limited owing to the small number of projects audited, the following tentative generalisations can be made. As later research has confirmed (see above) it was found that project design is often altered following submission of the ES. Surveillance at the sites showed that visual effects were consistently underestimated or just not stated, especially in terms of the number of affected properties or for settlements further away. However, mitigation measures were generally adhered to.

Recent project audit work

Toyota plant study

The Toyota plant study considered the economic, labour market, land use and environmental effects of the Toyota plant development at Burnaston, Derbyshire[19]. The ES was produced for an outline planning application, and interestingly the quality of the follow-up study is of a much higher standard than the earlier ES. In general the ES was unspecific about both the project timescale and socio-economic effects. The vagueness of the original socio-economic predictions makes them untestable even though the audit report provides a wealth of data on this. The ES did however underestimate the direct workforce by a small amount. Compared with the Structure Plan projections the audit report suggests that the development has not led to the demand for several thousand housing units, while the industrial space required by associated development in the county has fallen short by several hundred hectares. The audit report treats other issues in a more cursory way. The ES identified traffic effects as potentially significant, and the audit report confirmed that the construction phase clearly had a significant effect on traffic flows on the A38. The ES stated that emissions would not breach consent levels. However, water quality consent limits were breached during construction.

Windfarm construction audits

This study examined landscape and ecological effects, together with public attitude issues, for three windfarms at various stages of construction[20]. Although the emphasis of the work was more general than just the testing of ES predictions, it represents a useful follow-up study, examining construction effects which are often neglected in audit work. It also looked at the perception of environmental effects by those living nearby, using a control site where no windfarm applications had been made. A key finding was that the visibility of completed windfarms was greater than predicted with developments noticeable at distances greater than 15 kilometres. This is significant because zone of visual influence analyses are not normally carried out beyond a distance of 15 kilometres. In general terms the audit confirmed predictions that the ecological effects would be low. The social survey work found that the environmental effects were considered acceptable with windfarms being viewed in a positive light.

However, the findings should be interpreted cautiously as monitoring of visibility took place in winter, and the key finding was based largely on results from only one windfarm.

Ongoing project audit studies

The Energy Technology Support Group has commissioned several other windfarm studies. A project effects audit of the Cemmaes windfarm in Powys has been carried out. A range of effects, including visual, noise, ecological, traffic and economic outcomes, has been examined for all project stages. Techniques have been audited for visual predictions and ecological reinstatement. An audit report is due to be published, while a sociological effects study has already been published[21].

A visual prediction techniques audit is currently under way using eight windfarms. A preliminary finding is that the general extent of visibility is not as great as that suggested by the construction monitoring study (referred to above) partly owing to the effects of summer haze[22]. A before and after noise audit has been carried out for the windfarm at Delabole and the results are due to be published, while other completed work has involved testing ES predictions for visual effects, noise and electromagnetic interference at this windfarm[23]. This found that, despite there being a change in the type of turbines used, the predictions were broadly accurate, with the noise predictions confirming the 'best case' scenario in the ES.

Follow-up work for projects not subject to EIA Regulations

Windfarms have only recently been added to Schedule 2 of the EIA Regulations. However, all of the windfarms referred to above were dealt with under the EIA Regulations because the need for formal EIA had been agreed between the LPA and the applicants. The following sections report on major audit studies where the initial appraisal work was carried out before the EIA Regulations came into effect.

Sizewell B PWR construction: monitoring and audit of local socio-economic effects

An ES was not prepared for the public inquiry, which took place during the mid-1980s. However, predictions and mitigation measures were provided in a series of inquiry reports[24]. Construction of the power station began in 1987 and monitoring work has been supported by Nuclear Electric since 1988. The work is especially useful in the field of EIA because it relates to several weak areas in current practice: socio-economic assessment, construction effects and monitoring. Monitoring reports for the first six years of construction have now been published[25]. An important feature of the work has been the close attention given to monitoring the local employment effects as this underpins many related socio-economic effects. The study methodology is robust in the way monitoring data have been collected from a variety of sources at repeated intervals over a relatively long period. The perceived effects have also been monitored.

The overall finding from the study is that many of the predictions used in the Sizewell B public inquiry were inaccurate because of a considerable underestimate of the build-up of construction employment. However, there may possibly have been an overestimate of the secondary effects on the local economy[26]. It was forecast that about one-third of peak construction employment should go to local people, whilst the actual proportion was slightly higher. Appraisal work at the inquiry stage was less successful in recognising that construction noise would be perceived as a significant local issue. In general the surveys of local residents revealed more negative than positive perceived effects, with increased traffic (and worker disturbance) being viewed as the major negative effect. Increased employment and local trade were seen as the major benefits.

In addition to the audit of predictions the study has enabled the following: the compilation of a database to inform other assessments (such as that for a new PWR, Sizewell C, on an adjacent site) and better project management including checks on the implementation of conditions.

Road appraisal follow-up work

Trunk road effects audits were carried out in 1991 for the Transport and Road Research Laboratory by a consultancy team led by Rendel Planning[27]. Four trunk roads that were dealt with at inquiries between 1983 and 1986 were selected as case studies. One of the selection criteria for the case studies was that the traffic levels expected were broadly the same as those experienced, and this perhaps limits the representativeness of the findings. The predictions presented in *Manual of Environmental Appraisal* (MEA) frameworks were audited. Although relating to environmental appraisals that were undertaken before the EIA Regulations came into effect, the findings of this follow-up work are of particular relevance to EIA work for roads because early ESs (1988–1993) tended to be based on the MEA framework approach. For each case study a series of physical surveys was carried out (in most cases these were for noise, air pollution, ecology, traffic levels and land use changes). The research dealt with the longer term nature of some effects (e.g. ecological effects) by carrying out in-depth interviews with experts to substantiate whether the original predictions would prove to be correct. Questionnaire surveys were carried out to establish whether any unanticipated effects had arisen. As well as examining the perceived effects, the approach adopted was useful because it attempted to examine the underlying causes of prediction inaccuracy and also to establish improved procedures for monitoring road schemes.

In overall terms about 60% of MEA forecasts were found to be within 5% of the recorded effects based on existing MEA techniques and the perceptions of questionnaire respondents. Only 12% of all the MEA entries could be identified to be over 5% inaccurate. The remaining entries were basically unauditable owing to factors such as their imprecise presentation in the frameworks. The most frequent cause of forecast inaccuracy related to computational errors, followed by unforeseen changes in external factors (e.g. new buildings blocking views). Interestingly, in a few cases, inaccuracies in the original baseline surveys were identified as a cause of prediction error. It was found that the most important omissions of forecast effects in the frameworks related to the following: fumes and dust, traffic management effects and effects on a range of community facilities.

Manchester Metrolink audit

The Manchester Metrolink audit is a comprehensive project effects audit of the development of the light rapid transit system in Greater Manchester[28]. The actual effects of the scheme were assessed and compared with predictions made in 1983 in an environmental evaluation of the system options. A standardised approach was taken in reviewing the accuracy of each prediction. This was based on the importance of the effects in terms of determining whether the project should have gone ahead. In general the audit did not identify any unexpected effects, and the magnitude of several effects was actually lower. In particular, direct severance and visual effects during the operating stages in the city centre were found to be lower than predicted. Also direct noise and vibration effects during the operational stage for two of the lines were lower than predicted in one of the scenarios, but not in the other scenario.

EIA monitoring: some good practice maxims

The following examples of good practice have been drawn from recent research, particularly the contents analysis of ESs for monitoring proposals.

The findings from research into project description audits suggest that ESs should pay greater attention to the uncertainties involved in specifying actually what the final project will turn out to be like. Where late alterations in project design do arise, further EIA work will need to be undertaken. This should be documented in an addendum with further consultation on this being carried out. For example the design of the CCGT power station on the Isle of Grain was rephased, abandoning an open cycle stage (allowing oil to be used) in favour of a totally closed cycle design. A comprehensive addendum to the original ES was submitted[29]. This even acknowledged that the final design was still uncertain, and an assessment was carried out on alternative designs. For each environmental receptor the assessment work was based on its worst case project design. For example, the visual assessment was based on the design with the highest emission stacks, whereas the local air pollution assessment was undertaken on the stacks with the greatest local effects.

Predictions in ESs should be explicitly linked to monitoring where possible. It is notable that ES review packages, such as that of Lee and Colley (1990)[30], give little emphasis to how well different ES sections are related to each other; instead the approach advocated is to review the ES by dissecting it. Responses to monitoring results, in terms of mitigation, should also be specified in the ES. The use of trigger levels is an effective way of achieving this. For example in the ES for a new CCGT power station at Barking Reach it was predicted that the outflow from the cooling pipes into the Thames would not increase the localised temperature of the water above a critical threshold of 21.5 °C. Temperature monitoring in the vicinity of the pipes was proposed, and if it was found that the predictions were inaccurate, a standby air cooling system would be brought into operation[31].

Proposals for monitoring in ESs should establish the following: which environmental parameters will be used to monitor particular effects, who will be responsible for actually carrying out the measurements, where and how often readings will be taken, and finally details on how the results will be reported. Only a very few UK ESs provide all this information in the form of a monitoring programme. The ES for a port extension at Peterhead Bay provided such a programme as part of an environmental management plan[32]. The benefit of a monitoring programme in an ES is that it provides decision makers and consultees with a comprehensive overview, so that suggestions for improvement can be made[33].

Research findings from the comparison between monitoring proposals in ESs and monitoring arrangements in practice suggest that ESs should be more explicit about monitoring that may be required under other legislation and consent procedures. In general, examples of this can be found when the ES supports more than one type of application (e.g. planning consent and a discharge licence). Some of the larger consultancies are better at setting ESs within the context of other environmental legislation. This is because they are increasingly involved in work both before and after the development application stage, often for the same project.

Ideally baseline monitoring should start well in advance of project implementation. An adequate time series of measurements is required so that any effects audit is not misleading because of the natural variability of the parameters being measured. The best cases of this arise where an existing project is to be extended. For example with the Sedgehill landfill extension, a good baseline for landfill gas and leachate effects existed because these had been monitored for the original development[34]. However, before and after monitoring is not the only approach to effects auditing. Monitoring at control sites (similar sites unaffected by the development) can be compared with the effects monitoring, although this approach is relatively rare (possibly because it doubles the cost). For example in examining public attitudes to windfarm developments, surveys are often also carried out in areas well away from any windfarms. A survey into the perceived effects of the Delabole windfarm adopted both a before and after and a control approach[35]. Another example could be where water quality monitoring is carried out both upstream and downstream of a facility[36].

Monitoring frequencies should normally be greater during the earlier project stages. For example with the Calder Valley sewage incinerator it was proposed that environmental management audits should initially be carried out every six months but that later the frequency should be reduced to every three years[37].

Monitoring should perhaps be more comprehensive during the pre-implementation stages and narrowed down during later stages to focus on the most significant effects. For example with the Cardiff Bay Barrage, this approach has been taken to monitor the extent of flooding. Pre-project groundwater levels have been measured at 130 boreholes; however, during later stages measurements will be taken at about 35 boreholes in the most sensitive locations[38]. Monitoring arrangements should also be focused on those aspects of prediction and management where there is greatest uncertainty.

Where possible, more than one source of information should be relied on to monitor an effect. This allows the data to be verified, which is important because it needs to be established that the uncertainty associated with the monitoring is less than that relating to the prediction work. If regulatory agencies are also carrying out monitoring, the arrangements should be co-ordinated so that duplication of monitoring frequencies is avoided. For example with the Lount landfill, the developer proposed to monitor aqueous emissions into a nearby stream once a month. The NRA were also proposing to monitor each month and so it was agreed to phase the monitoring so that the frequency changed to once every two weeks[39].

The growing use of environmental site officers during construction is an effective means of improving liaison between the EIA team and the construction teams, as well as that between the developer and local interests. The Second Severn Crossing and the Blackwater Valley Road (Central Section) are both good examples of this approach. The site officer could be given the following roles: ensuring that commitments in the ES are fulfilled, auditing site environmental procedures, and reviewing environmental effects where changes in design have been necessary since the ES[40].

EIAs should be more closely linked to environmental management systems (EMSs). These require periodic 'environmental audits' of project operations. The EIA, a code of practice and any consent conditions imposed can all be seen as the initial building blocks of an EMS[41]. The EIA can be used to identify the effects to be managed, and baseline data in the ES can provide a basis for the EMS. The code of practice can be used to set up thresholds and goals, while the conditions could represent the start of a register of environmental standards to be complied with. Very few ESs refer to any future environmental auditing; however, the Calder Valley sewage incinerator mentioned above is a good example. The consultancy which undertook this EIA has been commissioned to carry out off-site air and ground monitoring every six months for a three year period[42]. The Billingham waste management facility ES provides another example of a proposed EMS[43].

EIA monitoring and audit: wider implications

Clearly the testing of predictions has major implications for the credibility of EIA as a process. Environmental interest groups (particularly at the local level) often take a cynical view of EIA. The argument is often made that developers overstate project benefits and down play negative effects in ESs. If this is the case, it could be partly due to contextual factors. EIA Regulations in the UK were introduced into existing decision-making procedures as a consequence of a European Directive. Continental consent procedures differ from those in the UK. On the continent, planning systems generally require comprehensive information and decision making is inquisitorial. In the UK, specific information is required by a planning system which itself takes a comprehensive view, while decision making is often adversarial[44]. When EIA is required in the UK, developers have to adopt a more continental approach which is comprehensive and less adversarial. The recent change in approach required by the EIA Regulations may have led to biased predictions in the UK, especially as formal review procedures are often not adopted. EIA monitoring and auditing are needed to help establish whether this situation may have arisen.

Monitoring and auditing can also contribute to the theoretical development of EIA in the UK. As formal EIA activity has only developed recently in the UK, research has not yet related practice to any theoretical context. EIA originated in the USA during the late 1960s, largely from rational systems theory. This prescribes that optimal decisions result if rational decision makers are presented with accurate and comprehensive information. One of the main aims of EIA as a procedural tool is to provide decision makers with better information and this stems directly from this theory. Other research is now being carried out into whether decision makers use EIA information rationally. EIA audit research examines the nature of the information provided. Together these new research directions may throw light on whether rational theory should continue to underpin EIA practice in the UK. Findings may suggest that the emphasis of EIA in the UK should be changed from trying to optimise decision making towards optimising post-decision management.

Conclusion

From the monitoring and audit work reviewed the following general points can be arrived at. Past research has shown that there are inherent problems in carrying out EIA audit work. Where predictions could be tested, approximately 50% were considered to be accurate. An important common finding was that very few unexpected effects were discovered, which suggests that the identification of effects is a robust feature of EIA. More recent research into visual and landscape assessment suggests that the extent of visual effects tends to be underestimated in ESs. However, visual mitigation measures do generally get implemented. Project descriptions in ESs can often have a short shelf-life owing to design alterations in later stages. Given the lack of any EIA regulations or guidance referring to monitoring, the finding that 30% of ESs include some form of monitoring proposal is encouraging, although these proposals tend to be focused on only a few effects. Preliminary research suggests that monitoring arrangements in practice are greater in number and may cover a more comprehensive range of effects for each project than is proposed in ESs.

The review of recent EIA audit work carried out by consultancies (involving quite a wide range of project types) raises several issues. In some cases the quality and rigour of the follow-up work is of a *higher standard* than the earlier assessment work. This may be a reflection of the increasing experience of practitioners and also a more focused remit. Consultants involved with the early EIA work are sometimes retained to carry out the follow-up work. This may raise issues relating to objectivity; however, it could be more appropriate in those cases where the ES work involved high levels of subjective judgement. Finally, most of the research and work reviewed shows a lack of emphasis on examining the *underlying causes* of audit findings. This is the key issue to be addressed if follow-up work is to provide an effective feedback.

Notes and references

1 Duinker, P N (1989) Ecological effects monitoring in environmental impact assessment: what can it accomplish?, *Environmental Management*, Vol. 13, No. 6, 797–805.
2 Tomlinson, P and S F Atkinson (1987) Environmental audits: proposed terminology, *Environmental Monitoring and Assessment*, Vol. 8, pp 187–198.
3 Commission of the European Communities (1994) Proposal to amend EC Directive 85/337/EEC, *Official Journal*, Vol. C130, No. 37, 12 May, Brussels.
4 Sheate, W (1994) *Making an Impact: A Guide to EIA Law and Policy*. London: Cameron May.
5 DoE (1989) *Environmental Assessment: A Guide to the Procedures*. London: HMSO.
6 DoE (1994) *Draft Guide on Preparing Environmental Statements for Planning Projects*. London: Land Use Consultants, HMSO.
7 DoE (1985) Circular 1/85: *The Use of Conditions in Planning Permissions*. London: HMSO.
8 Commission of the European Communities (CEC) (1993) Council Regulation (EEC) No. 1836/93 allowing for voluntary participation by companies in a Community eco-management and audit scheme, *Official Journal*, Vol. 168, 10 July, Brussels, pp 1–18.
9 British Standards Institution (1994) *Specification for Environmental Management Systems, BS 7750:1994*. Milton Keynes: British Standards Institution.
10 The Environment Information Regulations 1992, S.I. 1992 No. 3240, 31 December.
11 Bisset, R (1984) Post-development audits to investigate the accuracy of environmental impact predictions, *Zeitschrift für Umweltpolitik*, Vol. 7, pp 463–484.
12 Culhane, P J, H P Friesema and J A Beecher (1987) *Forecasts and Environmental Decision Making: The Content and Predictive Accuracy of Environmental Impact Statements*. London: Westview Press.
13 Buckley, R (1991) How accurate are environmental impact predictions, *Ambio*, Vol. 20, No. 3–4, May, pp 161–162.

14 Frost, R (1993) Planning beyond Environmental Statements, MSc Dissertation. Oxford: School of Planning, Oxford Brookes University.

15 Wood, C and C Jones (1992) The impact of environmental assessment on local planning authorities, *Journal of Environmental Planning and Management*, Vol. 35, No. 2, 115–127; Lee, N, N F Walsh and G Reeder (1994) Assessing the performance of the EA process, *Project Appraisal*, Vol. 9, No. 3, September, pp 161–172.

16 Bisset, R, *op. cit.*

17 Institute of Environmental Assessment (1993) *Digest of Environmental Statements*. London: Sweet & Maxwell.

18 Mills, J D (1992) The adequacy of visual impact assessments in Environmental Statements, MSc Dissertation. Oxford: Oxford Brookes University.

19 Ecotech Research and Consulting Ltd (1994) Toyota Impact Study summary, unpublished.

20 Chris Blandford Associates (1994) Wind Turbine Power Station Construction Monitoring Study, in association with the University of Wales for Countryside Council for Wales, February.

21 Energy Technology Support Unit (ETSU) (1994) Cemmaes Wind Farm: Sociological Impact Study, Market Research Associates and Dulas Engineering, ETSU, March.

22 Stevens, R (1995) Dulas Engineering Ltd, personal communication, March.

23 Wood, G (1994) An investigation into the environmental impact of windfarm developments, BA Dissertation. Cambridge: University of Cambridge.

24 Department of Energy (1986) *Sizewell B Public Inquiry: Report by Sir Frank Layfield*. London: HMSO.

25 Glasson, J, A Chadwick and R Therivel (1989–1994) Local socio-economic impacts of the Sizewell B PWR Construction Project, First to Sixth Annual Monitoring Reports. Oxford: Impacts Assessment Unit, School of Planning, Oxford Brookes University.

26 Glasson, J, R Therivel and A Chadwick (1994) *Introduction to Environmental Impact Assessment*. London: UCL Press.

27 Rendel Planning (1992) Techniques for environmental monitoring: an assessment of the accuracy of four MEA frameworks, Draft Final Report to Transport and Road Research Laboratory, unpublished.

28 Jones, C and N Lee (1993) *Post-Auditing in Environmental Impact Assessment: The Greater Manchester Metrolink Scheme*. Occasional Paper 37, Manchester: Department of Planning and Landscape, University of Manchester.

29 Applied Energy Services Ltd (1991) AES Medway Generating Plant Environmental Impact Statement Addendum. Prepared by Trevor Crocker and Partners, May.

30 Lee, N and R Colley (1990) *Reviewing Environmental Statements*. Occasional Paper 24, Manchester: Department of Planning and Landscape, University of Manchester.

31 Barking Power Ltd (1990) Barking Reach gas power project, Environmental Impact Statement. Prepared by Ashdown Environmental Ltd, December.

32 Peterhead Bay Authority (1992) West End of ASCo south base development, Environmental Impact Statement. Prepared by Peter Fraenkel BMT Ltd, April.

33 Petts, J and G Eduljee (1994) Integration of monitoring, auditing and environmental assessment: waste facility issues, *Project Appraisal*, Vol. 9, No. 4, December, pp 231–241.

34 Northumberland County Council (1988) Sedgehill landfill extension, Environmental Impact Statement. Prepared by Northumberland CC Waste Disposal Section, December.

35 Exeter Enterprises Ltd (1993) Attitudes to windpower in Devon and Cornwall, Report.
36 Northumberland County Council (1988) *op. cit.*
37 Yorkshire Water Authority (1990) Calder Valley sewage sludge incinerator, Environmental Impact Statement. Prepared by Environmental Resources Ltd, February.
38 Cardiff Bay Development Corporation (1988) Cardiff Bay Barrage Bill, Environmental Impact Statement. Prepared by Environmental Advisory Unit, November.
39 Midland Land Reclamation Ltd (1992) Lount landfill scheme, Environmental Impact Statement. Prepared by Golder Associates, June.
40 Hill, M (1994) Impact monitoring in EIA: the Second Severn Crossing. Paper at the Institute of Environmental Assessment's 3rd Annual Conference, September.
41 Allett, T (1993) From assessment to audit. Paper presented at the Conference EIA in the UK: Evaluation and Prospect, University of Manchester, April.
42 Yorkshire Water Authority (1990) *op. cit.*
43 Northumbrian Environmental Management (1993) Proposed municipal waste-to-energy facility on the Process Park, Billingham, Cleveland, Environmental Impact Statement. Prepared by Environmental Resources Management, August.
44 Cowan, A (1994) Local authority review and decision-making. Notes of lecture to MSc/Diploma course in environmental assessment, Oxford Brookes University, 22nd February.

CHAPTER 8

EIA AND POLLUTION CONTROL

Elizabeth Street

Introduction

Imagine the scene. It is one week before Christmas in 1990. The Development Control Officer is desperately trying to clear her desk before the holidays when two large planning applications with ESs are put in her in-tray: applications for gas-fired power stations, one for 1000 MW in East London (Barking Power) and the other for 600 MW on the Isle of Grain (AES Medway). Although these applications will be processed and determined by the Department of Trade and Industry, there is a need for Kent County Council (KCC) to review the applications and be assured that the County Council has no objections to the proposals. The information on air pollution impacts at first sight looks incomprehensible and seems to be contradictory. Simple mathematics suggest that if one is two-thirds the size of the other then the emissions from the two chimneys should be comparable, the smaller having two-thirds the emissions of the larger.

It was enough to ponder this over the Christmas break but there had to be an evaluation of these two applications. One application was downwind of the other and both were north-west of most of Kent. Prevailing winds suggested that there was likely to be an air quality issue. Cumulative air impacts needed to be addressed. A system would need to be set up which would allow KCC to develop an approach to cumulative air pollution impacts that was easily understood and could be applied to all future development proposals which were likely to have an impact on air quality in Kent.

Over the next 18 months a total of five applications for incinerators and four for power stations were to be received in the East Thames Corridor. This chapter will describe how this problem was dealt with in Kent, explaining the legislation, the need to consult with statutory consultees and other interested parties in the area of air pollution and how planning consent was granted for these two original schemes but not all the proposals for power stations and incinerators in the East Thames Corridor. Finally we explain how the Kent air quality management system has been developed and is being used to evaluate other proposals with air pollution impacts in Kent.

Finally in this chapter we outline how this experience has led to a widening of approaches to air quality modelling and monitoring which involves a partnership with the districts and the support of central Government and puts Kent in an ideal place to respond to the Government's latest announcement that local authorities need to develop air quality management systems.

There is no longer a need for Development Control Officers to be concerned about how to deal with the air quality issues of applications for power stations and incinerators in Kent.

Legislation on air pollution impacts

Under Article 3 of the EEC Directive 85/337 environmental impact assessment will identify, describe and assess 'the direct and indirect effects of a project including air'[1]. It was therefore correct that these applications for power stations should include information on air emissions and their likely impacts. EC legislation suggests that additional information may be needed to assess the cumulative impacts of development. It was therefore wholly appropriate that KCC should insist that the cumulative air impacts should be assessed.

When a planning application is accompanied by an EIA, the planning department at KCC undertakes a rigorous and systematic approach to the appraisal of the application which is divided into four parts:

- technical review of the ES undertaken by in-house experts or by consultants;
- evaluation of the response from statutory consultees and local interest groups;
- analysis of requests for additional information required from the developer and determining what should be requested;
- review and analysis of responses to any additional information supplied, this information being included in the committee report along with a recommendation to grant or refuse planning consent.

The technical appraisal of the ES for most planning projects can be done in house for most aspects of the environmental information. Maps of the environmental and planning constraints can be drawn up by staff within the planning department. Traffic impacts, noise impacts, archaeological and ecological concerns can all be addressed in house. Air and water quality issues are more difficult as the planning department does not have the expertise internally to deal with these issues and therefore it has to rely heavily on the advice of the National Rivers Authority (NRA) and Her Majesty's Inspectorate of Pollution (HMIP).

Authorisation on integrated pollution control

In the case of disposal of wastes to water, the developer has to apply to the NRA for a discharge consent license. When considering an application for an industrial process classified under the Environmental Protection Act 1990 (EPA) as needing authorisation for integrated pollution control (IPC), the developer has to apply for authorisation. This process is separate from the application for planning consent. Developers often apply for authorisation under IPC later in the development process than the planning application stage. Applications for IPC authorisation are concerned with the technology, industrial process and the limits which will be imposed on the plant for the hours of working and amount of pollution which is allowed to be emitted from the chimney or discharged to sewer/river or disposed of on the land. Generally speaking, developers will obtain outline planning consent before proceeding with HMIP and NRA consents.

Authorisation under IPC is based on establishing that two criteria related to the development proposal have been fully taken into account in the development of the industrial process and the disposal of wastes: that the process conforms to the 'best available technique not entailing excessive costs' (BATNEEC) and that in the disposal of wastes the 'best practicable environmental option' (BPEO) has been chosen.

The granting of authorisation under IPC is not part of the EIA process as outlined in the EEC Directive 85/337. The legislation is interpreted in this country through the Town and Country Planning Acts. EIA is only undertaken as part of the process of granting planning consent. Nevertheless, HMIP is one of the statutory consultees in the process of obtaining planning consent for an application accompanied by an ES. KCC therefore wrote to HMIP as one of the statutory consultees to ask their opinion of the ES.

Response of HMIP

When considering applications for power plants and incinerators, there is obviously a need to understand the production process to be used and consequent emissions which will have impacts on the land, water and air.

The DoE Consultation Paper on Planning Policy Guidance on Planning and Pollution Control (1992) pointed out that close consultation between the pollution control authority and the planning authority is therefore needed to ensure an early understanding of any revised requirements necessary in the judgement of the pollution control authority, and the reasons why alteration to the plant is essential.

At this stage in the development of HMIP authorisation procedures, HMIP was extremely hard pressed to deal with all the applications for authorisation. Their response to requests for their views on planning applications which were accompanied with an ES was to state that the application would be suitable for consideration for authorisation when an application was made under IPC. This cannot be taken to mean that the planning application has been considered in detail by HMIP; in fact very little consideration of the details of the application will be undertaken until the applicant formally submits an application for IPC authorisation. HMIP may wish to change the design and layout of the project, the height of the chimney etc. which will change the environmental impacts of the proposal. These details are not available at the planning application stage unless the developer opts to apply for authorisation under IPC and planning consent at the same time.

HMIP have environmental reference levels and a model to look at multiple emission sources. This suggests that if HMIP had communicated this type of information to KCC, and they had a statutory duty to comment on the ES, KCC could have responded to the applications more quickly and effectively, avoiding the expense of public inquiries resulting from refusal of planning applications due to insufficient information being made available to planning authorities during the processing of planning applications with environmental impact assessments. In the case of one of the applications to be considered in this chapter KCC planning subcommittee had to defer making a decision about the application until reassurance on air pollution impacts had been sought from HMIP.

Clearly, a system where HMIP was not responding to planning applications for power stations and incinerators, and providing information on air quality, was involving local authorities in considerable expense in processing applications where inadequate information was available to deal adequately with the application. In the case of the two power stations, the response was that the application would be suitable for authorisation and therefore no further information on the possible cumulative impact of the development proposals was forthcoming from HMIP.

KCC therefore objected to the Barking Power proposal as the ES accompanying this application had stated that background levels surrounding the site were already exceeding NO_X guidelines set by the EC. For the AES Medway proposal on the Isle of Grain, the planning subcommittee sanctioned money to be spent on hiring a consultant to review the air pollution impacts and to develop a North Kent Air Quality Model which would be able to assess the cumulative impacts of further development proposals in North Kent. Consideration of the AES Medway application was delayed while the model was developed and an assessment of the cumulative impact of the air pollution impacts had been considered.

AES Medway did apply for authorisation at the same time as they applied for planning consent and eventually when their proposal was run through the air quality model KCC was able to support the application to the Department of Trade and Industry.

The North Kent Air Quality Model

In developing the North Kent Air Quality Model it was recognised that the major point sources that needed to be considered were coal-fired power stations, oil-fired power stations, combined cycle gas turbine installations and waste incinerators.

These installations emit a range of substances to the atmosphere including particulates, carbon dioxide, carbon monoxide, metals, acidic gases and hydrocarbon compounds. It was decided for the purpose of the North Kent Air Quality Model to consider NO_X and SO_2 which are common to all installations. The two nitrogen oxides (NO_X) most commonly encountered as primary pollutants are nitric oxide (NO) and nitrogen dioxide (NO_2). NO is converted to NO_2 in the atmosphere principally through reactions with ozone. For the purpose of this study, the conservative view is taken that all NO_X is NO_2. In reality a more realistic estimate would be that 10% of NO_X emitted from a stack is NO_2 and that a further 10% is converted to NO_2 within approximately 1 kilometre of the stack. Therefore ground level concentrations of NO_2 due to a particular source may be represented by 20% of the NO_X concentration.

The area covered by the North Kent Model extends from the western boundary of the County of Kent with London, eastwards to the Medway estuary and from the River Thames south to the M20 motorway. The area covers some of the area of the District Councils of Dartford, Gravesham, Rochester upon Medway, Gillingham and Swale, Sevenoaks and Maidstone representing over 1600 square kilometres of land. The ground elevations vary from low lying flat terrain adjacent to the River Thames to the raised areas of the North Downs. It was felt that topography played an important part in localised pollution situations in Kent and therefore it was important that the model should take into account the topography of Kent. Consideration had been given to extending the INDIC[2] model from London to Kent. But at this time the London INDIC model did not take account of topography and therefore this suggestion was rejected.

Before KCC could evaluate the air pollution impacts of the AES Medway power station, the developers were asked to monitor background levels of NO_X and SO_2 for a 5 kilometre radius around the site, using 25 diffusion tubes for NO_X and five gas bubblers for SO_2. This was done for at least a month; if readings were considered to be unrepresentative the monitoring was continued for another month.

Little information on background levels of pollution in Kent was available at this time. It was therefore important that background monitoring was undertaken to see if the site compared with the predicted background data. It was recognised that this was only a rough estimation of background information.

Information on stack emissions and monitoring information were fed into the US National Environmental Policy Act ISC long term air quality model.

This model predicts the likely impact of the proposed development given that emissions will be from high chimneys. It uses the Gaussian Plume Dispersion Model[3]. The model extends across North Kent from Dartford to Sittingborne and takes into account the topography of the area. This is extremely important as the Thames basin forms an air sink in the area.

Before the model can be run the characteristics of the chimney size and height, together with the volume and type of emissions likely to arise from the process, must be known so that the model can adequately reflect the changes that will occur in air quality as a result of the new development. This is a very important part of the process of evaluating the cumulative impacts of the proposed development. These technical details summarise the information that the developer needs to submit to HMIP for authorisation and therefore give the planning department the technical details which allow a more comprehensive evaluation of the likely pollution impacts at the planning stage.

It was decided at this time to consider only the annual average concentrations of air pollution since the main focus of the work was to determine whether the development would have an adverse cumulative impact on Kent. Short term pollution incidents were not considered at this stage (Table 8.1).

Table 8.1 Data necessary to operate the model

ISCTL grid reference
Stack height (m)
Base elevation of stack (m)
Equivalent stack diameter (m)
Gas exit temperature (K)
Gas exit velocity (m/s)
Load factor (%)
NO_X emission rate (g/s)
SO_2 emission rate (g/s)

Background levels from existing air quality monitoring stations are fed into the model together with information about any new proposed point sources which may increase air emissions. The model indicated that background levels on the Isle of Grain for NO_X were around $25 \, mg/m^3$ and that the AES Medway power station would raise these levels to $27 \, mg/m^3$. We were therefore able to return to committee stating that there was no objection to the power station on air pollution grounds.

Further developments within the East Thames Corridor

Over the next 18 months there was a total of nine applications for power stations and incinerators in the East Thames Corridor.

Combined cycle gas turbine power stations

Applications for a total of four gas-powered electricity stations have been proposed in the Thames Gateway area. Working from east to west, the first application was at Greenwich for a small station of between 300 and 400 MW. This application was withdrawn.

Barking Power's, on the other hand, was an application for 1000 MW, the largest application for the generation of power in the East Thames Corridor at the time. It is also the development closest to the centre of London and therefore closest to the pollution high for nitrogen oxides to the east of London. The ES made it clear that this development was located in an area of London which already exceeded EC guidelines for background levels of nitrogen oxides. Kent objected to the application, but were not able to press the objection as the County Council did not border directly on the boundary of Barking. This station was granted planning permission and was under construction by January 1995. The application did give an opportunity to establish two air quality monitoring stations, one on site and another in Bexley, which were useful in developing a better understanding of the air quality issues related to the development.

Within Kent the application for AES Medway was granted planning consent for 600 MW and it also was under construction by January 1995. This was after the air pollution impacts of the development had been evaluated through the North Kent Air Quality Model.

The application for Kingsnorth power station, also on the Isle of Grain and for 600 MW, was granted consent in September 1994. Construction had not started by the beginning of 1995 and it was anticipated then that the developer would apply for higher generating capacity to between 700 and 800 MW.

Thus an additional 2500–22,000 MW of electricity will be generated from the Thames Gateway region making the Kent Gateway area a net exporter of electricity. This made KCC question whether this extra capacity was needed in energy policy terms. Would it not have been better to conserve energy rather than just increase capacity? The planning department wrote to the Department of Energy to ask whether these issues could be addressed. The response came back that it was up to the market to decide whether further electricity was needed.

Waste incinerators

By March 1995 there had been five applications for domestic waste incinerators in the Thames Gateway area. The combined heat and power domestic waste incinerator at Deptford has been granted planning consent and is operational, burning much of Lewisham's waste and generating a small amount of electricity. This was a successful planning application because it was seen as a good local solution serving the community by dealing with local waste and generating electricity.

Two applications for sewage sludge incinerators have been granted planning consent at Bacton and Crossness. These incinerators were introduced to overcome the problems of the EC Directive which prohibited the continued dumping of sewage sludge at sea. It was generally acknowledged that it was better to burn the sewage sludge than continue to dump it at sea or try to spread it as fertiliser on land. The incinerators were considered the best environmental option.

An application for a large domestic refuse incinerator by Cory was proposed at Belvedere in Bexley. This application went to inquiry and was refused consent on the grounds that access to the site was inadequate. Although extensive evidence was given on the likely air pollution impacts of the application, the Secretary of State did not comment on this aspect of the proposal in his decision letter. Following the inquiry KCC expected a new application to be made to progress this development in the future, the question of access having been subsequently addressed. Nevertheless, the problems associated with application for an incinerator in East London which will burn 1.2 million tonnes of domestic refuse have yet to be resolved.

National Power's proposal for a waste to energy plant at Northfleet

National Power proposed a waste to energy incinerator at Northfleet. The plant would take up to 700,000 tonnes of waste a year (almost all of Kent's domestic waste) by producing 49 MW of electricity. The application was not therefore processed by the Department of Trade and Industry (who process power plants of over 50 MW) but by Gravesham Borough Council. It was judged to be an 'S' case (a Kent shorthand for cases where strategic consultation with the County Council is required) by Gravesham Borough Council. The strategic considerations of the application were therefore considered by KCC.

The site was located along the Thames waterfront at a low level; access was restricted. It was envisaged that most of the waste would be brought in by truck from the A2. There were many considerations to be taken into account in the processing of the planning application. Gravesham Borough Council hired a consultant to undertake the technical appraisal of the ES. At KCC it was necessary to run the proposal through the Air Quality Model after background monitoring had been undertaken.

The background levels of NO_X were quite high in some areas, particularly along the A2 road, and this gave cause for concern about the location of a further source point of NO_X in the area. The model indicated that the incinerator would raise background levels to $49.7 \, mg/m^3$, $0.3 \, mg/m^3$ below the EC guidelines of $50 \, mg/m^3$.

National Power had decided not to apply for authorisation under IPC at the same time that they applied for planning consent. The committee report was therefore written to reflect the high levels of pollution likely to be found in the area and the fact that we were unsure at the time of writing the report whether the technology would be acceptable to HMIP. Members decided not to grant planning consent until they had received advice from HMIP about the air pollution impacts. National Power withdrew their application.

Refinement of the Kent Air Quality Model

Consideration of each of these proposals highlighted the value of Kent's Air Quality Model as a tool for finding out background levels of pollution and for aiding the decision-making process in EIA. In fact since these initial applications had been considered by the model, it had been run three more times to consider the air quality implications of proposals for power stations in the study area.

Two combined heat and power applications were considered for SCA Paper in Aylesford and Kemsley Paper at Sittingbourne, improving air quality in both cases by replacing existing boilers. The air quality implications of a liquefied gas power station also on the Isle of Grain were considered but a planning application was not forthcoming on this application.

The North Kent Air Quality Model had now considered a total of 12 applications for developments of power stations and incinerators in the area. Every time the model was run the information on background levels was updated and the model was altered as developments received or were refused planning consent. This meant that the model was unique and represented up to date information on changes in air quality in Kent. It was not possible for a planning consultant to replicate the Kent model since all the information which was fed into the Kent model could not be found out by a planning consultant. Therefore the Kent Air Quality Model was becoming an important tool for modelling predicted changes in air quality in North Kent.

HMIP report on air quality

In the meantime, HMIP produced a report on nitrogen oxide levels in the East Thames Corridor[4]. There are over 40 Schedule A IPC authorisations in Kent. These include all the major power stations and installations which are likely to have an impact on air quality. Many of these processes are to be found in the East Thames Corridor (about 30) and therefore it was extremely useful to have a report from HMIP on air quality in the East Thames Corridor. The report concludes that there is no imminent danger of a breach of the EC Directive limit as a result of NO_X emissions from the proposed new power stations and waste incinerators.

The results of the assessment on the relative contribution of industrial NO_x emissions are consistent with the established view that vehicles are the dominant source of NO_2 in urban areas. The greatest benefit to ambient NO_2 levels is therefore likely to come from control of vehicle emissions. Estimates made as part of this study demonstrate a potentially significant reduction (of 30%–50%) in NO_2 concentrations by the year 2000 as a result of the introduction of catalytic converters, assuming an annual rate of traffic growth of 1%–2%.

The longer term (post-2000) prospects for vehicle-derived NO_2 levels in the East Thames Corridor are much more difficult to estimate, particularly in relation to the growth and development which is expected to take place in the Corridor. In view of the possibility that a progressive increase in traffic growth could neutralise the benefits of catalytic converters in urban areas, long-term strategies should be addressed to limit the demand for road transport, and to encourage a model shift away from the private motor car in such areas.

This work highlighted the importance of looking at background levels of pollution and tackling the problems related to small emissions from smaller plants and the need to model and monitor pollution from cars. In fact the report concluded that between 70% and 80% of air pollution in the East Thames Corridor was due to motor vehicles.

PPG23: *Planning and Pollution Control*

The final version of the Planning Policy Guidance PPG23: *Planning and Pollution Control* tries to make clear what should be considered by the planning authority in the granting of planning consent and what should be considered by HMIP in the granting of authorisation under IPC.

The role of the planning authority is to ensure that the development is an acceptable land use. The material considerations which should be taken into account are:

- location, taking into account such considerations as the reasons for selecting the chosen site;
- impact on amenity;
- the risk and impact of potential pollution from the development in so far as this might have an effect on the use of other land;
- prevention of nuisance;
- impact on the road and other transport networks and on the surrounding environment.

On the other hand the pollution control system under part 1 of the EPA 1990 makes it clear that a business or process cannot operate without pollution control consent, licence or authorisation. Pollution of the environment is defined as:

due to the release (into any environmental medium) from any process of substances which are capable of causing harm to man or any other living organism supported by the environment[5].

The PPG recommends that local planning authorities consult HMIP on potentially polluting developments in order to take account of the controls exercised by HMIP. If possible planning and IPC authorisation should be applied for at the same time.

Planning applications which are accompanied by an ES are likely to include information on the likely impact on the environment of the proposed development. In these cases advice should be sought from HMIP. The PPG goes on to state:

> If ... the pollution control authority informs the planning authority that there are likely to be delays in reaching agreement before a pollution control authorisation or licence can be granted, the planning authority may seek to agree with the applicant to defer consideration of the application until it believes that the potential pollution problems can be overcome[6].

In other words, the planning and pollution control authorities should work together to overcome the likely polluting impacts of new large scale developments. In Kent we have attempted to achieve this by forming the Air Quality Liaison Group.

Air quality in Kent and the Kent Structure Plan

Another aspect of the work on air pollution which started directly from the EIA process was the preparation of the background papers for the third review of the Kent Structure Plan. The Air Quality Model had identified that some areas of the county had high levels of NO_x and this then became a consideration in the development of structure plan policies. Policy ENV19 states:

> Development will be required to be planned and designed so as to avoid or minimise pollution impacts. Where such impacts cannot be reduced to an acceptable level, or together with prevailing background pollution it would produce an unacceptable level, the proposed development will not be permitted[7].

Further information on background levels of air pollution in the county as a whole was provided by Warren Springs Laboratory. This provided emission levels of pollutants, including sulphur dioxide, nitrogen oxides, volatile organic compounds (VOCs) and carbon monoxide, for every 10 kilometre grid in the country. This information was mapped and indicated higher levels of pollution in Kent's major towns than in the countryside and unusually high levels of SO_2 in Folkestone and Dover. Analysis of the Standard Industrial Classification of Industries in these towns suggested that the pollution was not coming from industry in the town but possibly from shipping or from France. This possibility will be discussed below.

This study confirmed the need for the development of a county-wide air quality management system. It also became obvious that one system of air quality management needed to include the Department of the Environment, HMIP, District Councils and Health Authorities. An Air Quality Liaison Committee was set up to represent all these interests. This committee has since demonstrated the value of partnerships between central, county and local government.

This group commissioned Professor Bernard Fisher of the University of Greenwich to undertake a review of air quality models and advise the group on the best model for air quality management in Kent. Following Bernard Fisher's recommendations we were able to appoint consultants to develop an air quality model for the county. It was recommended that either the ISCL model, based on the US NEPA long and short term model, should be used or the ADMS system. In the end, we appointed Ashdown Environmental to develop the model based on the US NEPA system, which is the same system that we used for the North Kent Model and means that all the data are transferable to the new model.

The Kent-wide model will be based on much better information that the North Kent Model. There are three sets of information which form the basis of the Kent model:

1. the Emissions Inventory which has been compiled from HMIPs list of Schedule A and Schedule B processes and information collected from Environmental Health Officers from all the District Councils in Kent;
2. information on monitoring which has been collected from National Power's monitoring information, local authorities' monitoring systems and any other information that is available;
3. information on energy use based on information from SEEBOARD[8] and the oil companies.

Thus we have a much better indication of overall patterns of pollution and carbon dioxide production. The model will be further developed to look at sulphur dioxide, nitrogen oxides and PM10, and to include pollution from traffic. The council will then be able to review development proposals with air pollution impacts anywhere in the county and also to develop scenarios which will develop and review different transport options for the county, e.g. the effect of the new rail route through the county, the impact of the development of light rapid transport in the Medway towns, the effect of park and ride schemes in smaller towns in Kent. All these can now be assessed for their air pollution impacts.

The development of the model does not end there. The air quality management system will provide a focus for air quality monitoring in the county. This can be fed into the model to calibrate and update the model. Information on future planning decisions which will affect air quality will also be used to update the model.

Study of pollution across the Channel

Earlier work in the county, which looked at emission inventories, suggested that there were high levels of sulphur dioxide in Folkestone and Dover. This cannot be traced to local industry and is obviously not car related. It is therefore likely that this is due either to pollution from shipping or to pollution from France. These findings have given us the opportunity to develop links with experts in air quality in Nord-Pas de Calais. We have found this very productive. The French are very competent at monitoring; they have 45 monitoring stations in Nord-Pas de Calais alone. They are interested in finding out the likely change in pollution levels as a result of the Channel Tunnel and would also like to measure ozone levels.

Kent on the other hand has developed a competence in air quality modelling and uses the modelling as a planning tool. We are beginning to monitor but not to the same extent as the French and yet we have captured most emission data through our system.

Development of the Air Quality Liaison Group and meetings with our counterparts from France has meant that we are able to apply to the European Union under the INTERREG programme to develop our studies of cross-boundary pollution.

Conclusions

Kent's experience in air quality management

EC legislation required changes to the way that London's waste was handled. It could no longer be dumped at sea and therefore there was a need to look at alternative means of disposal for sewage sludge. Proposals for incinerators were responding to these changes and to market forces. Applications for new gas-fired power stations were a result of changes in gas pricing and spare capacity on the national grid. As a result of these changes a total of nine applications with potentially air polluting impacts were lodged and this meant that cumulative impacts had to be assessed.

EIA gave the legislative basis for considering these cumulative air quality impacts, while the introduction of the North Kent Air Quality Model provided the means through which the impacts could be assessed.

Since each applicant had to carry out air quality monitoring for SO_2 and NO_X, background air quality information was collected and enabled the model to be calibrated and updated.

It soon became apparent that a model for north Kent was not going to be adequate and that a model for the whole of Kent taking into account pollution from London and France was necessary.

The development of the Air Quality Liaison Group allowed all levels of government and different professional groups to aid in the development of a comprehensive modelling and monitoring system for Kent.

Linking the system into EIA has meant that we have been able to charge developers for the cost of running the model for each proposal, reducing the cost to the local authority and ensuring that there is no dispute over the validity of the modelling information. This is accepted by the determining authority if the developer uses the Kent Air Quality Model.

To summarise, we have gone from a totally bewildering approach to air quality impacts where each developer uses a different model and estimates impacts differently to a system which means that we can be systematic and look at the smaller impacts which do not trigger EIA but nevertheless have a considerable impact on air quality, namely the motor car.

New initiatives in air quality management

On 19 January 1995 the Government announced their commitment to bring cleaner air to towns and cities by regular assessments of air quality by local authorities[9]. This includes the establishment of national air quality standards for nine pollutants; early legislation on a new role for local authorities and the creation of air quality management areas where air quality falls short of targets; also a 20 point action plan on transport was proposed.

It has been suggested for example that local authorities will be able to close town centres to traffic when pollution levels are high. Kent authorities will be in an ideal position to respond to the Government's new initiative as a result of the work that has been put into modelling, monitoring and collecting an emission inventory through the Kent Air Quality Liaison Group.

Local air quality management and development plans will be closely related. Land use planning can make relatively little contribution to immediate improvements in air quality, but over the longer term the development planning system is central to policies which are consistent with the concept of sustainable development. The Government have reiterated their commitment to environmental appraisal of plans as suggested in PPG12. It is suggested that the appraisal should include a review of the effects of policies on air quality and that it is the explicit duty of the local authority to review air quality periodically.

The DoE also announced that it would be reconsidering the advice offered on planning and pollution control in PPG23. It is to be hoped that the new legislation and the creation of the Environment Agency can ensure that a partnership can be forged between planning permission and authorisation under IPC so that we can seriously develop pollution and land use planning to ensure sustainable development in the future[10].

Notes and references

1 Directive on assessment of the effects of certain public and private projects on the environment (85/337/EEC). Brussels: Commission of the European Communities, 1985.

2 INDIC is the trade name of a model, as are ISC, ISCLT and ADMS which are mentioned later in the chapter.

3 The Gaussian Plume Dispersion Model was developed by the famous mathematician Karl Friedrich Gauss (1777–1855) to demonstrate how emissions from factory chimneys behave in the atmosphere.

4 Her Majesty's Inspectorate of Pollution (1993) *An Assessment of the Effects of Industrial Releases of Nitrogen Oxides in the East Thames Corridor.* London: HMSO.

5 DoE (1994) PPG23: *Planning and Pollution Control.* London: HMSO.

6 *Ibid.*

7 Kent County Council (1993) The Third Review Kent Structure Plan Deposit Draft. Kent County Council Planning Department, Maidstone.

8 SEEBOARD refers to the South East Electricity Board.

9 DoE (1995) *Air Quality: Meeting the Challenge. The Government's Strategic Policies for Air Quality Management.* London: HMSO.

10 Since the writing of this chapter, the Government has developed and published a National Air Quality Strategy.

CHAPTER 9

LESSONS FROM EIA IN PRACTICE

Joe Weston

Introduction

The title of this chapter is purposely presumptuous in that it is the claim of this book that lessons can be drawn from the evidence and experiences recorded here. From the evidence presented here, and other recorded trends, we can draw some conclusions about the nature of EIA practice in the UK. In this chapter we examine that evidence and assess the UK's EIA system in terms of a comparison with other systems and notions of good practice and the theoretical framework examined in the Introduction.

As was explained at the very beginning of this book, the evidence and experiences recorded here are a snapshot of the EIA process and its impact on the UK planning system. That snapshot has focused upon a fixed period of time, from the introduction of formal EIA in 1988 to the time of writing in 1995. It would be dangerous to overemphasise the implications for the future of EIA simply on the basis of the evidence presented here and yet, together with the changes that are taking place even as we write, some predictions can be made.

Comparative assessment of UK EIA

The process

Notions of 'good practice' tend to relate the use of the EIA process to the theory of EIA discussed in the Introduction to this book, i.e. the iterative, rational and objective process advocated by Munn, Walthern and many others. Wood (1995) argues that EIA systems can be compared with a list of criteria based largely upon the stages of the process which were discussed in the Introduction to this book[1]. While it may be useful to compare systems with the theoretical framework of EIA a comparison of one system against another is of less utility. Such a comparative assessment requires, firstly, that there is complete international acceptance of what constitutes a 'good' EIA system and there is no evidence that such agreement exists. Under the criteria Wood (1995) establishes, the UK system falls short of 'best practice' in terms of scoping, a consideration of alternatives and impact monitoring. While most academics working in the field, and many practitioners, would agree that these are vital, if not fundamental, components of any EIA system, the UK Government, and presumably those other governments whose systems do not meet those criteria, would appear not to agree. Indeed Wood (1995) accepts that a move towards 'best practice' depends upon 'political endorsement' rather than any more rational acceptance of what is or is not a 'good' system[2].

It is therefore very difficult to make an objective comparative assessment of the 'quality' of EIA in the UK because the system here is unlike the system as it is operated in most other countries. As was argued in the Introduction, the UK has only a partial EIA system, when measured against the 'ideal' components of the EIA process, and therefore it cannot easily be judged against others or indeed the theories of what constitutes good quality or best practice. The UK system has been tacked onto an existing complex planning system that has its own long-standing rules, procedures and traditions and EIA has become part of that planning system. Where there are no existing planning systems or where EIA is introduced as a whole decision-making process it is almost certain to be different from the UK's system. The system of EIA adopted under the USA's NEPA, for example, is very different from the UK's, largely because the Act created a whole new decision-making process. The NEPA system includes mandatory scoping, an assessment of alternatives and ES review. However, the USA is a federal nation with a high degree of autonomy devolved to the states. These individual states have their own EIA systems which, as with California, can differ considerably from the NEPA system.

Different nations, even different levels of government within nations, have their own priorities, agendas and levels of environmental concern. These differences are certain to reflect not only on the environmental management measures they adopt but also on their commitment to them.

Since the 1970s the use of EIA has been spreading throughout the world and as a process is being adopted in a variety of forms. EIA is also increasingly becoming a requirement of international funding agencies when they are considering support for infrastructure and other projects in developing countries. Yet many developing countries, particularly in Africa, have few real legislative frameworks in which EIA can operate[3]. In those countries, systems have to be developed to accommodate the requirements of an external funding agency and hence EIA is not even an indigenously developed process. The World Bank, the International Finance Corporation, African and Asian Regional Development Banks and the Organisation for Economic Co-operation and Development all require EIA for funded projects and provide guidance on EIA procedures; and many consider the most comprehensive of these to be that provided by the World Bank in its Operational Directive 4.01 (1991)[4]. Here EIA includes the production of an ES which provides details of initial consultations, full details of the project and all its potential impacts, alternatives, mitigation measures and an executive summary . For major 'high risk' or 'contentious' projects the

World Bank requires an environmental advisory panel, comprising of internationally recognised environmental specialists, to be convened to oversee the scoping and review of the EIA. They advise both the Bank, as lender and project appraiser, and the borrower, the government proposing the project, on all aspects of the EIA process including the report or ES[5]. Not only, therefore, is EIA imposed from outside but also the system and the people who make the key decisions on what should be considered by the process are also largely drawn from outside the country where the project, and the EIA, are to take place.

In Australia we find a different approach again. Generally the Federal Government delegates many powers, including environmental protection, to the individual states so that, as with the USA, even within a single nation state we find different systems. A review of the Commonwealth Environmental Protection (Impact of Proposals) Act in 1995 suggested there should be a greater role for the Australian National Government where projects were likely to have national or international implications[6]. However, the individual states remain substantially in charge of the system. The 1986 Western Australian Environmental Protection Act, for example, makes no formal requirements on the content of an ES; it does, however, according to Wood and Bailey (1994), 'expect' them to contain:

- a non-technical summary;
- details of the technical information used and how this information was interpreted;
- details of the basis for the prediction of impacts as well as the impacts themselves;
- details of how the issues raised in the project guidelines (produced by the Environment Agency) are addressed[7].

Wood (1995) notes that the 1986 Western Australian system made environmental considerations central to decisions on project authorisations and that since then political pressure has considerably weakened the system[8].

The New South Wales Environmental Planning and Assessment (Amendment) Act 1994 requires a public exhibition of the ES before approval can be granted and projects subject to EIA even include contaminated land remediation works[9].

In some countries, the USA and Denmark and others, it is governmental agencies or the determining 'competent' authority which carry out the EIA and not the developer as is the case in the UK. Other countries, the Netherlands, Belgium, Canada, Malaysia and Indonesia, require mandatory EIA review and have created national agencies which, in theory, provide an independent intermediary between the developer and the competent authority[10].

We could continue tediously reviewing the different approaches and different systems in existence to demonstrate a very simple point: all EIA systems are unique as they are linked to particular domestic circumstances or land use and development decision-making processes. The adopted system will reflect both the individual nation's, or indeed internal region or state's, concept of what EIA is and the legal, constitutional and even cultural framework in which land use decision making takes place. Wood's (1995) EIA evaluation criteria identify only one model, that of Western Australia, which meets all the requirements of a full EIA system and that model is itself being altered by political rather than environmental considerations[11].

We cannot make other than value judgements as to whether one system is better than another and it would be extremely difficult and even misleading to judge any one system against another. We can say that the UK system, when assessed against the theoretical iterative stages of the EIA process, is lacking in a number of fundamental areas and that in that respect it does fall short of what most would accept as 'best practice'. However, the truly significant point to be made from any comparative study is that one of the key strengths of EIA as a process is that it can be adapted to fit virtually any land use or other environmental authorisation systems whilst retaining many of its most important features.

The UK and the EU

If we cannot objectively measure the UK's system against those adopted by other nations perhaps we should really be examining the system within the context of the EU. After all EIA only came into being in the UK, as a formal requirement, as a result of an EU Directive which was supposed to be implemented uniformly across the community as a whole. Much was made in the Introduction to this book of the cool reception the Government in the UK gave to formal EIA. Yet despite the UK Government's initial reluctance, it has, at least, implemented the EU requirements in a form which arguably follows the letter if not the spirit of that Directive. On the other hand the implementation of the EIA Directive across the community as a whole has been, to be generous, varied. Many EU states did not have the sophisticated planning system necessary to copy the UK and simply add EIA onto existing decision-making processes. Some states, Holland, Ireland and France for example, already had formal EIA requirements and experienced problems adapting their systems to the requirements of the Directive. Belgium was going through a complex process of constitutional reform just when they were required to implement the Directive. Belgium's move towards a federal state slowed down the whole policy and planning decision-making process and hence the implementation of the Directive. In Italy implementation required passing national laws that for a whole variety of reasons were delayed so that EIA was for some considerable time based only on Prime Ministerial decree[12]. Implementation in Greece was even more problematic and eventually the Government was indicted before the European Court of Justice for failing to implement the Directive[13]. La Spina and Sciortino (1993) suggest that in the Mediterranean states of the EU there has been little enthusiasm for implementation and that this, and the 'scope for delay and buck passing between central and local government', permitted by the vagueness of the Directive, has, in some cases, made the EIA measures 'completely ineffective'[14].

The accusation of taking a minimalist approach to the requirements of the Directive cannot be laid solely against the UK either. In a 1994 German Federal Administrative Court ruling it was held that it was necessary for a plaintiff to demonstrate that a decision on a project would have been different, if an EIA had been carried out, before that decision could be quashed[15]. That ruling is not dissimilar to the position taken by the courts and planning Inspectors in the UK. In fact it could be seen as being a more onerous condition to place on objectors to schemes that have not been subject to EIA. In such cases the objector would almost need to carry out an EIA to test the validity of the decision before mounting a challenge.

In comparison with many of its EU partners, therefore, the UK could be seen as almost a paragon of virtue in its introduction of EIA. Yet we should remember that the EU is not simply a collection of trading nations; it is made up of many different peoples of very different cultures, traditions and values. The way the peoples of the EU approach environmental issues, let alone the implementation of legal decision-making processes, will understandably vary. The Directive is, after all, like any piece of legislation, open to interpretation and we saw in the Introduction how the UK has always favoured a literalistic interpretation of law and has implemented the Directive on that basis. Salter (1992a) believes that the UK's literal interpretation of the Directive neglects many aspects of what it was trying to achieve. In particular he points out that the UK's EIA Regulations:

> specify only direct and indirect effects and do not make it clear that the description of the likely significant effects should cover secondary, cumulative, short, medium and long term, permanent and temporary, positive and negative effects of the project in accordance with paragraph 4 of Annex III (of the Directive).... One cannot assess effects without looking at the forecasting methods used. One cannot study measures used to avoid, reduce or remedy those effects without reviewing the main alternatives studied by the developer in conjunction with reasons for choices made in project selection[16].

Jorissen and Coenen (1992) have argued that there is a need for guidance on EIA procedures throughout the EU to avoid the problem of different countries interpreting the Directive in different ways. They argue:

> Clear guidance on screening and scoping procedures, on identification of all the relevant impacts, on determination of the significance of these impacts, on the choice of methods used for prediction and survey, on existing data sources, and on the communication of the findings, would improve practice[17].

They also argue that the absence of a clear definition of EIA adequacy within the Directive permits developers to take a minimalist approach which at present can only be countered by the ability of the competent authority to demand more. That ability is often lacking because of the nature of the domestic planning system and the cultural, political and legal relationships between levels of decision making. The amendments to the Directive agreed by the EU's Environment Ministers in 1995 are unlikely to improve the situation as no significant changes have been made which would automatically result in more information being provided.

So we have to accept that even if the primary legislation which introduced EIA is common to all members of the EU the actual system and process adopted is likely to vary for a whole range of complex reasons.

Assessing quality

The environmental statement

One simple measure of the quality of EIA is the quality of the ES produced as part of the process. The DoE have taken this approach with both the Manchester University study of ES quality in 1991 and the more recent work carried out by Oxford Brookes University[18]. The basic argument for this approach is that if you improve the quality of ESs then, over time, the overall quality of the EIA process will also improve. There is no universal agreement on this assumption and some believe that it is wholly misleading to base an assessment of UK EIA on the quality of statements. Street (1993) sees the assessment of ESs as simply a snapshot view of the EIA process which largely ignores the fact that the ES is only one element of the environmental information which needs to be taken into account. A more comprehensive measure of the quality of the process is seen as an assessment of the quality of the information finally laid before the decision makers. Furthermore as Braun (1993) argues, poor quality ESs can be redressed by the consultation process which will bring in information from other sources and the demand for further information from the developer[19]. Perhaps a further test of quality would be assessing the final outcome of the process, i.e. whether the EIA process has resulted in better projects being built. That would of course be difficult to assess, yet a 1995 survey of environmental and planning consultants which had carried out EIAs showed that over 70% believed that the introduction of EIA into the UK had resulted in at least some improvement in environmental protection[20].

However, the quality of ESs has become the focus of a great deal of academic and practice attention and the DoE does advocates the production of high quality comprehensive ESs[21]. The ES is also the main public document produced during the EIA process and provides both the public and statutory consultees with the basis of their own assessment of a project. As the ES is such a crucial part of the whole EIA process it would seem reasonable to base at least some emphasis on the importance of its quality.

The Oxford Brookes University study into ES quality was perhaps more sophisticated than the earlier work in that it did ask questions about 'quality for whom'. This is an important issue for a poor quality ES may in fact work in the best interests of those opposed to a project. As we have seen in this book, development proposals often result in a campaign against them. The ES can become the focus of this campaign and weaknesses in the statement can provide objectors with the ammunition they need to gain support for their cause and to allow them to investigate the issues more thoroughly to further weaken the credibility of the developers and their consultants. Consequently a developer who takes the minimalist approach and produces a document which is little more than a justification of the proposed development may find that this particular tactic has serious drawbacks. It is therefore possibly in the best interests of developers to ensure that an ES is as comprehensive and objective as possible.

The most recent evidence, from the Oxford Brookes University study, suggests that the quality of ESs has steadily improved since the introduction of the process in 1988. Yet most of the published evidence still suggests that the quality of ESs varies considerably both within EIA systems and between systems[22]. Indeed, this variation was one of the key findings of the EU's five year review of the EIA system across the community[23]. The now quite extensive literature on the subject suggests that the causes for poor quality ESs are:

- lack of experience of producers and reviewers of ESs;
- lack of objectivity of ESs and the use of statements as a 'justification' of a project or action;
- lack of institutional or legal powers to demand higher quality;
- lack of specific guidance on the content of an ES.

Salter (1992b) argues that the quality of an ES also depends upon a number of interrelated institutional factors including:

> the attitude and ability of the person seeking consent, the competence and interest of the public, the interest of central government and the interest of the relevant authorities and consultees concerned[24].

Experience

The one issue which keeps emerging as a factor in determining quality is the issue of experience. The Oxford Brookes University study found a clear link between the experience of both the consultant and the local authority and ES quality and Skehan (1993) saw in the Irish EIA system an 'observed correlation' between ES quality and the experience of consultants and planning authorities[25]. This position is supported by the work of Lee and Dancey (1993) who also found in Ireland evidence that short ESs, those of less than 25 pages, tended to be of inferior quality to longer statements.

However, Lee and Dancey (1993) also make clear that just as a long ES may not necessarily be of good quality, the experience of the producer is also no guarantee of quality[26]. In France this variation in quality is seen to exist between large, national and controversial projects and smaller local projects, with the more controversial projects having better quality ESs. The suggestion here is that the promoters of larger projects will tend to have more experience in the field and of course more resources available to produce good quality ESs[27].

Experience is important to all facets of the process and is not limited to the experience of the producer of statements. West *et al.* (1993) argue that although there are a large number of highly trained scientists and researchers in the developing world they tend to have little experience of working in the multidisciplinary teams that Michael Lee-Wright suggests in Chapter 2 are necessary for the production of good quality ESs[28]. Kakonge and Imevbore (1993) develop this issue of 'experience' further by arguing that it is not just inexperience in personnel terms which hinders good quality ESs but the absence of the body of environmental knowledge and data which is built up with experience[29].

Yet even the availability of experienced 'experts' cannot on its own result in good quality ESs. The Ministry of the Environment for Luxembourg, where ESs for major projects tend to be carried out by large and experienced German, French and Swiss consultancies, noted that ESs still contained many fundamental deficiencies such as an absence of any assessment of alternatives[30].

Objectivity

Chapter 5 highlighted the importance of reliable, objectively produced and presented environmental information for the success of the EIA process. Furthermore the DoE's *Evaluation of Environmental Information for Planning Projects: A Good Practice Guide* (1994b) makes clear that when local authorities review a submitted ES they should check to ensure that the 'overall findings are clearly presented in an objective statement'[31].

One obvious check on objectivity is the relationship between the producers of the ES and the promoters of the project. In the Flanders and Wallonia regions of Belgium evidence of a lack of true objectivity and independence in ES production has been related to the fact that the 'consultant remains financially dependent on the developer'[32]. In Denmark it is the competent authority which prepares the statement and not the developer. Even here there is evidence of a lack of objectivity where an authority is politically resistant to a particular project[33].

Ginger and Mohai (1993) make clear that lack of objectivity is a major issue even under the much respected USA's NEPA system. They take the view that in many cases the ES is a 'tool for justifying agency decisions' and that the reason for this is that the ES is produced after the relevant agency has already focused on a particular action or project[34]. In other words the EIA process tends to begin after major decisions have already been taken, just as they were in both case studies examined in Chapter 5.

Some, including the CPRE, have argued that the best way of achieving objectivity and good quality ESs is to introduce a formal review stage when an independent body decides whether or not the ES is adequate[35]. Some EU states (Italy, Belgium and the Netherlands) do have independent ES review bodies; however, there has been little real work on the overall impact of these bodies on the quality of ESs. Evidence from Belgium suggests that a lack of resources makes adequate review difficult. In Wallonia members of the review body have even had to carry out ES reviews on a voluntary basis in their own time[36].

Kakonge and Imevbore (1993) make a link between the need for institutional frameworks and the experience and powers of agencies to fully enforce regulations and perform reviews of ESs[37]. This certainly appears to be the case in many developing countries. Abracosa and Ortolano (1987) observe that in the Philippines the National Environmental Protection Council has neither the political power nor the resources needed to force development agencies to comply with its requirements[38]. Under the New Zealand system the Parliamentary Commission for the Environment retains the right to intervene to ensure that the environmental assessment reports are adequate, yet Wood (1993b) believes that the Commission's lack of resources will inevitably mean that intervention will only take place in exceptional cases[39].

Many who argue for independent review in the UK tend to see the new Environment Agency created under the 1995 Environment Act as the most appropriate organisation for this role. However, if, as the evidence from elsewhere suggests, the success of independent review depends upon the powers, resources and will of the relevant agency then proponents of such a system may be sorely disappointed. The Secretary of State for the Environment published guidance on the likely approach of the new agency towards its functions in October 1994. That approach was stated to be the 'achievement of environmental goals without imposing unnecessary burdens on industry and the public and taking proper account of costs and benefits' and 'cost effectiveness and value for money for those who pay its charges and for tax payers as a whole'[40]. On this evidence independent review by the Environment Agency may be a backward step.

In the absence of an independent review body in the UK the role will continue to fall to the competent authority. According to the DoE's publication *Good Practice on the Evaluation of Environmental Information for Planning Projects: Research Report* (1994a) local planning authorities carry out this review by way of a simple checklist[41]. It is true that the Lee and Colley review package, or variations thereof, are used and in some cases planning authorities commission environmental consultants to carry out the review for them. Whether a local authority carries out the review in-house or commissions consultants the objectivity of that review can also be questioned by the developer. The very nature of the relationships involved in the EIA process makes any independence difficult and easily criticised.

Given the adversarial nature of land use planning in the UK, and the competing and conflicting interests which are at the centre of the process, it is difficult to see how true objectivity can ever be achieved in EIA. We have seen throughout this book that the planning system is essentially a political decision-making process. In that context it is perhaps asking too much to expect a supposedly rational planning technique to remain untarnished by that political process.

Guidance

It has already been argued that the guidance published by the DoE in 1989, together with the advice in Circular 15/88, gave rise to the potential for a minimalist approach. Since the introduction of EIA a whole host of 'best practice' guidance has emerged. This ranges from the use of review criteria as a benchmark for the production of ESs to more direct guidance like English Nature's *Environmental Assessment Handbook* (1992), the CPRE's *Environmental Statements: Getting Them Right* (1990), the handbooks produced by County Councils such as Kent and Cheshire and internal guidance produced by major companies like ICI[42].

The DoE's *Evaluation of Environmental Information for Planning Projects: A Good Practice Guide* (1994b) rightly emphasises the need to see the ES in the context of the required environmental information and the process as a whole[43]. However, the guide is only aimed at those responsible for assessing the environmental information; it is not a best practice guide for those preparing a statement or carrying out an EIA. The more recent *Preparation of Environmental Statements for Planning Projects that Require Environmental Assessment: A Good Practice Guide* (1995a) may not win prizes for having the most snappy title but it does provide a far better starting point for those undertaking EIA than the original 'Blue Book'[44].

Advice on EIA is also provided in the Planning Policy Guidance Notes (PPGs) published by the DoE. Current PPGs have been published since the introduction of the EIA Regulations and virtually all have sections on EIA, as do many of the Mineral Policy Guidance Notes (MPGs), and, in the main, these only deal with the regulatory requirements for EIA. Of all the PPGs perhaps the most comprehensive advice on EIA is in PPG22: *Renewable Energy*. Not only does it discuss the requirements of the Regulations but it also makes some interesting statements about standards.

> The principle is now well established that the polluter should pay the cost of meeting acceptable environmental standards and the EPA provides that effects should be minimised by the use of the 'best available technique not entailing excessive cost' (BATNEEC). These standards are set at a given level, although site-

specific interpretation of such standards may be agreed. However, the national standards should generally be regarded as the minimum. Applicants should build into the appraisal of new investment projects the cost of meeting required environmental standards[45].

Annex 9 of PPG23: *Planning and Pollution Control* explains the requirements for EIA and has this to say about ESs:

2 ... The information included in the environmental statement is likely to be similar in many cases to that which may be provided in support of an application for pollution control authorisation.

3 The aim of an environmental statement will be to provide a full and systematic account of a development's likely effects on the environment, including those which are subject to pollution controls, and the measures envisaged to avoid, reduce or remedy significant adverse effects[46].

MPG3 provides a more detailed set of standards in respect of environmental impacts resulting from coal mining and colliery spoil disposal. The 'specific impacts' (visual, noise, blasting, dust, water, transportation, land use and built heritage, nature conservation, subsidence, tips and related structures) are described in some detail, including matters which need to be assessed for each section[47]. MPG6 also has a brief section on EIA and points out that with mineral workings 'The duration of the proposed workings is also a factor to be taken into account'[48]. MPG7 provides a fairly detailed reference list which includes works on EIA for the mining and minerals industry[49].

Most forms of guidance are very helpful but they lack any statutory backing and a developer can still produce the very barest of assessments to comply with the Regulations. The other problem with guidance, a problem for EIA as a whole which is often overlooked, is the unique nature of the projects subject to the EIA Regulations. That uniqueness arises because of the individual nature of the project itself, the receiving environment, the type, size and wealth of the developer, the policies, attitude and resources of the local planning authority and the interests and environmental perceptions held by the public. As we have seen throughout this book these individual characteristics are defining features not only of the projects but of the use and practice of EIA.

The UK Government gave a commitment as early as 1990 to produce new guidance on the preparation and review of ESs and the DoE commissioned much research into the requirements of such guidance[50]. As discussed above, that guidance was finally released in 1994–1995 and it is too early here to assess its impact. However, when guidance is no more than advice it is likely to be interpreted to fit the individual circumstances and requirements of the project, developer or planning authority. After all, even when tested against the minimalist standards of the DoE's 1989 guidance many EIAs have been found wanting and yet they still conform with the requirements of the Regulations.

The quality of ESs varies throughout the EU and beyond – it is not just an issue for the UK's EIA system – and the explanations for the production of poor quality ESs are much the same as in the UK. However, one explanation for variation in quality may be unique to the UK and its adversarial planning system. In a political process such as the UK's development control system all the parties involved have strategies for influencing the decision makers. If it is inevitable that a project will be subject to public inquiry it may be in the best interests of a developer to produce a minimalist ES at the application stage and reserve the details for the formal setting of the inquiry before an independent Inspector. It is therefore difficult to examine the issue of ES quality outside the context of the political nature of the planning process.

Problems, issues and lessons in UK EIA

Project screening and scoping

Despite amendments to the Regulations, the publication of new guidance and the development of practice-based experience, the scope for a minimalist approach remains and is unlikely to be affected by the revised Directive. Yet Peter Bulleid's chapter demonstrated that even with a set of Regulations and policy guidance which allows for significance to be interpreted as narrowly or widely as one likes, both developers and local authorities still seem keen to ask for and produce ESs. With all the resource costs involved in the process there appears to be little resistance to EIA in practice. There could be many reasons for this but public relations, the politics of planning, must be high up the list. Refusing to produce an ES is not going to endear your project to an already sceptical if not hostile public and local authority. Similarly failing to ask a developer to provide an ES may smack of collusion to an increasingly politically astute local electorate. Furthermore if a developer needs to address questions over ecological, landscape, noise and traffic impacts anyway they might just as well produce that information in an ES as in dribs and drabs as the application progresses through the system.

Even if the number of projects covered by the Regulations is not widened we can therefore expect, on current trends, more not fewer EIAs in the future. As Glasson (1995) puts it: 'The bubble is unlikely to burst'[51].

Determining the coverage of those EIAs is a different matter. The revised Directive may, if the UK implements that part (which is discretionary), simply ensure that local authorities provide their requirements for an assessment when asked to do so by the developer. This is not the mandatory scoping exercise proposed in the initial draft of the amendment and it is difficult to see how this change will make any significant difference to the EIA process[52].

Scoping is the key to EIA success and it requires the active participation of consultees, local authorities and the public. The public, and sometimes the local authority, tend to be excluded for tactical reasons and the ability of consultees to respond adequately to requests for information is dependent upon the resources, structure and attitude of the organisations. As we have seen in many of the cases examined here the response of HMIP to consultation by developers and local planning authorities has not always been helpful, particularly where projects are not of a type which require prior authorisation by HMIP. Should the new Environment Agency suffer from the same resource, staffing and structural problems as HMIP then the quality of EIA scoping is unlikely to improve.

Participation and consultation

A great deal of the focus of this book has been on public participation and consultation and on the whole the system has been found wanting. It is no coincidence that consultation and participation are such significant features of the book – after all even the DoE in the original 'Blue Book' recognised that one of the main emphases of the EIA process is consultation and public participation[53]. For most proponents of EIA, early consultation and full public participation are fundamental requirements of best practice and yet few EIA systems have truly participatory public involvement in the assessment process[54]. Andrew McNab has shown here how difficult it is to provide any truly participatory process within the UK's adversarial planning system and, from the cases reviewed here, we can identify two main problems.

Firstly the public are largely seen as 'the enemy', not simply by the developer but often also by local authorities. The public do not, on the whole, participate in the UK's EIA process; rather they react, often with hostility, to development proposals and on the whole object to them. Very seldom, if ever, do we see petitions of thousands of names supporting planning applications – any planning application, let alone those for major projects requiring EIAs. A developer's perception of the public cannot help but be clouded by the type of problems identified both by Andrew McNab and Richard Read. Little wonder that many developers prefer, on the whole, to keep their powder dry and carry out the minimum requirements of the Regulations.

For local authorities the situation is less clear cut. They are, after all, servants of the public and are, or should be, operating the planning system in the public interest. The trouble is that the public do not always understand the restraints that exist within that simple duty. Issues like national need, government advice and the difference between material and non-material planning considerations are not only a complete mystery to many people but are seen as excuses put up by bureaucratic planners to allow a developer to get away with environmental 'destruction'. When the developer and the planning authority are the same, as with the abattoir case discussed in Chapter 5, any vestige of trust goes out of the window.

With that kind of background it is difficult to see how any best practice EIA public participation exercise is going to further the interests of either the developer or the planning authority. It may be possible to involve the public in a fully participatory role where there are projects that have a level of general support. Yet, for the majority of projects, far from aiding the project design process early public involvement is more likely to scupper the proposal completely.

The second issue is the risk of blight caused by early consultation. An example from south Oxfordshire springs to mind. Three years in advance of any planning application Thames Water commenced a public participation and consultation exercise on its proposals for a 33,000 million gallon reservoir south of Abingdon. The site lies in flat open countryside in the heart of the Vale of White Horse District. Indeed the flat plain in which the site is located is the defining feature of the Vale of White Horse. The proposed reservoir would lie within 25 metre high embankments which would rise out of the landscape, dominating five villages. Farmland and a dozen or so homes would disappear and the proposed five year construction period, with thousands of lorries, site workers, noise and dust, is likely to disrupt the lives of all the villagers living close to the site.

Thames Water's consultation process invited comments on the scheme, and its EIA scoping document, from local people as well as statutory consultees. Halfway through the process the company rescheduled their plans and put back the submission of the planning application a further two years.

Informal discussions with local estate agents suggest that there is little evidence that this process has had any real impact upon house prices. Yet the uncertainty over the future of the project must have caused the lives of hundreds of people to be disrupted. Not only are they faced with the disruption caused by the construction and the environmental consequences of the project itself, they are also faced with years of uncertainty about the eventual impacts on their lives and homes. That uncertainty, and the blighting effect it would undoubtedly have, would be magnified many times over if, as some have demanded, Thames Water had been forced to identify, publicly, the 50 odd alternative sites it claims to have investigated[55].

Decision making

What is the role of EIA in the planning system and how much weight should be given to the contents of an ES when planning decisions are made? Basically the EIA is a provider of information and the weight given to 'environmental issues' has not materially changed. It is not EIA which makes an environmental factor of more or less weight, it is the policy background in which planning decisions are made. As we have already seen, many of the 'environmental effects' reported in an ES are not normally considered material considerations, particularly where they are controlled by other legislation. In other cases an environmental effect may be material and yet only attributed marginal weight in the decision-making process. For example, while ecological impacts are material considerations they are only given any significant weight when those effects are on a Site of Special Scientific Interest or other national or international designation.

Even where environmental factors are material considerations the effects upon them have to be balanced against the policy background to the proposed development. Section 54a of the Town and Country Planning Act 1990[56] makes the development plan[57] the prime consideration in determining all planning applications. In assessing any development the first place a decision maker needs to look is the development plan and not the ES. It is also important to remember here that PPG1 still establishes a basic presumption in favour of development so that development plans cannot be couched in too negative terms. However, Section 54a may provide an opportunity to link these other issues with EIA and to strengthen its importance. Policies within the plan which seek to protect and enhance the natural environment, if they survive the plan adoption process, would make those issues material to the decision. A similar approach can be adopted with air pollution where the plan can seek to protect the amenity of the area through pollution control policies. Section 54a can also be used to raise the importance of EIA. For example, in its draft Local Plan the Vale of White Horse District Council had a policy which required the developer to submit an ES to independent review before submission[58].

In Chapter 6 we looked in some detail at public inquiry decisions and from that review it is possible to identify trends in decisions which may have long term impacts upon the EIA process.

Firstly, where a proposed development is one to which Schedule 2 of the 1988 Regulations could be seen to apply and no ES has been submitted it is unlikely that an Inspector will require the inquiry to be postponed until an ES has been submitted. Inspectors take the minimalist line and simply seek to ensure that the environmental information is taken into account in the decision-making process.

There is also the important issue of the use of the ES during the inquiry. The ES is submitted with the planning application and may be anything up to two years old by the time the case goes before an Inspector. The evidence heard at the inquiry may therefore be more relevant to the proposed scheme, which will have altered during the processing of the application, than the ES. That evidence is more likely to be focused upon the council's reasons for refusing the application than was the ES and contain more up to date information. It is not surprising therefore that evidence at an inquiry, which is subjected to cross-examination, is often attributed more weight than an ES.

Cross-examination can highlight weaknesses in commonly used methodologies, particularly when the methodologies are attempting to predict impacts which are subjectively experienced such as odour, noise or visual intrusion. In some cases conclusions drawn from the methodologies employed in EIA are contradicted by published standards or guidance and in such cases such standards, particularly when they are provided by recognised 'expert' national bodies, are afforded more weight than the ES.

Finally, and very significantly for local planning authorities, there is the right of local authority witnesses to criticise an ES at an inquiry. That 'right' may be forfeited, or at the very least weakened, if the council's officers had not made any criticisms of the ES during the processing of the application or requested more information under the terms of the Regulations. Where an ES is not challenged or questioned by the local planning authority during the consideration of an application, at appeal an Inspector may take the view that the planning authority accepted the findings of the ES.

These are important lessons for practitioners and should be considered throughout the EIA process.

The shifting goal posts

There has undoubtedly been some significant changes to the planning system since the introduction of EIA in 1988. Some, like the introduction of EU environmental policy principles as well as new environmental laws, have been far reaching and at the same time difficult to assess in terms of their overall impact on planning and EIA. Others, like the creation of the Environment Agency, are still very recent and it will be many years before their impact can be assessed.

Policy changes

There are many policy factors which are likely to influence the EIA process and the content and quality of ESs. The strict legal requirements as laid down by legislation, regulation, the courts and planning appeal decisions are not the only influences on the system. EIA in the UK takes place within the framework of the development control process and as such an ES is a planning document and is likely to be framed in such a way as to take account of, and be based upon, material planning considerations. Chief among those considerations will be the policies of the relevant development plan and the policies of national government as set out in Planning Policy Guidance Notes, Mineral Policy Guidance Notes and Department of the Environment (Welsh and Scottish Office) Circulars.

There are numerous sections within the PPGs and other government pronouncements which set out their commitment to environmental issues and to the concept of sustainable development. For example PPG1 reminds developers and local authorities of the main principles behind the Government's environmental policy:

> The Government has made clear its intention to work towards ensuring that development and growth are sustainable.... The sum total of decisions in the planning field, as elsewhere, should not deny future generations the best of today's environment[59].

With this guidance now firmly at the heart of land use planning, we can expect to see, and perhaps should demand to see, ESs containing statements on a project's ability to meet the requirements of sustainable development. Having said that, however, we must heed Winter's (1994) concern that:

> Any environmental statement must address the likely impact of a relevant development on the list of environmental subjects set out in Schedule 3 of the Regulations which includes.... Many of the issues covered will relate to 'critical natural capital' and are thus core areas of concern for sustainable development but there is no obligation on the part of the LPA, having taken account of the environmental statement, to give it overriding importance[60].

Significantly, perhaps, the concept of sustainable development, together with other Government environmental policies such as 'the polluter pays' and 'the precautionary principle', have evolved and come into force since the introduction of the EIA Regulations in 1988. Indeed, their introduction into the planning system through the PPGs has largely only taken place since 1991. This is also true of some of the standards introduced through the Environmental Protection Act such as BATNEEC and 'best practicable environmental option'. As has been seen in this book, these standards are being used in EIAs as a test of the acceptability of predicted impacts and this trend is almost certain to continue despite the problems discussed in Chapter 5. However, the integration of the requirements of IPC authorisations into ESs, as suggested by the revised Directive and PPG23, may have very significant implications. Many of the requirements of IPC authorisation are not material to planning applications and yet are important features of best practice EIA. Under IPC it is necessary to consider, amongst other matters, alternatives, risk, ability of the operator to comply with conditions of authorisation, cumulative impacts and monitoring arrangements – in other words, the type of information local authorities and the public often ask for but are denied as not being material to the planning application.

Organisational changes

We have to ask how much real commitment the Government has to sustainable development when set against what is actually happening out there in the country. Local government reorganisation looked at one stage to be bringing strategic planning in the UK to a virtual halt. The much watered down changes have resulted in a mixture of different systems of local government which makes it difficult to see how the jigsaw will fit together. The structure of local government is important for the development of SEA and for the way project EIA is carried out. Most ESs so far submitted have been for county matter applications and the Regulations make provision for consultation with the district in which the application site is located. This allows for the bringing together of a strategic and local view on the development and good ESs should address both the local and more strategic impacts. But if there is only a unitary authority, only those local views may be involved and the strategic issues – transport, resource management and alternatives (sites and processes) – may not be addressed as fully.

We have already discussed the new Environment Agency and have suggested that it will have a crucial role to play in EIA. It remains to be seen how well it performs that role but the signs are not particularly encouraging when one considers the way the Government seeks to define its responsibilities, one of which being:

> to encourage regulated organisations to respond to the requirements of the Agency in ways which minimise their costs and where possible help any advantages to the competitive position of the UK as a whole to be exploited[61].

A further feature of the development of EIA in the UK lies in the fact that it has taken place wholly under the policies and priorities of a Conservative Government. This may not continue to be the case and Labour or Liberal Democrat administrations may change the policy and organisational structure under which EIA is carried out. It remains to be seen whether this will be for better or worse.

Some concluding thoughts

We must start with a cautionary approach to the future of EIA in the UK. The current trends do not seem to give much room for over-optimism. Yet we have come a long way since the 1970s when most of the issues EIA attempted to deal with were minority concerns which politicians regarded as peripheral to the main goals of economic growth. Today we do have the principles of sustainable development and the precautionary approach to environmental protection within the planning process and developers do now have to address the environment far more than ever they did before the introduction of EIA. The EIA process has brought other benefits such as more environmental monitoring, the development of sophisticated prediction methodologies and the environmental assessment of development plans. Despite these undoubted benefits it remains difficult to claim that in the UK the EIA process has its own intrinsic objective of environmental protection. Here it is a process which, although arguably more structured and thorough, is little different from the development control process for non-EIA projects. Indeed less than 25% of consultants surveyed in 1995 were of the view that EIA had made a significant impact upon the UK's development control system and 70% of those who had been involved in public inquiries believed that the ES had been treated little differently from evidence in non-EIA inquiry cases. As one respondent to that study argued, EIA cases are less than 0.07% of the total number of planning applications dealt with in the UK each year and as such are unlikely to have had more than a marginal impact on the system as a whole[62].

EIA does provide and make public information on environmental impacts at a much earlier stage and in a more comprehensive manner and this is a significant improvement and perhaps its major achievement. Yet it has not changed the fundamental principles of the UK development control decision-making process. The nature of that process is legalistic, political and discretionary. For all the work by the very many participants in the EIA process, the decision makers can put to one side the environmental impacts, having taken them into account, and base their decision on a wholly different agenda.

This book has never claimed to be anything more than an examination of the UK's EIA system as it has been. It has not been an attempt to predict the future and yet, despite the yet to be implemented amendments to the EU Directive on which UK EIA is based, we can at least say that, without fundamental change to the political and legal foundation of the UK development control process, the future is unlikely to be very different from the past.

Notes and references

1 Wood, C (1995) Lessons from comparative practice, *Built Environment*, Vol. 20, No. 4, 322–344; Wood, C (1995) *Environmental Impact Assessment: A Comparative Review*. London: Longman Scientific and Technical.

2 *Ibid.*

3 Kakonge, J O and A M Imevbore (1993) Constraints on implementing environmental impact assessments in Africa, *Environmental Impact Assessment Review*, Vol. 13, 299–308.

4 World Bank (1991) Operational Directive 4.01: Environmental Assessment, World Bank.

5 Haeuber, R (1992) The World Bank and environmental assessment: the role of non-governmental organisations, *Environmental Impact Assessment Review*, Vol. 12, 331–347.

6 Jones, B (ed) (1995) Current Survey, *Environmental Liability*, Vol. 3, No. 1. ppcs 1.

7 Wood, C and J Bailey (1994) Predominance and independence in environmental impact assessment: the Western Australian model, *Environmental Impact Assessment Review*, Vol. 14, 37–59.

8 Wood, C (1995) *op. cit.*

9 Jones, B (ed) *op. cit.* ppcs 2–3.

10 Glasson, J, R Therival and A Chadwick (1994) *Introduction to Environmental Impact Assessment*. London: UCL Press, pp 153.

11 Wood, C (1995) *op. cit.*

12 Jorissen, J and R Coenen (1992) The EEC Directive on EIA and its implementation in the EC member states, in Colombo, A G (ed) *Environmental Impact Assessment.* Dordrecht: Kluwer Academic, p 3.

13 La Spina, A and G Sciortino (1993) Common agenda, southern rules, European integration and environmental change in the Mediterranean states, in Liefferink, J D, P D Lowe and A P J Mol (eds) *European Integration and Environmental Policy.* London: Belhaven Press, pp 224.

14 *Ibid.*

15 Jones, B (ed) *op. cit.* ppcs 8.

16 Salter, J R (1992a) Environmental assessment – the question of implementation, *JPL,* pp 3113–3118.

17 Jorissen, J and R Coenen, *op. cit.*

18 There have been a large number of articles discussing the quality of ESs, many of which are based upon the work at Manchester University. For a discussion of that work see Lee, N and D Brown (1992) Quality control in Environmental Statements, *Project Appraisal,* Vol. 7, No. 1, 41–45. The most recent work was carried out by Oxford Brookes University's School of Planning which was published as DoE (1996) *Changes in the Quality of Environmental Statements for Planning Projects.* London: HMSO.

19 Street, E (1993) Notes from the coal-face on environmental assessment, *Planning* 1022; Braun, C (1993) EIAs: the 1990s. The view from Marsham Street. Paper presented at the Conference EIA in the UK: Evaluation, University of Manchester, 6 April.

20 Weston, J (1995) Consultants in the EIA process, *Environment Policy and Practice,* Vol. 5, No. 3.

21 DoE (1994a) *Good Practice on the Evaluation of Environmental Information for Planning Projects: Research Report.* London: HMSO.

22 Nelson, P (1995) Better guidance for better EIA, *Built Environment,* Vol. 20, No. 4, pp 280–293.

23 Wood, C (1993a) EIA in Europe – results of the five year review. Paper presented at the EIA Conference, Bloomsbury Hotel, London, 25–26 November.

24 Salter, J R (1992b) Environmental assessment: the challenge from Brussels, *JPL,* pp 14–20.

25 Skehan, D C (1993) EIA in Ireland. Paper presented at the EIA Conference, Bloomsbury Hotel, London, 25–26 November; DoE (1996) *op. cit.*

26 Lee, N and R Dancey (1993) The quality of environmental impact statements in Ireland and the United Kingdom: a comparative analysis, *Project Appraisal,* Vol. 8, No. 1, 31–36.

27 Commission of the European Communities (1992) *Report from the Commission of the Implementation of Directive 85/337/EEC.* Brussels: CEC.

28 West, C, R Bissett and R Snowden (1993) Developing countries EIAs. Paper presented at the EIA Conference, Bloomsbury Hotel, London, 25–26 November.

29 Kakonge, J O and A M Imevbore (1993) *op. cit.*

30 Commission of the European Communities, *op. cit.*

31 DoE (1994b) *Evaluation of Environmental Information for Planning Projects: A Good Practice Guide.* London: HMSO.

32 Commission of the European Communities, *op. cit.*

33 *Ibid.*

34 Ginger, C and P Mohai (1993) The role of data in the EIS process: evidence from the BLM wilderness review, *Environmental Impact Assessment Review,* Vol. 13, 109–139.

35 Council for the Protection of Rural England (1992) *Mock Directive.* London: CPRE.

36 Commission for European Communities, *op. cit.*
37 Kakonge J O and A M Imevbore, *op. cit.*
38 Abracosa, R and L Ortolano (1987) Environmental impact assessment in the Philippines: 1977–1985, *Environmental Impact Assessment Review*, Vol. 7, 293–310.
39 Wood, C (1993b) Antipodean environmental assessment, *Town Planning Review*, Vol. 64, No. 2, 119–138.
40 Quoted in Tromans, S (ed) (1994) *Environmental Law Bulletin*, No. 9, November, London: Sweet & Maxwell: see also discussion of the Agency's Draft Management Statement in *Environmental Law Monthly*, Vol. 4, No. 5, May 1995.
41 DoE (1994a) *op. cit.*
42 Cheshire County Council (1989) *The Cheshire Environmental Assessment Handbook: Planning Practice Note No. 2.* Chester: Cheshire County Council; Council for the Protection of Rural England (1990) *Environmental Statements: Getting Them Right.* London: CPRE; English Nature, The Countryside Council for Wales and Scottish Natural Heritage (1992) *Environmental Assessment Handbook.* London: NCC; ICI (undated) *ICI Group Guidelines for the Environmental Impact on New Projects.* London: ICI; Kent County Council (1990) *Environmental Assessment Handbook.* Maidstone: Kent County Council.
43 DoE (1994b) *op. cit.* p 1.
44 DoE (1995a) *Preparation of Environmental Statements for Planning Projects that Require Environmental Assessment: A Good Practice Guide.* London: HMSO.
45 DoE (1993) PPG22: *Renewable Energy.* London: HMSO.
46 DoE (1994c) PPG23: *Planning and Pollution Control.* London: HMSO.
47 DoE (1994d) MPG3: *Coal Mining and Colliery Spoil Disposal.* London: HMSO.
48 DoE (1994e) MPG6: *Guidelines for Aggregates Provision in England.* London: HMSO.
49 DoE (1989) MPG7: *The Reclamation of Mineral Workings.* London: HMSO.
50 Nelson, P, *op. cit.*
51 Glasson, J (1995) Environmental impact assessment: the next steps?, *Built Environment*, Vol. 20, No. 4, 277–279.
52 Environmental assessment rules leave much to member states, *ENDS Report 252*, January 1996.
53 DoE/Welsh Office (1989) *Environmental Assessment: A Guide to the Procedures.* London: HMSO.
54 Clarke, B D (1995) Improving public participation in environmental impact assessment, *Built Environment*, Vol. 20, No. 4, 294–308.
55 Village fury over reservoir, *Abingdon Herald*, 13 May 1993.
56 Section 54a was inserted into the 1990 Act by the Planning and Compensation Act 1991.
57 The 'development plan' comprises the full statutory plan framework, i.e. the adopted Structure and Local Plan, or Unitary Development Plan, and will also include Waste and Mineral Local plans. See paragraph 17 of DoE (1992) PPG1: *General Policy and Principles.* London: HMSO.
58 Vale of White Horse District Council (1993) *Local Plan: Draft for Consultation.* Abingdon: Vale of White Horse District Council.
59 DoE (1992), *op. cit.*
60 Winter, P (1994) Planning and sustainability: an examination of the role of the planning system as an instrument for the delivery of sustainable development, *JPL*, pp 883–900.
61 DoE (1995b) *Guidance to the Environment Agency under the Environment Bill on its Objectives.* London: HMSO.
62 Weston, J (1995) *op. cit.*

INDEX